Ashis Nandy and the Cultural Politics of Selfhood

Thank you for choosing a SAGE product! If you have any comment, observation or feedback, I would like to personally hear from you. Please write to me at <u>contactceo@sagepub.in</u>

—Vivek Mehra, Managing Director and CEO,
SAGE Publications India Pvt Ltd, New Delhi

Bulk Sales

SAGE India offers special discounts for purchase of books in bulk. We also make available special imprints and excerpts from our books on demand.

For orders and enquiries, write to us at

Marketing Department
SAGE Publications India Pvt Ltd
B1/I-1, Mohan Cooperative Industrial Area
Mathura Road, Post Bag 7
New Delhi 110044, India
E-mail us at <u>marketing@sagepub.in</u>

Get to know more about SAGE, be invited to SAGE events, get on our mailing list. Write today to <u>marketing@sagepub.in</u>

This book is also available as an e-book.

Ashis Nandy and the Cultural Politics of Selfhood

CHRISTINE DEFTEREOS

SSAGE www.sagepublications.com
Los Angeles • London • New Delhi • Singapore • Washington DC

First published in 2013 by

SAGE Publications India Pvt Ltd
B1/I-1 Mohan Cooperative Industrial Area
Mathura Road, New Delhi 110 044, India
www.sagepub.in

SAGE Publications Inc
2455 Teller Road
Thousand Oaks, California 91320, USA

SAGE Publications Ltd
1 Oliver's Yard, 55 City Road
London EC1Y 1SP, United Kingdom

SAGE Publications Asia-Pacific Pte Ltd
33 Pekin Street
#02-01 Far East Square
Singapore 048763

Published by Vivek Mehra for SAGE Publications India Pvt Ltd, Phototypeset in 10.5/12.5 Utopia by Diligent Typesetter, Delhi and printed at Saurabh Printers, Pvt Ltd.

Library of Congress Cataloging-in-Publication Data

Deftereos, Christine, 1974–
    Ashis Nandy and the cultural politics of selfhood/Christine Deftereos.
        p. cm.
    Includes bibliographical references and index.
    ISBN 978-8132110453 (hardback: alk. paper) 1. Political psychology—India. 2. Psychoanalysis—India. 3. Secularism—India. 4. Toleration—India. 5. Nandy, Ashis. I. Title.
    JA74.5.D446   2013   306.2—dc23   2012049755

ISBN: 978-81-321-1045-3 (HB)

The SAGE Team: Neelakshi Chakraborty, Rohini Rangachari Karnik and Nand Kumar Jha

For my parents who taught me that the different ways of seeing others couldn't always be found in books. For Alex, who sees everything.

There are possible ways of looking at the person, to which the modern world has few clues. These possible ways cannot be explained away as mystifications or as romantic invocations of the past. Indeed, it is we who have been living in a make-believe world that ignores other concepts of the boundaries of the Self and which a huge proportion, perhaps even a majority of the world, still lives.

Ashis Nandy
***Freud, Modernity and Postcolonial Violence* (2004)**

And to venture even further: if we were not all translators, if we did not unceasingly lay bare the foreignness of our inner lives – its departures from the stereotypical codes we call national languages – in order to transpose this foreignness into other signs, would we have a psychical life at all, would we be living beings?…speaking an 'other language,' in other words, is quite simply the minimum and primary condition for being alive.

Julia Kristeva
***Intimate Revolt: The Powers and Limits of Psychoanalysis* Volume 2 (2002)**

Contents

Preface

The health of a democracy can be measured, amongst other things, by the culture of its public debate and its range of dissenting views. Ashis Nandy's contribution to public debate and dissent, and his ongoing research on Indian democracy point to a resilient and regenerative pluralism. Despite the intensity of ongoing challenges to the Indian political imaginary of 'Unity in Diversity', by the ethno-nationalist agenda of Hindutva ideology and continuing debates over the politics of inclusion, and claims to 'Indianess', Nandy's prognosis remains unchanged. As a radical democrat one finds in his work a commitment to official and, importantly, unofficial expressions of democratic pluralism that disrupt accepted meanings of how pluralism is both understood and recognised. This commitment to 'alternatives', whether in the form of alternative socio-cultural configurations or those 'other selves' that exist outside the legitimate secular criteria constituting the modern 'entitled' Indian subject, is demonstrated in the theoretical spaces his work ventures into and the political responses he advocates.

The reclaiming of pluralism in its myriad cultural, political and psychological forms, alongside the pursuit of alternatives, comes at a cost. This cost can result in more than just an unpopular stance, subject to the self-referential nature of academic quibbling. The attempts to criminalise and silence the voice of the critic by the Gujarat government in 2008 demonstrate just how threatening Nandy's alternatives, notably his anti-secularism, remain even thirty years on. A detailed engagement with his anti-secular thinking is often overshadowed by the political consequences of this position, and there remains a curious silence, or as Amit Chaudhuri aptly describes 'unvoiced disagreements' (Chaudhuri, 2004a: 1) even from scholars who are critical of secularism. The legal case also raises important questions about the nature of the Indian state, the relationship of the critic in public culture, the role of political and cultural criticism and the modes of dissent that are audible within society. Although the initial charges against Nandy have been dismissed, there remains relatively little engagement with the constitutive features of Nandy's dissenting anti-secular thought, and how a modern Indian secular post-colonial scholar arrives at such a seemingly counter-intuitive position.

This book offers a critical analysis of Nandy's work by focusing on how dissent manifests in his cultural and political criticism, starting with his anti-secular position. It explores how Nandy, 'as a true dissenter' as he is often described, resists all dominant frameworks of knowledge, critiquing and reconstituting not only the conditions of dissent, but also the methods used to arrive at such a destination. Nandy's predilection for border crossings, whether intellectual, disciplinary, cultural or otherwise, point to a radical thinker who resists conventional classifications. Characterising how dissent is actuated in the voice of the critic 'who dare[s] to defy the given models of defiance' (Nandy, 1987a: vii) is therefore an attempt to capture and trace the dynamism of this profoundly political, subversive and anti-disciplinary thinker. As this book argues, Nandy's approach and his identity as a critic cannot be understood through a prescriptive formula of 'how best to read Nandy' or by searching for a locus for his contrarian interventions within a disciplinary method. Such an approach would depoliticise Nandy's profoundly political opus and close the door on the 'politics of awareness' that his work urgently alerts us too. Rather, detailing the way 'meaning' and 'knowledge' is *ruptured* and *regenerated* under the defiant gaze of the critic opens up an important space for contextualising and working through the alternatives advanced in his work. These alternatives may be *necessarily* provocative and confrontational, as is the journey undertaken to arrive at them.

One of the consistent criticisms levelled at Nandy is his critique of 'modernity' and his confronting emphasis on the cultural and psychological sources of resistance and creativity located in the traditions of the non-modern or pre-modern world. This repeated emphasis on the 'non-modern' or 'pre-modern' and the un-historicized invocation of a pre-colonial past remain bitterly divisive points of debate. For instance, to speak of a pre-modern 'natural tolerance' or a 'tolerable ethnocentricism' without contextualizing such concepts reproduces an epistemic violence that represses India's widely documented pre-modern history of violence. A deepening of Nandy's anti-secular thinking is needed here, in order to explore how such categories or, rather, typologies are invoked in his work and what function they perform within the critique. Again, questions need to be asked as to how and why the modern secular critic actuates such a provocative 'return' and to what extent this advances the political objectives of defiance and awareness structuring his work. Such a task necessitates an appreciation of how the postcolonial identity of the critic is negotiated, including the way Nandy 'works through' the complex terrain of cultural politics of selfhood, as a feature of his method. How are the shadows or latent anti-modern selves that frequent Nandy's work and threaten to radically disrupt dominant and homogenising accounts of subjectivity and human experience, worked through in the voice of the modern critic? And, does the Freud that Nandy savagely applies through the psychoanalytic focus underpinning his distinctive cultural and political criticism not also reveal the dynamic workings of a 'Savage Freud'?

This book responds to such questions by exploring how psychoanalysis informs Nandy's dissent and the method he adopts to generate such confronting alternatives. In detailing what is characterized as a *psychoanalytic mode of revolt* operating in the voice of the critic, this reading also suggests that Nandy's approach destabilizes existing psychoanalytic modes and forms. Here, the self-described 'political psychologist' and 'intellectual street fighter' come face to face not only with the psychology of politics but also with the politics of psychology, affirming why Nandy is one of the most original and confrontational Indian thinkers of his generation. It is intended that this book will contribute to an ongoing critical discussion of Nandy's work and the alternatives his work invites, despite the provocative, challenging and counter-intuitive nature of many of his interventions. If anything, the defensive structures that can foreclose a deeper engagement with these ideas point to the necessity for collective confrontation, self-reflection and self-awareness. Such a task is urgently needed to counter the dangers of what Nandy warns is a growing 'global culture of common sense' (Nandy, 2004a) and to reclaim a dissenting 'analytic attitude' essential for cultural and political criticism. This dissenting 'analytic attitude' is equally vital for safeguarding pluralism, including the pluralism of 'other selves' that linger even as disruptive debris within the politics of selfhood, in the world's largest democracy.

Acknowledgements

In the early stages of discovery and thinking through my intellectual curiosity in Ashis Nandy's work, I had the opportunity of meeting him on several occasions between 2005 and 2007 and recording our discussions in New Delhi and in Melbourne. I extend my gratitude to Ashis for his generosity and openness in sharing his thinking, and bringing many of his ideas to life. I am equally grateful for the welcome that Uma Nandy always extends to me, and who, together with Ashis, re-affirms that cross-cultural exchange can never purely be an intellectual exercise.

Extended thanks to my colleagues and friends at the University of Melbourne, where this work was first conceived, and to the encouraging editors and staff at SAGE Publications.

Introduction
Intellectual Street Fighting—From the
Symptomatic to the Psychotherapeutic

Ashis Nandy as a Confronting and Contested Figure

A shis Nandy is undoubtedly one of the most important Indian thinkers of his generation. Described in India as 'bigger than most pop stars', his voice is synonymous with original critique and a presence in public and academic debates. (Sardar, 1997: 47). A prolific contributor for over thirty-five years to cultural, social and political criticism, his distinctive interventions across a range of topics remain uncompromising. These include Nandy's consistent critique of western modernity; the political culture of the Indian state; the postcolonial condition; Indian selfhood and the 'secret and latent selves' that frequent his work and threaten to unsettle identities; the politics of knowledge production, including the epistemic violence of colonial dispossession; an increasing global and homogenising 'culture of commonsense'; and the Indian middle classes whose uncritical complicity in this culture becomes subject to a range of lively 'Nandyanisms.' This confrontational subject matter, along with what are often regarded as Nandy's outrageous ideas and perspectives, establish him as a highly contested intellectual figure. Notwithstanding the scathing 'anti-secularist manifesto', first detailed in *Seminar* in 1985, Nandy's writings provoke, securing his position as one of the most passionately divisive yet important contemporary Indian thinkers. Even in the acrimonious debates on Indian secularism where Nandy is at his most polemic, his critique of the role of the secular ideal within Indian political culture and in the formation of political identities cannot be ignored. These debates may be short-circuited by the existing crisis of secularism and the territorial anxieties that inform intellectual exchange, but his persistent forewarnings of the distortions that the ideology of secularism produces remain as relevant as they did when they first appeared.

Equally enduring is Nandy's strident critique of the role of religion in secular politics and the symptomatic rise of Hindu fundamentalism espoused by organisations like the Rashtriya Swayamsevak Sangh (RSS) and the Bharatiya Janata Party (BJP). Nandy remains resolute in his outspoken comments on the rise of the Hindu Right even in the face of attempts by critics to conflate his anti-secular position with these political forces. This is notable in the debates of secularism where Nandy's critique is often over-determined by the political stakes of his work. Even within the Left, where a number of scholars have voiced their own lengthy attacks on secularism, Nandy's distinctive 'brand' of anti-secularism produces defensive responses that can simplify his arguments in ways analogous to the political rhetoric circumscribing these debates. While often referenced as a leading anti-secular voice in India, such a title is riddled with complexities, including what the constitutive features of Nandy's anti-secularism are, and how the modern postcolonial secular scholar arrives at such a destination. Just like the latent anti-secular selves explored in Nandy's work disrupt a dominant Indian political imaginary, the multiple voices of the modern Indian critic also deserve careful consideration.

More recently, it is Nandy's critique of the political culture in the State of Gujarat under the Hindu nationalist leadership of Narendra Modi that has proved consequential. In 'Obituary of a Culture', Nandy's characterisation of Modi as a 'classic, clinical case of a fascist' (Nandy, 2002c: 3), following an interview with him, ominously set the scene for the unfolding of the tragic events that followed in Gujarat. It also set the scene for the legal proceedings launched against Nandy six years later in 2008, in response to his article published in *The Times of India*, commenting on Modi's re-election and the radically altered Gujarati political culture under his leadership. Nandy's criticisms of the Modi government were consistent with his earlier forewarnings of the government's authoritarian political motives. If critics had been in doubt of Nandy's political allegiances with the Hindu Right given his anti-secular stance, then the criminal case against him reaffirmed an ideological division, alongside an attempt to censure dissent. The criminal case attracted international condemnation, as a global network of scholars and activists responded, supplementing the public demonstrations and debate in India. Adding to the media attention was the way Nandy's ideas regarding the authoritarian tendencies of the Indian state were put to trial, in effect becoming a living test case for his arguments. The attempt to censor Nandy's voice in this way is ironic, given that confronting the encoded politics underpinning the audibility of dissent is a reoccurring theme in his own work.

The attempt to criminalise the voice of the critic raises important questions about the role of the public intellectual in India. If, as Nandy claims, the legal proceedings 'are just an attempt to silence people like me', then what is so confrontational and threatening about Nandy and his work[1]. The question beckons an understanding of what kinds of provocations, confrontations and disruptions his work invites, and what form these take, along with larger systemic issues regarding a State increasingly intolerant of dissent, the health of Indian democracy, and the psychological and political defences underpinning national priorities. While the charges against Nandy have been dismissed, the threat that the critic of the State poses still lingers. This is evident in what can be described as a climate of state-sanctioned censorship against public intellectuals and activists. This includes the life imprisonment of human rights activist and paediatrician Dr Binayak Sen in December 2010, and the 2011 sedition charges against Arundhati Roy for her comments on Kashmir. While Nandy's threat differs, the role of public dissent and debate, including the mode through which dissent is advanced as both audible and tolerable, is a live issue.

The Indian publication, *Outlook Magazine*, describes Nandy as 'India's most irreverent Social Scientist' (Reddy, 2007: 1). The contested significance attached to Nandy's irreverence is detailed in the number of responses he and his work generate. Representations vary from acknowledging Nandy as the founding voice of 'modern Indian criticism', to less celebratory depictions of an intellectual who is 'unclassifiable' (Tharamangalam,1995: 460; Lal, 2005: 16). The volume of this mixed reception is all the more arresting given that, as Vinay Lal points out, Nandy is 'not strictly an academic or professional scholar' (Lal, 2000: 20). As a trained clinical psychologist, his interest in political psychology, psychoanalysis and social criticism emerged early on in his career. Nandy's entry into the research culture of the Centre for the Study of Developing Societies (CSDS) in Delhi in the late 1970s, where he has been based for over forty years, secured his involvement in Indian intellectual life. While the intellectual and political independence of CSDS has been scrutinised, Nandy continues to contribute to the vibrancy of the Centre and the international dialogues it cultivates. His position as a writer who does not align himself with existing scholarly debates, and remains outside of the teaching machine, leaves him vulnerable to criticisms regarding his academic credentials. With the exception of a brief lectureship in

America during the Indian Emergency, Nandy's profile is marked by his research contributions, activism and numerous writings that confront and transcend distinct disciplinary methods and perspectives.

Nandy's longstanding publishing relationship with Oxford University Press in India demonstrates his commitment to an Indian intellectual culture. Nandy appears then to be the 'non-player'—the contrarian figure who resists playing by the established rules of the game, a figure widely referenced in his work for its disruptive and creative potential. It would be a misrepresentation to dismiss Nandy as a non-player, who rejects outright all academic protocols and rules of engagement, without accounting for the political implications of such a title. Like the savage outsider he references, 'who is neither willing to be a player or counter-player', Nandy's own relationship to knowledge is not so straightforward (Nandy, 1983a: xiv). The disruptive and creative impact of the savage outsider needs to be considered alongside the dissenting ideas and methods that underpin his political efforts to rupture given models of defiance. Vinay Lal's succinct description, 'defiance of defiance', captures something of Nandy's aptitude for confrontation in his writings, adding weight to the political imperatives of the non-player (Lal, 2000). The question though of how this defiance is arrived at and advanced in Nandy's work remains profoundly threatening and destabilising for a number of critics. This anxiety over how best to locate and represent his thinking is exacerbated by the alternative and open-ended perspectives he provides, which equally resist disciplinary classification and closure. If disciplinary fidelity or even interdisciplinarity is a measure of scholarly acumen, then Nandy's defiance as a non-player and the ambivalence that his work embraces continue to disturb.

The deceptive simplicity of Nandy's writings unburdened by the weight of epistemic abstraction or fidelity is a source of territorial anxiety and debate. Nandy's self-characterisation as both 'intellectual street fighter' and 'political psychologist' adds to this, running the risk of trivialising the wider significance of his contributions. Whether the intellectual street fighter functions as a latent shadow self or a secret self to the political psychologist or vice versa, both self-descriptions reveal the politics informing his approach to knowledge and critique. For instance, the reflexivity of his writings on the politics of dissent is often eclipsed by his position as the ultimate dissenting enfant terrible within Indian academia. Much of this tension can be explained by Nandy's relationship to disciplinary knowledge and more specifically his critical encounter with political psychology. While the combat of 'intellectual street fighting' may absolve Nandy of adhering to academic protocols, this is received critically within the field of Indian political psychology where scholarship is measurable in self-referential ways. Consequently, Nandy's outsider status carries over into the field of academic psychology where his dissident place within its historical trajectory has been secured (Kumar, 2006: 236). Along with fellow dissident, the eminent psychoanalyst Sudhi Kakar, Nandy's appropriation of psychoanalysis and the perspectives this generates challenge the boundaries of critical psychology, though in different ways to Kakar, whose use of psychoanalytic concepts is, arguably, more explicit. The field in India is marked by a disjuncture between the mainstream and largely cognitive-based interpretations of psychology and what are deemed to be alternative and dissenting perspectives, such as those advanced in Nandy's and Kakar's work. This division is related to the somewhat uncritical relationship that the social sciences in India have had with inherited Western traditions of scholarship. The field of psychology in India exemplifies this with what is described as 'mainstream validational' research and 'oppositional-indigenous or reactionary and nativist' perspectives (Crooks, 1994; Kumar, 2006). These demarcations are radically critiqued in Nandy's writings and reveal the distortions of a colonial legacy and continuing colonising logic. The creative and disruptive potential of the 'non-player', or the 'political psychologist as non-player' is another reminder of the ongoing need to critically confront and challenge the limits of disciplinary knowledge. While the problem of epistemic violence is afforded greater complexity in Nandy's work, charges of a reactionary nativist agenda inform representations of him, affirming the contestation surrounding his interventions.

Part of Nandy's provocations can be explained in these terms, as the voice of the postcolonial critic produces a moment of forced engagement with the politics of inherited knowledge systems and colonial dispossession. Adding to this self-reflexive task is the voice of the 'intellectual street fighter' and dissident political psychologist whose psychoanalytic focus facilitates an analytical encounter with the past, including the past that survives in the present. Dipesh Chakrabarty rightly acknowledges Nandy's sensitivity in addressing the role of India's undesirable past, and the tensions and contradictions that Indian modernity presents for the postcolonial critic (Chakrabarty in Lal, 2000). Chakrabarty emphasises that 'it is only rarely that Indian intellectuals have addressed this problem in a self-conscious manner though it often erupts in what they write about the past' (Chakrabarty in Lal, 2000: 250). Nandy's continuing 'return' to the past includes the past that survives in the present, not only within historical time but according to the rhythms of psychic life. This is demonstrated in his attentiveness to the constitution of Indian selfhood, the colonised minds of the victim and perpetrator, processes of identification, issues of agency and resistance and the ambivalence that he retrieves within an Indian political imaginary. The divisions like those found within the field of Indian psychology between validational and indigenous thought then belittle the dynamic interplay between the past–present in human subjectivity and cultural processes that Nandy's work so carefully addresses, and which resist disciplina ry closure.

It is equally Nandy's nonconforming appropriation of psychoanalysis, seldom accounted as a defining feature of his work, that enables him to produce such open-ended perspectives. Psychoanalysis provides a language through which to explore the way the past manifests in the present within psychic life, in addition to understanding how power and ideology inform human subjectivity, in tracing 'the psychic life of power' (Butler, 1997). This for Nandy necessitates the dialectical relationship between outer and inner incentives and manifestations of power. Nandy reads and applies psychoanalysis as a method of critique, tool of demystification, subversion and critical analysis. While Kakar's efforts can be distinguished from Nandy's in his unambiguous use of the psychoanalytic model of symbolisations, such as dream work and interpretation, Nandy's approach appears inherently vague and inconsistent. His rejection of psychoanalysis's acultural universalising motives, as a tool for social engineering instituted and practised within certain schools of psychoanalytic thought, further troubles the utility and application of psychoanalysis for social analysis. Under Nandy's gaze, 'as savage outsider' psychoanalysis functions as a tool for disruption and critique and not as a psychotherapeutic technique of normalisation arriving on the coat-tails of colonialism in India. The use of psychoanalysis as a tool of social engineering in producing the 'ideal' colonial subject in colonial India is widely documented in his work. This, however, is not the only legacy that psychoanalysis carries forward. For Nandy, psychoanalysis as a critique along with its distinctive 'analytic attitude' can also function as a weapon against the accepted certitudes that his work so vigorously challenges and warns against.

Even within the field of postcolonial studies, where Nandy's use of psychoanalysis and intellectual border crossings is celebrated, claims of his reactionism and nativism persist. For instance, his emphasis on a pre-modern Indian 'natural tolerance' or 'tolerable ethnocentrism' as cultural and psychological categories of resistance and survival, remain sensitive points of contention given the pre-modern history of violence in India, especially against Dalits and women. Even his appropriation of psychoanalysis as a postcolonial critique detailed in *The Intimate Enemy: Loss and Recovery of Self under Colonialism* (1983) appears amorphous, in comparison to the directives of post-colonial theory from within the American academy. Many important issues are raised in Nandy's work, but even less resolved, leaving an open question as to how the encounter between psychoanalysis and the postcolonial critic unfolds in the work of the 'non-player' or 'savage outsider'.

Nandy's critical relationship with knowledge production, his sensitivity to the psychic traumas of the colonial legacy, including its continuities and distortions within contemporary Indian life, remain under-theorised in mainstream psychology and sociology in India. This active defiance of well-guarded scholarly boundaries ensures that Nandy's border crossings, and re-positioning of the boundaries of debate, are often met with resistance and vitriolic criticisms. These are exacerbated by his distinct capacity to engage with subject matters and frames of knowledge that are otherwise relegated to 'the realm of unmentionable' (Kumar, 2006: 251). His predilection for confrontation and intellectual perspectives that challenge the limits of their own production amounts to what in Foucauldian terms can be described as a politics of discomfort. The effects and affects of these play out in both the horror and fascination that he and his work elicit, leaving many questioning the significance of Nandy as a critic beyond his characteristically oppositional voice or status as provocateur.

This book addresses these issues of reception, representation, and the relationship between ideas and methods by characterising dissent in Nandy's cultural and political criticism. It explores Nandy's distinctive confrontations along with the psychoanalytic focus underpinning his writings. It is through the dissenting voice of the 'intellectual street fighter' and political psychologist, and the directives of the 'non-player' and 'savage outsider', that the role of psychoanalysis in his cultural and political criticism is explored. This includes the way psychoanalysis, with its emphasis on the decentred subject, can function as a disruptive tool against the dangers of homogeneity, closure within accounts of human subjectivity, and within the cultural politics of selfhood. Taking into account Nandy's emphasis on the productivity of what is marginal, identity forms, individual and collective processes of identification within political life remain dynamic and ambivalent. It is in this relationship between self and society and within what Judith Butler calls 'the psychic life of power' (Butler, 1997) that the politics of the 'non-player' and his critique is explored. If the task of accounting for the horror and fascination that Nandy's work attracts is to be taken seriously, then it is not only the ideas but also the method through which social and political criticism is generated that needs to be detailed.

Nandy is at his most challenging in his invitation to confront the cultural and psychological viability of the ideology of secularism in India. The debates on Indian secularism, and what is widely accepted as the crisis of secularism in India, provide the starting point for detailing the confrontations and disruptions Nandy invites. As a site for contested meanings over India's modernity, the debates reveal the intense contestation surrounding questions of 'Indianness' and the political culture of the modern secular postcolonial State. Tracing Nandy's argument from its inception in 1985 with 'An Anti-Secularist Manifesto' to his most recent writings on the authoritarian developmentalism of Hindutva demonstrates the continuity of his position. Moreover, the intensity of this material proves useful for understanding the relationship between ideas, critique, method and, by extension, identity and subjectivity. Nandy's critique of secularism allows for a detailed analysis of these relationships as they are addressed in his work and identity as critic. What is so confrontational about Nandy's critique of secularism and what does this position reveal about the critic's tools of analysis? Further, on what grounds are Nandy's contributions to these debates contested, deemed problematic and with what consequences? Nandy summarises his confrontation with secularism in terms of the disjuncture that exists between the ideology of secularism instituted in the apparatus of the modern Indian state and peoples' everyday lived experiences.

As he states, 'people have categories of identification and I do not see why those categories have to be reticent to accord the visions of secularism. when those categories have served your purpose perfectly well…and what is so sacrosanct about the concept [of secularism]?' (Nandy and Deftereos, 2005d: 23). Central to Nandy's confrontation are the ways that the ideology of secularism forecloses existing categories of identification. This growing disjuncture between official accounts of a modern secular self with unofficial accounts of 'other selves', and the tensions this produces are a reoccurring concern. So, too, are the ways of middle class Indians living lives structured through Western categories of identification, including a politically instituted concept of toleration and national belonging. The diminished range of politically recognised identities in public life, the simplification of human subjectivity and the policing of boundaries over who can claim 'Indianness' remain under threat in contemporary Indian life. Characterising Nandy's confrontation with secularism necessitates an understanding of the way the ideology structures Indian political culture and establishes politically recognised and legitimate identities.

Makarand Paranjape observes, 'Secular modernity, admittedly, becomes the number one enemy in most of Nandy's work, bearing the brunt of much of his ire' (Lal, 2000: 239). The intensity of his ire in confronting the operation of the secular ideal is demonstrated in the controversy his work continues to produce in public discourse and academic debates. Don Miller acknowledges the consequences of Nandy's scandalous confrontation in becoming 'intimate enemy number one', well before the recent attempts to publically criminalise Nandy's identity (Miller, 1998). Miller's play on words here, referencing Nandy's *The Intimate Enemy*, reveals the vehement threat and disruption that an anti-secular position represents within Indian political culture. The image of Nandy as 'intimate enemy' also provides two important avenues for analysis. First, how the concept of an intimate enemy, an enemy who is within—and consistent with the psychoanalytic focus underpinning his work—is notably constitutive of the self, including the identity of the critic, informs Nandy's method of critique. For instance, what does this turning against an intimate self or even a dominant part of one's self imply for the identity of the critic and the methods used to arrive at this confronting destination? How is such a seemingly counter-intuitive approach connected to the ways the postcolonial identity of the modern secular Indian critic is negotiated or worked through? As Nandy affirms, 'What's the point of saying Indian's suffer from a range of pathologies if one exempts oneself from criticism by cleverly defining oneself as an enlightened liberal declassed exception?' (Darby, 2005: 54).

Second, what consequences does being 'intimate enemy number one' have for understanding the role of the critic and the significance attached to Nandy's confronting and contested identity? Within the discursive field of the debates on Indian secularism Nandy becomes subject to a series of over-determined responses and representations, the accounts of which seldom detail the constitutive features of his anti-secular position and, instead, respond to the threat and provocation of such a radically confronting alternative. Consistent with these processes of emphasising the voice of the critic in threatening and disruptive terms, much criticism of Nandy and his work is done by demonstrating his anti-secular and anti-modern commitment. From this perspective Nandy is represented as 'spearheading the emerging culture of academic anti-secularism in India' (Baber, 1996: 317). The philosopher Akeel Bilgrami responds to Nandy's threat and disruption by questioning his capacity to even contribute to the debates on secularism. In Bilgrami's account, Nandy does not even get 'to the terms of meaningful debate about secularism, but dangerously derail[s] it' (Bilgrami, 1994: 1749). Whether these claims made about him are accurate representations is a secondary concern. Such debates are organised around the reception of Nandy's arguments and ideas, including the threat and disruption his work carries forward intellectually and the political consequences of his claims. Typically, they ignore the methods, including the psychoanalytic focus Nandy adopts to arrive at such a confronting destination. The location of agitation and fascination for critics is partly located in Nandy's *willingness* to pursue such an alternative. What can also be overlooked is why and how he is able to transcend a dominant secular *ideal* and confront and work through these accepted identities, meanings, fantasies, projections and ideals that underpin Indian political culture. This willingness and capacity to confront and work through the constitutive features of an *ideal* and *idealised* modern secular Indian identity, is central to understanding the controversy attached to his work and identity as the 'non-player', or 'savage outsider'.

The willingness to raise these sensitive and complex issues, even if this necessitates *becoming* an intimate enemy, is consistent with Nandy's aptitude for entering into the psychoanalytic processes of confrontation and working through them. This psychoanalytic focus of working with and working through the formation of subjectivity, and politically recognised processes of identification produces a self-reflexivity that can disarm critics. Such a confronting task is deeply imbedded in the radical questioning of the constitutive features of the modern Indian self. This self-reflexivity though, disarming as it may be, provides an entry point for engaging with Nandy's method and the profoundly political, subversive and anti-disciplinary nature of his interventions. Nandy does more though, than identify and confront dominant homogenising processes of identification that foreclose the complexities and ambivalence of human subjectivity and experience. He also advances an approach of working through the complications that such confrontation brings. This book argues that Nandy's approach to dissent mirrors the dynamic processes of this psychoanalytic encounter. There are strong affinities between *working through* in a psychoanalytic therapeutic experience and the way Nandy *works through* the cultural and psychic resistances that otherwise block an appreciation of the damage and distortions that the ideology of the Indian secular state has entailed. From such a perspective Nandy's border crossings are intimately connected to this capacity to work through cultural resistances and defence mechanisms, dominant fantasies and projections.

In detailing and characterising this psychoanalytic focus, Nandy's self-identification as a political psychologist with a psychoanalytic orientation is taken seriously alongside that of the 'intellectual street fighter'. Consistent with Nandy's resistance to all dominant forms of knowledge, his use of psychoanalysis resists a specific disciplinary locus or fidelity to a particular school of psychoanalytic thought. Nandy's appropriation of psychoanalysis is dynamic as it offers a critique of the politics of psychology alongside the psychology of politics. His work, for example, carefully attends to the ambivalence of identity categories, the boundaries constituting the dominant and latent selves that inform his work, by turning to the dialectic between outer and inner incentives, to the border between culture and psyche in order to address cultural and political concerns. The extent to which his work might itself be a departure from the prescriptive claims of certain psychoanalytic schools of thought needs to be taken into account. The question though, is not whether Nandy's use of psychoanalysis falls short or deviates from existing theories, but the way psychoanalysis facilitates the processes of *confrontation* and *working through* which is central to this method of critique. This dissenting appropriation of psychoanalysis, as one would expect from such a thinker, manifests through a *psychoanalytic mode of revolt* operating within Nandy's work, one that enables him to generate alternatives that remain thoroughly political, subversive and anti-disciplinary.

Focussing on the role of psychoanalysis in his work executed in non-conformist ways reveals the deep continuities that play out across the breadth of Nandy's writings. Although, on the surface level, Nandy's writings move us through a range of themes: the role of imagining the Indian village in Hindi films; the politics of widow immolation in the practices of *Sati* during colonialism; the postcolonial condition; critiquing poverty and the violence of development; exploring the audibility of dissent; Indian and Pakistan relations;

Indian nationalism; the game of cricket in India, to name a few, yet, despite the appearance of these distinct themes, there is a consistent psychoanalytic impetus that informs the range of his scholarship. As Nandy explains:

> Frankly, many people tell me about the range of my work...but...I would think the range is somewhat narrow in the sense that my primary concern has always been human subjectivity. What makes a human being click? ... What are the inner dynamics of a person? What or how is the person configured? How is the self configured? That has always been my primary interest and in that sense my concerns are not really changed because it is only in a different condition or context that I am looking at it. And even within that, you might have noticed that two broad areas of human endeavor have always fascinated me: human destructiveness and human potentialities. These two extreme areas; and human potentialities including human creativity, and much of my work flows from this as an oscillation between these two. (Nandy and Deftereos, 2005a: 4)

In accepting Nandy's commitment to exploring human subjectivity and human experience, this book explores how a psychoanalytic mode of revolt operates within these terms. In addition, the directives repeatedly found within his work reinforce the need to continue to defy the features of dissent alongside 'a politics of awareness.'

The efforts to make over Nandy as a criminal figure, an intimate enemy, are all the more arresting given the international recognition and praise he has received. The international accolade granted to Nandy in 2007, a few months prior to the incident in Gujarat, reinforces the intense contestation that surrounds him and his work. In being awarded the prestigious Grand Prize of The Fukuoka Asian Cultural Prize, the selection committee acknowledged that 'Professor Ashis Nandy is one of the leading social and cultural critics in not only India but also the whole of Asia' (Darby, 2008: 1). This reinforces the view of Nandy as an important intellectual figure whose resonance extends beyond India. The committee also recognised that 'he has been a socially committed intellectual who has actively participated in grassroots actions, and therefore, is called the Conscience of India' (Darby, 2008: 1). That Nandy can be understood as the conscience of India is an image that takes on a deeper level of significance. To be recognised as an intellectual figure that functions as the voice of the cultural or political conscience is suggestive of a psychoanalytic orientation. In Edward Said's work, the intellectual functions as 'a kind of counter memory, with its own counter discourse that will not allow conscience to look away or fall asleep' (Said, 2004: 142). Said's description alerts us to the ethical imperative and antagonism that conscience bestows upon the function of critique and more importantly, the identity of the critic.

Extending on this motif of an 'auto-critical' moment, conscience also performs an important function in the formation of the subject. In addressing this connection, Judith Butler writes that

> conscience is the means by which a subject becomes an object for itself, reflecting on itself, establishing itself as reflective and reflexive. The "I" is not simply one who thinks about him—or herself, it is defined by his capacity for reflective self-relation and reflexivity. (Butler, 1997: 22)

Butler's comments affirm the importance of the role of psycho-analysis in Nandy's work and his identity as 'the conscience of India'. In critiquing the making of identities and of Indianness in Indian political culture, Nandy demonstrates autonomy of thought by theo-rising the complexities of human subjectivity and the contingency of boundaries within these processes of subject formation. He also demonstrates self-criticism and self-reflexivity in and through his approach. These features are already present in the voice of the po-litical psychologist. Notwithstanding his dissident status within the Indian field of psychology, it is curious that the psychoanalytic focus of Nandy's work is seldom afforded the detailed consideration it de-serves. Especially so, given that it has much to reveal about his ideas and method, including how the modern secular critic arrives at his controversial anti-secular position. This work directly responds to these concerns, including Nandy's ability to generate anxiety, fas-cination and horror or what amounts to 'a politics of discomfort', but which coincides with the promise of rupture, a working through and regeneration, the effects of which are evident in the recovery and regeneration of meanings and knowledge, including rupturing and regenerating accounts of self and society. The shift in focus from critical readings of Nandy's scholarship and contested intellectual identity to a reading in which the psychoanalytic dimensions of his work are detailed allows for a more complex understanding of the 'multiple selves of the critic'.

THE MULTIPLE SELVES OF THE CRITIC

Existing scholarship about Nandy has largely assessed his work and significance by emphasising the critical and dissenting features of his approach. While these efforts are certainly important and the value of these perspectives is not disputed, these responses are lim-ited in their ability to account for the role of psychoanalysis in his writings. Emphasised in these existing accounts are the critical ideas in Nandy's work, his non-conformist ways, maverick style and commitment to 'alternative information orders and knowledge systems' (Lal, 2000: 15). While theorising that this autonomy of thought and mode of critical intervention is crucial, doing so through a psychoanalytically informed approach provides a very different account of how dissent is actuated in the voice of the critic. A number of examples from scholarship written about Nandy can be cited to illustrate this point of difference between critical and psychoanalytically informed readings.

The first comprehensive text addressing Nandy's work is Vinay Lal's edited *Dissenting Knowledges, Open Futures: The Multiple Selves and Strange Destinations of Ashis Nandy* (2000). This follows a special edition of the journal *Emergencies* published in mid-1997. Lal's critical exploration of Nandy's intellectual identity and significance is detailed in his extensive interview with him. Here, Nandy's oppositional modus operandi and his 'defiance of defiance' are emphasised as characteristic of his scholarship. Lal's phrase astutely acknowledges the way in which Nandy's criticisms themselves undo usual radical criticisms, challenging the constitutive conditions of dissent and its audibility. The second part of the text brings together a collection of seven essays by authors collated as 'Critical Perspectives on Ashis Nandy'. These critical essays demonstrate the multiple ways that his identity and significance as a critic can be understood and represented. This is a central theme established in the text, and undoubtedly important for exploring the raison d'être of the critic. Lal acknowledges that Nandy's 'politics of discomfort' come packaged in his 'multiple selves and strange destinations' (Lal, 2000). The image of a multifaceted identity is supplemented further with what Lal suggests is Nandy's openness to imagining futures. This connection between subjectivity and the open-ended characteristic of Nandy's approach remains undertheorised despite noting its value. Similarly, according to Lal, Nandy's intellectual debates invite us into distinctively strange destinations. However, exactly what constitutes their strangeness is not fully explored, nor the methods that Nandy adopts in order to arrive at them. While a strong psychoanalytic correlation can be established between concepts of strangeness, the confronting, threatening and disruptive critical readings alone cannot adequately account for these features.

The concepts of openness and open-endedness in Nandy's work equally demand theorisation and are not entirely distinct from what Lal notes are the multiple selves at play. Does this multiplicity, for instance, not denote a deeper, more psychoanalytic concern regarding a divided or decentred subjectivity? Can critique that leads us into strange destinations, or the multiple selves of the critic be defined with any great certainty or permanence? These features of openness are equally central to theorising questions of reflexivity and self-reflexivity within his work and identity as critic. Critical readings do not account for what Nandy elsewhere reveals to be the distinctively psychoanalytic features of this openness. Commenting on this openness, he notes that interpretation is a projective test.

> People read what they want in my work. I never close my work, at least too closed. I like open-endedness so that not only can people see me in that, [but] so that people can also put themselves into it. That has always been part of my effort. (Nandy and Deftereos, 2005a: 27)

It is worth emphasising that the psychoanalytic focus is already present in his work and in the voice of the political psychologist. This, though is not necessarily followed through, leaving Lal affirming, but not adequately accounting for, the effects of this openness. Similarly, Lal does not adequately explore how this dissenting mode or the counter-hegemonic attitude to structures of knowledge that Nandy employs is generated. Lal draws our attention to Nandy's revealing dedication in *Traditions, Tyranny and Utopias: Essays in the Politics of Awareness* (1987a) reinforcing his commitment and alliance with the voices 'which defy the given models of defiance' (Nandy, 1987a). Lal, and here he is not alone, is focused on quantifying and qualifying this defiance, rather than noting the self-reflexivity of the comment. Further overlooked is the reflexivity and self-reflexivity of the title of the text, in which Nandy's efforts are articulated within an intellectual and political commitment to a politics of awareness. This provides yet another opportunity for exploring the psychoanalytic features of such a task, including the role of self-criticism and self-reflexivity in producing a critical awareness.

This oversight is also evident in Makarand Paranjape's essay published in Lal's edited text. In Paranjape's case, perhaps, the missed opportunity carries a different weight given the focus he provides for his reflections. In his essay 'In the Interstices of Tradition and Modernity: Exploring Ashis Nandy's Clandestine and Incommunicable Selves', a psychoanalytic intention is evident in the title. This is further supplemented by what he states is his interest 'in investigating the kind of self-representation and self-engineering—to use Nandy's words again—that go on in his work' (Paranjape in Lal, 2000: 234). These parameters of investigation, fascinating as they are, are ultimately found wanting.

This is due to the absence of a psychoanalytic framework in which to develop and elaborate on these concerns. Paranjape steers this questioning into different terms, making much of what he sees as Nandy's modern dilemmas in espousing tradition. Again, this is an important, if not contentious connection to make and in Paranjape's reading, essential to understanding Nandy's meaningful critical interventions. Just how this is made possible in Nandy's writings and perspectives is explained by the ways that he 'rehabilitates Gandhi', notably as 'an inveterate dissenter' (Paranjape in Lal, 2000: 237). While Gandhi, as an intellectual directive, is present in Nandy's work, this does not evidently explain his own aptitude for meaningful intervention. Paranjape ultimately turns his attention to critiquing Nandy for not being 'traditional or spiritual enough' instead of questioning his secular modern identity (Paranjape in Lal, 2000: 239). This is an interesting deconstructive device and rebuttal to the charges laid against Nandy by critics for his retreat into a romanticised cultural traditionalism and anti-modernism. If Nandy is a modern secular scholar, how is his own modernity defended against or more importantly, confronted and worked through in order to affirm what Paranjape claims is his 'sustenance from non-modern sources?'(Paranjape in Lal, 2000: 239). Such questions bring us back to the complex terrain of the cultural politics of selfhood, including the way the postcolonial condition is confronted and worked through in the voice of the critic.

Dipesh Chakrabarty acknowledges that it is rare for the tensions between tradition and modernity implicit in the modern Indian intellectual to be addressed in such a self-conscious manner as Nandy achieves. According to Chakrabarty, Nandy 'more than anybody else in India has drawn our attention to the questions the very idea of tradition poses to all modernisers/cultural critics of the subcontinent' (Chakrabarty in Lal, 2000: 250). While Chakrabarty engages with these tensions critically, in terms of demonstrating how this 'problem of the undesirable past—configures itself in Nandy's work', the self-consciousness of these efforts, or rather the features of self that facilitate these methods of self-consciousness, remain uncharted (Chakrabarty in Lal, 2000: 250). Simply stated, the self-reflexivity and insight generated by Nandy's approach while acknowledged as significant, remains unexplained. Chakrabarty, therefore, falls short of characterising the features of this internal dynamic and its significance for deepening our understanding of Nandy's confrontations.

Ziauddin Sardar in his reading of 'The A B C D (and E) of Ashis Nandy' describes Nandy's intellectual aptitude as representative of a thinker who is a polymath, for his 'thought and scholarship is one long quest for alternatives to the dominant modes of everything! But it would be out of character if Nandy's alternatives were located within prevailing boundaries, or the search itself followed a common path' (Sardar in Lal, 2000: 13). Sardar acknowledges that Nandy's critical impetus cannot be reduced to a simple formula or contained within a disciplinary locus. To attempt to do so would be antithetical to the dissenting alternatives his work points us towards. Sardar comments on a number of these alternatives and the value we might attach to them, but the reasons as to why Nandy is able to actuate these counter-hegemonic perspectives are not fully developed. This maverick attitude that Sardar applauds is ultimately accepted as a personality trait and stylistic device.

Similar representations are evident in interviews conducted with Nandy. One such example is from the Iranian philosopher Ramin Jahanbegloo in his interview with Nandy published as *Talking India: Ashis Nandy in Conversation with Ramin Jahanbegloo* (2006). Jahanbegloo begins by characterising Nandy's intellectual significance in terms of his contribution to a dialogue of cross-cultural and cross-political studies. Yet, as he points out, the pathways this dialogue advocates is not determined by Nandy's local or international profile, or his localised and international interests. Rather, it is marked by a distinctively dissenting impetus. Jahanbegloo describes this in terms of an 'acute critique of all homogenisation projects and the imposition of a cultural grid on another culture' (Nandy and Jahanbegloo, 2006: viii). Nandy's antipathy to the artifice of absolutising the relative differences between cultures is well-documented. But again, how is this sensitivity developed as a feature of the methods of the critic? Phillip Darby, in an interview reflecting on Nandy's intellectual significance reiterates his critical disposition. Darby suggests that what 'interests Nandy are to disturb set opinion, or conventional understandings of things, so there are both *shocks and excites*' (italics mine, Deftereos, 2007:5). What distinguishes Darby's comments from these critical readings is his acknowledgement of the effects and affects that Nandy's work elicits. In noting these affects, Darby gestures towards the dynamic rupture that Nandy's work invites, one which proves a useful starting point for the analysis undertaken here.

While a dissenting impetus is already established in these critical readings, there is a greater complexity at play that Darby describes as a visceral reaction. This reaction is not limited only to the reception of Nandy's work and the response of the reader. That which is experienced as a reaction, as an effect and affect, also informs the self-criticism and self-reflexivity that Nandy demonstrates in his work. While these critical reflections are valuable contributions for understanding the significance of Nandy's work, accounting for the psychoanalytic focus of his work provides a more complex account of his methods. What is commented on very effectively as the external effects of his work, such as the democratisation of knowledge and the pluralisation of knowledge systems, cannot be removed from the internal dynamics emphasised in this analysis. Nandy's mode of intervention, explored as a psychoanalytic mode of revolt, has much to reveal about how these external and internal dynamics operate within his work and his identity as critic. The positioning of the border between the inner world(s) of the subject, what can be termed the psyche, and the outer world(s), that which can be noted as culture, is carefully attended. The way this border between internal and external processes is positioned in the formation of the subject is a central feature of this task for it tells us something about the way individual and collective selfhood is formed. It is this dynamic interplay between internal and external processes, and the recovery of the possibility of a dynamic interplay between psyche and culture, that is preserved in Nandy's writings. This adds another dimension to understanding Nandy's predisposition for border crossings and challenges us to re-position the boundaries of debate with his alternative interventions. The closure of this dynamic interplay and the defence of a dialectical understanding of outer and inner powers in forming the self and society are central features of his work.

A PSYCHOANALYTIC READING OF SELF AND SOCIETY

In addition to the emphasis placed on Nandy's critical and dissenting features, the psychoanalytic focus of his work is discernable. This is illustrated, in a more obvious way, in the titles of his essays and books where Nandy's receptiveness to psychoanalytic themes and concerns is apparent. These titles reveal an emphasis on the secret selves that inform and disrupt 'official' accounts of selfhood and culture, the presence of conscious and unconscious processes and his concerns with agency, modern oppression and forms of resistance. For example, in not necessarily listing these titles but in noting some of the phrases used, this commitment is if not established then at least made upfront. Phrases like 'possible and retrievable selves', 'a politics of awareness', 'the secret politics of our desires', 'the intimate enemy', 'loss and recovery of self', 'the savage Freud', and 'time warps: silent and evasive pasts' gesture towards the dynamic interplay across the borders of outer and inner life.

D.R. Nagaraj's description of Nandy in the introduction to *Exiled at Home* (2005a) establishes this further. Nagaraj portrays Nandy as 'a chronicler of the existential unconscious against the political conscious, a historian of the quotidian against meta-narratives of socio-political engineering' (Nandy, 2005a: ixx). That Nandy's work draws our attention to the complexities of these processes and chronicles its unfolding, sheds a different light on the 'multiple selves' that inform his work and the 'multiples selves of Ashis Nandy' to which Vinay Lal alerts us. This is reinforced by Nandy himself whose self-representations as a political psychologist and 'intellectual street fighter' are not mutually exclusive but central to the tasks of chronicling and recovering multiple selves in his work, and even the multiple selves of the critic.

Worth noting is the role of Nandy's training as a clinical psychologist in India in the 1970s which he describes as being 'heavily psychoanalytic at that time and heavily anti-quantitative'. He continues: 'You know I started my life as a formal psychologist with a heavy Freudian slant, well Freudian meta-psychology at least, if not Freudian psychology [as understood] in proper conventional psychoanalysis, so in any case it was part of the picture' (Deftereos, 2005b: 3). The historical trajectory of the discipline of psychology in India suggests that psychoanalysis has at best had a peripheral role in the development of this scholarship. This point is reinforced by Nandy's dissident status within the field, in part explainable by the critical impetus informing his explorations into the politics of psychology and the psychology of politics.

Consistent with Nandy's thoroughly critical approach is the way his dissenting gaze is cast upon his reading of psychoanalysis itself. As is characteristic of his thinking, there is a double meaning or legacy that defines the history of psychoanalysis in India, as both a colonial technique of socialisation and a disruptive tool for critique. As a colonial tool of social engineering, psychoanalysis arrived in India on the coat-tails of imperialist urges to re-code the colonised subject in the imago of the ideal European man. The arrival of psychoanalysis in colonial India, as writers such as Christiane Hartnack, Amit Ranjan Basu, Sudhir Kakar, and Manasi Kumar have detailed, was itself a highly contested endeavour (Hartnack, 2001; Kakar, 1992; Kumar, 2006). Nandy too explores this contested role of psychoanalysis in

India in his essay on the first Indian psychoanalyst Girindrasekhar Bose, titled 'The Savage Freud: The First Non-Western Psychoanalyst and the Politics of Secret Selves in Colonial India'. Nandy draws on the figure of Bose to navigate the contested *arrival* and role of psychoanalysis. Under the leadership of Bose, the founder and first president of the Indian Psychoanalytic Society from 1922 to 1953, psychoanalysis played an important function within Indian society. Challenging the acultural and universalising drives within psychoanalytic thought, Nandy acknowledges the hybridisation of the discourse in its colonial setting. In the colonies, he states,

> was the scope to construct a Freud who could be used as a radical critic of the savage world and, at the same time, a subverter of the imperial structures of thought that had turned the South into a dumping ground for dead and moribund categories of the Victorian era. (Nandy, 1995b: 136)

The dual function is also consistent with Nandy's reading of colonialism, itself a site of contested meanings, fantasies and projections, implicating the coloniser and colonised, including the colonising and colonised cultures into complex processes of identification, transference and counter-transference. Like colonialism itself, the importation of psychoanalysis in Colonial India was not a straightforward or unidirectional encounter of assimilation and domestication. Although an available technique of social engineering utilised by colonial elites, psychoanalysis was equally a tool of demystification and criticism.

As Nandy explains,

> psychoanalysis also had to serve as a new instrument of social criticism, as a means of demystifying aspects of Indian culture that seemed anachronistic or pathological to the articulate middle classes, and as a dissenting western school of thought that could be turned against the West itself. (Nandy, 1995b: 83)

It is in this reading of psychoanalysis, as a dissenting and disruptive tool, that Nandy's approach can be found. Consistent with Nandy's modus operandi of dissent, psychoanalysis in his work does not follow a prescriptive reading of Freudian depth-psychology, or follow the intellectual pathways of established Freudian and post-Freudian schools of thought. This too, perhaps, explains why the psychoanalytic focus of his thinking remains undertheorised. Nandy's self-professed de-professionalised approach to psychoanalytic theory and concepts also defies rigid readings of psychoanalysis as 'the talking cure' offering a normative framework of selfhood. He notes that psychoanalytic concepts in his writings are not always 'recognised as psychoanalysis proper!' (Nandy and Deftereos, 2005a: 8). This de-professionalised application of psychoanalysis is consistent with Nandy's confrontation with homogenising and standardising approaches to knowledge. To adopt Phillip Rieff's expression, the 'analytic attitude' that Nandy demonstrates and further refines is best understood as a dissenting analytic attitude, one which is firmly grounded in the postcolonial encounter. It is also situated in the dynamism of the Freudian analytic enterprise in its application as a mode of social criticism rather than preserved within a fixed disciplinary locus.

Other reasons for the undertheorised role of psychoanalysis in his work include deeper and more complex resistances to psychoanalysis and psychoanalytic methods of cultural analysis. These include the current 'neo-colonial backlash' (Kumar, 2006) from cultural and social science theorists questioning the validity of psychoanalysis, in addition to its dissenting status within the Indian field of political psychology. Deeper resistances to the analytic experience itself also match Nandy's arresting confrontation of being 'at the edge of psychology'. The drive 'against analysis' (Derrida, 1998) may well be the shadow self of psychoanalysis as Jacques Derrida acknowledges in Freud's discussion of resistances. For Derrida, these inbuilt criticisms are played out by the repetition compulsion within psychoanalysis itself, demonstrating the complexity that these processes of confrontation and working through entail.[2]

To characterise the psychoanalytic focus of Nandy's writings as a psychoanalytic mode of revolt, and to detail how this produces dissenting perspectives, is therefore not a task of establishing a theory or disciplinary locus that Nandy fits into. It would be inconsistent with Nandy's reflective self-relation to knowledge production and commitment to radicalism to foreclose the dynamism of the Freudian analytic encounter. How Nandy's work might itself be understood as a postcolonial encounter with psychoanalysis and a reworking of and departure from the disciplinary locus of psychoanalysis needs to also be taken into account. While the historical trajectory of psychoanalysis in India as a therapeutic practice and mode of social criticism is important, understanding Nandy's own postcolonial encounter with psychoanalysis as both a product of and critical deviation from this trajectory is equally so. It is within this context that this book characterises and details the psychoanalytic mode of revolt in which to locate Nandy's intellectual sensitivity for the positioning of external and internal boundaries—the boundaries between culture and psyche—his sensitivity for theorising the complexities of human subjectivities, his attentiveness to the inclusions and exclusions operating in power relations and in processes of identification. The psychoanalytic mode of revolt also provides a deeper engagement with Nandy's consistent concern with the ways in which dominant and official accounts of politics and political identities can foreclose alternative expressions and accounts of self and society.

Nandy warns against the dangers of standardisation and homogenisation—features that have a distinct psychoanalytic component. This includes the standardisation of psychoanalysis itself, as certain schools of Freudian psychoanalysis have frozen the dynamism of Freud's discoveries. It is this psychoanalytic commitment across Nandy's work, including his critique of secularism, that directs his confrontation with the boundaries of politics and Indian democracy. For as he warns, deeply imbedded defences within a society, like the critical defence of the secular ideal within Indian politics, can 'limit the play with self-definitions, ego boundaries and identity fragments, that is needed to unleash the potentialities of a culture of participatory democracy' (Nandy, 2002c: 4). This includes the self-critical and self-reflexive capacity 'to play with one's past-as-part-of-one's-self', especially when that past is 'not conveniently dead' (Nandy, 2002c: 4). Nandy responds to these concerns by *rupturing* established dominant meanings and defences, and *regenerating* meaning by reclaiming the pluralism within human experience and within Indian democratic culture. This is the task of politics. As he states 'not only must politics work with—and work out—the contradictions in human subjectivity, that subjectivity in turn concretises, perhaps better than any action, the state of politics in a society' (Nandy, 1980a: vii).

Politics is for Nandy an engagement with human subjectivity. This includes questioning how the subject is formed, how the boundaries of selfhood are constituted through cultural and political processes, concepts of agency and resistance, processes of identification, and how ideologies are instituted in psycho-social processes through what the philosopher Judith Butler notes are processes of subjection. Butler's 'psychic life of power' thesis addresses the complexities of subject formation in relation to ideology and power. Drawing on an Althusseurian reading, Butler details the psychic dimensions of power and ideology in forming the subject, and in positioning the boundaries between self and other. According to Butler the psychic life of power and of ideology operates through processes of subjection in the very *making* of the subject. This process denotes something more than simply internalising or taking on characteristics of external power, for subjection to power marks the very process of *becoming* a recognised subject. This emphasises an interesting paradox, in that although external to the subject, 'subjection is nevertheless a power assumed by the subject, an assumption that constitutes the instrument of that subject's becoming' (Butler, 1997: 11). Such readings of subjectivity address the positioning of the boundaries in the formation of the subject, in addition to the contingency and ambivalence of the boundaries, between self and other, public and private, secular and non-secular, psychology and politics.

A similar argument is to be found in Nandy's analysis of the inner and outer workings of power and oppression across the various themes he covers. In Nandy's work, exploring the effects and affects of power operating within individual and collective accounts of human subjectivity are central to the confrontations he enters into. These issues are present in a number of places in his work. For example, in a collection of essays offering a cultural and psychological biography of the modern Indian nation state, published as *The Romance of the State: And the Fate of Dissent in the Tropics* (Nandy, 2002a), this psychoanalytic reading of politics is evident. In the preface to the text, Nandy suggests that the concept of politics he is interested in and contributing to is the dynamic interplay between external and internal processes, in theorising politics at the borders between culture and psyche. As he explains in the text, 'the essays in this book explore the vicissitudes of the idea of the modern state under different cultural and psychological conditions' (Nandy, 2002a: ix). In doing so, he also opens up alternative conceptual spaces through which to rupture and regenerate the boundaries of inclusion and exclusion operating in politics. Nandy, consistent with this approach, thus claims that 'politics is nothing less than a means of redefining a society's selfhood by renegotiating the distribution of power and the legitimacy of existing centres of power in different domains of life' (Nandy, 2002a: ix).

This definition of politics, marked by sensitivity for the psychic dimensions of power, is evident in earlier writings. *The Savage Freud and Other Essays on Possible and Retrievable Selves* (Nandy, 1995b), which can be read as a prequel to *The Romance of the State* (Nandy, 2002a), establishes this commitment. In the text, methods in support of a Freudian depth psychology (although applied in Nandy's idiosyncratic way) are established amidst a psychoanalytic exploration of possible and retrievable selves that can destabilise the positioning of the boundaries constituting politics. In address-ing politics as an ontological condition, theorising possible and re-trievable selves takes on a distinctively psychoanalytic focus. This includes exploring how the politically recognised subject is formed and the inclusions and exclusions operating within the cultural poli-tics of selfhood. This awareness and sensitivity for the positioning of boundaries adds a greater complexity to understanding the 'border crossings' that Nandy's work invites us into. Nandy's approach here, it should be noted, is not marked by an emphasis on retrieving 'lost' selves, or even 'authentic' selves as certain critics have accused him of. Rather, it is in recognition of the fact that human subjectivity is itself an ambivalent process of *becoming* and fixed identity claims, includ-ing those made in defence of a modern secular Indian self, Hindu Self or even non-modern self, are not entirely possible. The residue of those 'other selves' are not so easily cast away given that repression itself finds recourse in unconscious processes. Accounting for these 'other selves', or even 'secret selves' repressed or visible, is central to the possibility of rupturing and recreating human subjectivity.

The question remains though as to how Freud, as the psychoana-lytic directive, appears within Nandy's critique, and furthers the op-eration of this method. What does the expression *The Savage Freud*, the title of the text, actually refer to? Does this title, for instance, re-flect upon the psychoanalytic methods and identity that Nandy might claim as his own? Are Nandy's non-conformist methods, including his non-conformist Freudian methods, being referenced as savagely applied? Or, is Nandy as the non-Western Indian scholar representing himself through an internalised colonial mirror as the savage subject? These questions demand a more sustained characterisation of these psychoanalytic methods, including Nandy's self-reflexive musings. Equally important is an understanding of how Nandy as the savage Freud, and savage outsider, invites us into processes of confrontation and working through them in his work as a psychoanalytic mode of revolt. Despite criticisms regarding Nandy's alleged anti-modernism, culturalism and romanticism for a pre-modern India, he maintains:

> The author of these essays...is not the offspring of village India...He is a child of modern India, looking for a language of social criticism that will not be entirely alien to a majority of Indians who have been increasingly empowered by an open political process, however, imperfect that openness. (Nandy, 1995b: ix)

Following this passage, the clues for these possible and retrievable selves, including his own, are to be found in Nandy's celebration of the pluralism within Indian democracy and Indian culture. The voice of the radical democrat is, however, not necessarily inconsistent with these psychoanalytic themes and methods that Nandy demonstrates. Nandy's work invites us into a mode of cultural criticism that provides a space for reflexivity and self-reflexivity, to journey into the cultural politics of selfhood and into the complexities of human subjectivity and cultural codes. It is an open invitation into processes of confrontation and of *working through* that mirror the psychotherapeutic journey of rupturing and regenerating human subjectivity. In doing so, it is also an open invitation to journey into Nandy's alternatives, including 'other' cultural and political configurations, 'other' selves and 'other' expressions of 'Indianness' that exist as our doubles, albeit latent within psychic, cultural, political processes. How this invitation is actuated in the psychoanalytic mode of revolt that informs Nandy's corpus and the horror and fascination that accompanies such a task comprises the primary focus of this inquiry. This book critically explores Nandy's open invitation, the confronting questions his work raises and the alternatives he offers. In doing so, it affirms the importance of this polemical Indian thinker, whose work resonates well beyond an Indian context, and whose voice should not be ignored even as it continues to divide.

THE STRUCTURE OF THE BOOK

This book details and characterises the mode of dissent in Nandy's work as a psychoanalytic mode of revolt. In tracing the features of this approach, this inquiry turns to a range of psychoanalytic concepts to demonstrate the psychoanalytic focus of Nandy's thinking, as well as exploring how this mode of revolt might destabilise psychoanalytic modes and forms too. Psychoanalysis applied savagely through the critical gaze of the political psychologist and 'intellectual street fighter' may not always be recognizable as 'psychoanalysis' but it does provide a focus through which to confront and work through deeply held projections, introjections, fantasies and ideals. Although these interventions destabilise and rupture dominant norms, earning Nandy the title of 'intimate enemy', or as even being 'at the edge of psychology', there is an equally strong defence of pluralism accompanying these undertakings. Nandy's thinking is in this sense a warning against the intimate enemy of foreclosure, one in which the dynamism of human subjectivity, the public dialogue over 'Indianness' and the disruptive potential of critique itself is foreclosed. Exploring how Nandy's psychoanalytic mode of revolt warns against the dangers of foreclosure is central for understanding how resistance and defiance remain dynamic live issues within his work.

Chapter 1, 'The Pathologies of Secularism', explores how the psychoanalytic focus underpinning Nandy's critique of secularism takes form. Starting with Nandy's 'scandalous' attack on secularism with his 1985 essay, 'An Anti-Secularist Manifesto' details Nandy's confrontation with the ideology of secularism critiquing its cultural and psychological viability. Nandy argues that the imported Western ideal of a secular nation state is largely incompatible with existing home grown concepts of tolerance and social cohesion. While this distinction is the focal point for critics of his work, and a repeated point of contention in the debates on secularism, Nandy's anti-secular position cannot be simply dismissed as an anti-Western tirade. In taking seriously the 'psychic life' of the ideology of secularism and its constitutive role in the formation of the modern secular Indian subject, Nandy carefully demonstrates the processes of subjection, the making over of the 'ideal' secular subject within Indian political culture. While processes of subjection are necessary for the formation of the subject, the ideology produces identity forms or typologies that are not conducive to the internal aims of secularism, namely safeguarding tolerance and a secular Indian political culture. This is where the pathologies of secularism are to be found in the production of adversarial identities, validated by a secular political culture, but that provide the very political conditions for conflicts. Nandy's anti-secular position is contextualised in these terms, as an attempt to confront and work through the ideals, projections and distortions that the ideology of secularism produces.

Chapter 2, 'Containing Indianness: Secularism versus Hindutva?', expands on Nandy's critique of secularism and his forewarnings of its crisis by detailing the rise of Hindu nationalism in Indian politics in the mid-1990s. In following the arguments Nandy advances in a number of writings, especially his collaboration on *Creating a Nationality: The Ramjanmabhumi Movement and Fear of the Self* (1995), the rise of Hindu militancy and the collective defences of the movement over who can claim 'Indianness' are located within the complexities of human subjectivity and within Indian political culture. For Nandy, the claims to 'Indianness' advanced by Hindu Nationalists and the promise of national unity and security that accompany their claims forecloses the ambivalence and contradiction of Indian traditions and culture, and identity, more broadly. The narrowing and policing of the boundaries of national identification, the 'inclusions and exclusions' witnessed in Indian politics, are explored here as symptoms of the adversarial identities that secularism fosters.

Nandy's ability to confront, challenge, and work through the cultural and psychological viability of the secular ideal and the pathologies of secularism remains, even thirty years on, thoroughly divisive and widely critiqued. Chapter 3, 'The Conceptual Battleground of Anti-Secularism and Culturalism', explores the horror and fascination that Nandy and his anti-secular thinking receive within academic and public debates on secularism. This includes how the political stakes of his work are understood, and represented, especially from within the Left where critical voices of Indian secularism have emerged alongside a curious silence regarding Nandy's 'brand' of anti-secularism. Two separate readings of this discursive field of reception demonstrate this point. The first is a discussion of two key critics of Nandy's work written during the late 1990s, and the second considers a heated public exchange that took place in 2004. This field of reception of both fascination and horror with Nandy's anti-secular interventions culminates in the attempts in 2008 to criminalise the 'intimate enemy'. What is consistent across these examples is that the location of agitation and fascination for critics is in Nandy's willingness to confront accepted identities, meanings, fantasies, projections and ideals operating in politics, and in doing so radically challenge the constitutive features of modern Indian secular political culture and selfhood. Nandy's border crossings, or rather his disruption of the boundaries of debate, remain profoundly destabilising, as these exchanges demonstrate his efforts to reposition the boundaries of debate and the boundaries of inclusion and exclusion operating within politics more broadly.

Chapter 4, 'Critique at the Threshold of Politics', critically details the autonomy of thought that distinguishes Nandy's interventions into the debates on secularism starting with his only two responses to critics. The autonomy of thought that Nandy demonstrates with his calls for a 'post-secular awareness' is informed by the method of his dissent. The self-critical and self-reflexive features of his approach may appear counter-intuitive for the modern secular critic, but nonetheless point to a significant feature of his approach. This turning inwards, in questioning one's own deeply held assumptions and processes of identification, is a feature of Nandy's psychoanalytic focus. Equally important are the ways he confronts the fear and threat of democratic pluralism, including the anxiety that 'people's choices' can represent, along with the pluralism within human subjectivity and human experience. Nandy's ability to cross a range of borders, intellectual, cultural and otherwise, whether in the form of rejecting the secular 'ideal' or in re-positioning the boundaries of debate, is also explored.

In Chapter 5, 'Revolt and the Role of the Critic', a deeper engagement with Nandy's idiosyncratic use of psychoanalysis and his identity as critic is explored. Drawing on psychoanalytic theory, notably Julia Kristeva's work on the revolt that takes place in the psychoanalytic psychotherapeutic encounter of the analytic experience, reveals that there is more at play to Nandy's capacity to enter into processes of confrontation and *working through*, his 'autonomy of thought' and dissenting analytic attitude. A reading of Nandy's characteristic de-professionalised gaze provides insight into the methods of the political psychologist in not only the psychology of politics but, more importantly, the politics of psychology. In characterising Nandy's mode of dissent as a *psychoanalytic mode of revolt*, the dynamic rupturing of dominant and homogenising structures of knowledge and meanings and the regeneration and recovery of 'alternatives' are located firmly within internal psychoanalytic processes. Revolt in its psychoanalytic context locates Nandy's capacity to surpass existing forms of defiance, alongside a series of internal processes which necessitate *confrontations* and a *working through* of the boundaries of his own postcoloniality in order to generate critique. This method of revolt, rupture and regeneration constitutes the foundation for Nandy's aptitude to defy accepted norms of defiance. These issues are evident in Nandy's essay, 'Shamans, Savages and the Wilderness: On the Audibility of Dissent and the Future of Civilizations', reprinted in *Bonfire of the Creeds* (2004a) as is the extent to which the metaphor of the shaman, and by extension the voice of the critic, is a figure *in revolt*.

Chapter 6, 'The Psychotherapeutic as a Mode of Social Criticism', addresses the integrity and permanent features of this psychoanalytic mode of revolt. This is explored in a detailed reading of how this structures Nandy's interventions in two examples of his work. The first revisits the representation of Nandy as 'intimate enemy', and the important interventions into the psychological and cultural conditions of colonialism and postcoloniality in *The Intimate Enemy: Loss and Recovery of Self Under Colonialism* (1983a). The second example looks at five shorter articles written in Indian newspapers between 2005 and 2007 and the way the operation of this psychoanalytic mode of revolt enables Nandy to enter into a permanent play with national fantasies, by rupturing and regenerating the 'idea of India'. Nandy's method as discussed presents a paradox for the critic of the State. For, in not reproducing established national norms, Nandy runs the risk of being de-authorised, yet it is precisely this risk and the pursuit of this risk that enables him to enter into processes of revolt. The psychotherapeutic effects and affects of Nandy's method and the alternatives, including the alternative political imaginings his work invites us to venture towards, are also considered.

'Re-Imaginings in the Cultural Politics of Selfhood' reinforces the need to account for the psychoanalytic focus of Nandy's interventions alongside a more critical assessment of the polemical opus of this important Indian thinker. Psychoanalysis under Nandy's critical gaze functions as a disruptive, political, subversive and anti-disciplinary tool of analysis. Nandy's invitation through the psychoanalytic mode of revolt opens up spaces for dissent and 'a politics of awareness', the possibility to re-imagine the cultural politics of selfhood, though in ways which remain permanently dynamic and contestable. To accept Nandy's wager to rupture and regenerate that which is accepted as commonsense is a reminder of our own ongoing possibility for revolt, a capacity fundamental to all human subjectivity and social and political criticism.

NOTES

1. http://ashisnandysolidarity.blogspot.com.au.
2. For a discussion on resistances to psychoanalysis, refer to Derrida's discussion of how resistance is itself a feature of the analytic experience. Derrida analyses five organised types of resistance, three emerging from the ego and a further two brought into play through the functioning of the Id and the Superego. See Derrida, J. (1998) Resistances to Psychoanalysis. Stanford: Stanford University Press.

PART A

The Pathologies of Secularism

1

The Pathologies of Secularism

Nandy's critique of secularism is primarily a confrontation with the cultural and psychological viability of secularism in India. Detailed in the essay 'An Anti-Secularist Manifesto' published in 1985 in *Seminar*, the cultural and psychological viability of secularism is made apparent through the psychoanalytic approach that Nandy adopts. This psychoanalytic focus is central to the anti-secular claims advanced in his critique. Nandy challenges, and ultimately rejects, the ways in which the pursuit of a secular ideal within Indian political culture works to foreclose subjectivity, concepts of Indianness and concepts of tolerance in specific ways. The making of the subject into politically recognised modern secular identities within Indian political culture is central to this task. For Nandy, this is where the crisis of secularism or, as he prefers, the pathologies of secularism are to be found: in what Judith Butler terms 'the psychic life of power' (Butler, 1997). In Butler's text, *The Psychic Life of Power: Theories in Subjection* (1997), the psychic life of power and ideology operates through processes of subjection in the *making* of the subject. The psychic life of power operates *in* and *through* these processes of *becoming* a subject. Butler's conceptual framework is useful for understanding the argument Nandy makes about subjectivity and the making of political identities within Indian political culture. Although not necessarily articulated within these terms, Nandy's analysis of the ways in which the political subject and political citizen are formed and made over within a dominant and normative secular political culture speaks directly to these processes of subjection.

What is equally significant about Butler's account of the formation of subjectivity is that this subjection to power is paradoxical. In Butler's reading, subjection signifies 'the process of becoming subordinated by power as well as the process of becoming a subject' (Butler, 1997: 2). Butler emphasises the necessity of subordination for subjectivity and in turn, the identity of the subject for being secured. Submitting to power is a fundamental condition for becoming a subject and central to the ontological security derived from these processes of subjection. In Nandy's critique, this paradox characterises the way in which political identities are formed, and the inclusions and exclusions that result from these processes. It is here that Nandy's anti-secularism is detailed and worked through: in the ways in which these inclusions and exclusions operate to consolidate a dominant and normative Indian political culture and political identities. Nandy's confrontation with secularism also demonstrates an intellectual sensitivity to the ways in which the boundaries between secular and non-secular, public and private, tolerant and intolerant are cast. Where Butler provides a language for explaining these processes of subjection, Nandy critiques the ways that these processes operate in Indian secular political culture. Nandy's critique of the way identities, political culture and politics are constituted in relation to a dominant secular ideal is central to this task.

Julia Kristeva's work is also useful for understanding the ways that these processes of subjection operate within Nandy's critique of secularism, and demonstrate the confrontational features of his anti-secular position. Kristeva's account of processes of *becoming* or subject formation, and her emphasis on the importance of the positioning of the boundaries of subjectivity, including the precariousness of these boundaries, is relevant for detailing the argument that Nandy makes about the formation of the subject and of political culture. Kristeva's contributions to psychoanalytic theory and her own account of processes of *becoming* are well-documented and widely critiqued. Equally well-documented is her application of psychoanalysis to political theory, and political processes.[1] However, it is Kristeva's concept of the abject that details the importance of the positioning of the boundaries of subjectivity and border points. In *Powers of Horror: An Essay on Abjection* (1982) Kristeva theorises at length the positioning of boundaries (the inclusions and exclusions) that take place in the formation of subjectivity, or within processes of becoming. Although these processes of inclusion and exclusion are necessary in order for the boundaries of selfhood to form, these processes are precarious as denoted by Kristeva's concept of the *abject*. The concept of the *abject* in her analysis captures that which must be cast away and repudiated in order for the boundaries of subjectivity to be secured. The *abject* and *abjection* are concepts which belong to pre-symbolic and hence, formative stages of subject formation. What is of interest are the ways in which she emphasises the precariousness of these processes, located as they are within pre-symbolic stages of subject formation. The abject provokes an affective state, of fascination and horror, as that which both lures and repels. Moreover, it is representative of a highly threatening and disruptive dynamic, a dynamic that *can* and *has* the potential to return us to pre-symbolic states. It references that which must *necessarily* be cast away in these processes of becoming, *despite* its fascination and *because* of its horror, in order for subjectivity to be formed and the boundaries of selfhood secured. Therefore, that which is representative of the abject is profoundly disruptive and threatening. The abject is that which re-affirms and reminds us of the precariousness of these processes, especially the positioning of the boundaries of selfhood. The abject within Kristeva's account carries forward the very real and potential threat of disrupting subjectivity. The dangers and the threat of the abject are in its disruption of subjectivity: that which can return us to the borderlands of signification as neither subject nor object. The abject carries forward fascination, accompanied by threat (both real and perceived), disruption, ambivalence and even the loss of identity.

The concept of the abject is applied in this chapter to theorise the way Nandy confronts the positioning of boundaries, and the inclusions and exclusions operating within the psychic life of power. In critiquing these processes of subjection operating within the secular ideal, Nandy's analysis emphasises aspects of Indian culture and concepts of selfhood, including Indianness deemed threatening and disruptive to this ideal. What is radically confrontational about his anti-secular position is this psychoanalytic focus on aspects of selfhood and of Indianness that have been abjected from view in pursuit of this secular ideal. This is where Nandy's anti-secularism is advanced, through this psychoanalytic questioning of these processes of subjection operating in Indian politics. In Nandy's account, the secular political subject instituted and authorised as an ideal political subject brings to the fore a number of tensions between these processes of becoming and existing concepts of selfhood and Indianness. These are explored in 'An Anti-Secularist Manifesto' as tensions between the psychic life of a dominant secular modernity and a pre-modern or non-modern cultural self. For Nandy, the non-modern cultural self still exists, albeit latent in Indian political culture today. To this extent, addressing these processes of subjection is significant for

Nandy's critique of modernity and what he cautions are its increasing homogenising and standardising effects. These processes of subjection and compliance, Nandy argues, are an inherited Western secular ideal, bringing to the fore a crucial dynamic which needs to be *worked through*. For Nandy, confronting and ultimately rejecting the ideal is central to the production of critique, his anti-secular position. He describes this task as one that necessitates an intellectual sensitivity for external and internal processes, the positioning of the border between culture and psyche, and in doing so, reveals something of his method of critique. Nandy states that 'this is a very heavy psychological effort in the sense that the pre-modern India that you carry within you, is I see in tension with the modern Indian, the living. So it is that level which I am negotiating and that language of negotiation is psychological...' (Nandy and Deftereos, 2005b: 4).

Whether this cultural self or pre-modern self can be entirely cast away or abjected from view through these processes of subjection operating within Indian political culture is dubious. Therefore, that which has been repressed from view, or cast away, in establishing the normative political subject and a normative concept of toleration, forms an important part of his reading of Indian politics. This includes confronting the limits and limitations in pursuing this official secular ideal; the ways in which ambivalence within subjectivity is foreclosed in the making of political identities; and the ways in which concepts of tolerance within Indian culture are overshadowed by a dominant and official secular mode of tolerance. Nandy's capacity to identify, confront and work through these issues exemplifies the psychoanalytic focus, and the intersection between psychoanalysis and political theory structuring his critique of secularism.

THE LIMITS OF STATE SECULARISM AND 'OFFICIAL' TOLERANCE

'An Anti-Secularist Manifesto' was first published in 1985 in *Seminar* and reprinted in *Romance of the State* (Nandy, 2002a).[2] The essay distinguishes between two different meanings of secularism that exist in contemporary Indian political culture. The first definition is traditionally a Western account, in which the ideology of secularism is defined by the separation and freeing of politics from religion. To this extent, Nandy's critique of secularism is not removed from debates on modernity. Following Gandhi's lead, this definition of secularism is an external inherited Western political ideal, the normative assumption operating being that the more secular a state is, the more tolerant it will be. It is argued that this secular ideal is integral to concepts of social and political amity and in safeguarding an official concept of tolerance in Indian political culture. Within this inherited ideal, the sacred is understood as having no role to play in expressions of tolerance within public life, and even less to contribute to the sphere of politics and democratic process.[3] This sensitivity to the pre-modern and modern India enables Nandy to claim that there is another definition discernable. This recognition of the tension and ambivalence present in modernity enables him to claim that there is a second, more local definition of secularism discernable, although latent within Indian culture and society today. This non-modern Indian meaning, derived from the traditions and cultural practices of the Indic civilisation, has survived as a reminder of alternative processes of identification and social and political organisation. From this perspective secularism is understood not in opposition to the sacred, but in opposition to the pathologies of intolerance, ethnocentrism, xenophobia and fanaticism. Nandy's analysis thus distinguishes between an inherited concept of secular modernity and existing non-modern or pre-modern modes of identification and social and political organisation. Much is made of the fact that this 'inherited' concept has been part of India's official postcolonial identity. This distinction generates a series of tensions, particularly between official modern and non-official non-modern expressions of subjectivity, which for Nandy need to be addressed.

These tensions between a traditional and modern self, which characterise the post-colonial condition, are not necessarily eradicated by the ideology of secularism or the secularised society it promises. Rather, for Nandy the ideology of secularism and the distortions that it promotes demonstrate its ineffectiveness in attending to these issues. These concerns regarding India's postcoloniality though do need to be worked through if the viability of secularism is to be seriously addressed. Equally important is an understanding of the way in which these tensions have been overplayed in Indian politics. For Nandy, these tensions have been appropriated by the Indian state to consolidate authentic concepts of tolerance, of Indianness, and Indian modernity. What is problematic about this is that secularism, as a dominant and imposed ideal, forecloses expressions of subjectivity and tolerance. According to Nandy, other expressions of subjectivity and tolerance, particularly non-modern forms, exist latently and, more importantly, constitute the underside of Indian political culture. Since the European meaning of secularism is conceptually laden with its historical foundations elsewhere, it can have little relevance to the concepts of tolerance and Indianness he wishes to theorise. As Nandy claims, 'the European meaning of secularism would make little sense to the average Indian rooted in a religious world view and not exposed to the kinds of debate the church-state divide produced in pre-modern Europe'. According to Nandy, this claim was recognised by the anti-colonial Indian elite, including freedom fighters, who saw the need for broad-based mobilisation, while acknowledging the incompatibility of this Western meaning of secularism for their religious society (Nandy, 2002a: 35).

The Indian meaning, in contrast to this, acknowledges that even when a State claims to be tolerant of religions, this does not necessarily lead to religious tolerance in society. Official secular tolerance instituted *in* and *through* the secular Indian state may safeguard the survival of a political community in times of crisis, or in the short term. It is, however, the Indian community and peoples which ensure its coherence, meaningfulness and lifeline over a longer period of time. For Nandy, the meaning attached to tolerance is deeply imbedded within the individual and collective psychological and cultural practices of everyday Indians. To this extent, these pre-modern or non-modern expressions of tolerance and accounts of selfhood have much to contribute. Nandy acknowledges that both definitions of secularism have co-existed within Indian political culture. However, 'one could [previously] follow the logic of the second, more local meaning of secularism in Indian politics, while paying lip-service to the first'. This is no longer the case and 'in recent years, the nature of the democratic process in India is forcing the political actors to choose between the two meanings' (Nandy, 2002a: 35). Whether this can be considered a choice is debatable, given that changing dynamics within Indian politics have consistently reinforced a dominant ideal advanced by the Congress Party that 'secularism is India's destiny' (Gandhi, 2002).

What Nandy takes issue with is that this destiny, including its foundations and its viability, remains largely unchallenged. The debates of secularism that do take place, even within the context of what is now widely accepted as a crisis in Indian secularism, tend to focus upon how this destiny should unfold.[4] Most conceptual arguments are focused upon re-instating this ideal and, hence, the dominant status of the secular ideal within political culture remains unchallenged. The dominance of a secular modernity as the only possible political ideal, along with the viability of this ideal, is therefore radically undermined.

Nandy rejects this ideal, and in the process distinguishes himself from these existing perspectives consolidating a secular India. In Nandy's analysis, the fact that the Indian state is able to play the role of the impartial arbiter with respect to the question of tolerance is naïve and 'now a pious hope' (Nandy, 2002a: 35). The rejection of this ideal, including the pursuit of this ideal as destiny, is supported by an additional claim. For, despite the rapid growth of the power of the Indian state, and processes of secularisation over the last two decades, there are distinct limits to state secularism.

It is in response to this official definition of a Western concept of secularism, and the means by which its dominant and normative status is achieved, that Nandy's confrontation and subsequent anti-secularism can be located. This secular ideal and destiny have subjugated individual and collective consciousness and the expression of subjectivities in particular ways. Again, it is worth emphasising that for Nandy these are complex historical, cultural and psychological issues. He proceeds by acknowledging that, 'since Indians first began to borrow this ideology in the 1830s, the ideology has also dominated modern Indian consciousness' (Nandy, 2002a: 36). This precarious relationship between a pre-modern and modern consciousness has, at times, been exhausted by the state. As Nandy explains, the Indian state has actively intervened and even legislated to enforce modes of compliance with this secular consciousness and processes of identification. The assumption operating, and that Nandy claims still has currency today, is that the ideology of secularism in its more absolutist mould would 'cut down to size' India's more vocal minorities unwilling to conform to the ideal.[5] Alternatively expressed, these processes of subjection operating within the psychic life of secularism would successfully, and completely, make over minority identities. To what extent though have these processes succeeded in making a modern secular Indian political culture? Are there limits to these processes of social engineering and the secularisation of Indian society?

Nandy offers a response to these questions by confronting the 'embarrassing fact' that there is a growing suspicion of the Western concept of secularism and receptiveness to non-secular ideas to religious and cultural tolerance (Nandy, 2002a: 36). That this is an embarrassing realisation not only in India, but also within Western societies demonstrates the ways the ideal cannot be achieved. This suspicion is evident in the dissenting accounts of tolerance and concepts of Indianness that have not disappeared from view, but that exist as threatening reminders. They are dissenting, peripheral and even latent views and practices, because they exist outside of the established normative boundaries of an Indian secular culture. Constituted outside of Indian secular culture, these views and practices are officially outside of politics. Situated at the borderlands of political culture, these dissenting views, values, practices and subjectivities remain deeply threatening and disruptive to established norms. For Nandy, these dissenting views and practices are deeply imbedded in practices of religious and cultural amity. These accounts of toleration are less mechanically imposed because they co-exist alongside accounts of Indianness, seldom recognised as having political value. What is significant is that such concepts of tolerance are actuated not through an external and abstract ideology, but are intimately connected to the boundaries of alternative expressions of selfhood. It is recognition that unlike official accounts, as the work of Don Miller suggests, 'toleration can wear so many entirely other faces'. As he suggests, 'It [tolerance] may be confusion, uncertainty, doubt; it may be fear, deference, weakness, compliance; it may be self-confidence, assurance, mastery; it may be paternalism, even derision; it may be neglect; it may be preordained to bear' (Miller, 1992: 172).

This reading of tolerance performs two important functions within Nandy's analysis.

First, it locates the question of tolerance within the complexities of subjectivity, and by extension within the self/other dyad. The tolerance for others and how that tolerance is expressed, including its limits, refers to an internal capacity connected to the complexities of subjectivity. Tolerance for others is constituted in relational terms and as something predicated upon the positioning of the boundaries of self. For Nandy, it is also situated within the expressions of Indianness that he wishes to retrieve and bring back into view. This dissenting tolerance, he claims, is an already present feature, internal to Indian culture and traditions.

The second role that this concept of tolerance performs in this critique is to radically challenge the viability and efficacy of these externally and mechanically imposed concepts of toleration. Despite official accounts, for Nandy the question of tolerance operating in Indian society has less to do with abstract political ideals and ideological formations. Instead, tolerance is situated within questions of subjectivity. The psychoanalytic features of this argument, including Nandy's intellectual sensitivity for theorising at the level of these external and internal boundaries, are unequivocally made. It is worth restating the point that Nandy's dissenting account of tolerance, for others and otherness, can be distinguished by its analytic foundations. For as he affirms, 'it is closer to the concept of understanding, and presumes cultural interdependency of the kind which encourages that tolerance of others because that tolerance represents the tolerance of less acceptable aspects of one's own self' (Nandy, 2002a: 36).

Before the potential merits of this psychoanalytic reading of tolerance can be assessed, along with its threatening and disruptive features, the ways that the secular ideal operates and defines politics need to be characterised more fully. How does the ideology of secularism and its claims of official toleration define politics? How does the ideology of secularism define political identities and processes of identification operating in Indian politics? Moreover, how does Nandy 'work through' this growing suspicion of the ideology of secularism in order to confront the boundaries underpinning political culture? How does Nandy confront and work through the inclusions and exclusions that define a dominant Indian political culture and political identities, central to his anti-secular position advanced?

MAKING THE IDEAL POLITICAL SUBJECT

Consistent with the psychoanalytic focus of 'An Anti-Secularist Manifesto', Nandy builds the argument that the real power of ideology is found within processes of subjection, which is in the making of the subject. In Nandy's analysis Indian political culture is formed through the operation of this secular ideal and through processes of subjection. As he states,

> this India does have sufficient exposure to the ideology of the state to be able to internalise the concept of secularism and sections of it are willing to go to any length to ensure that the concept is not questioned...[for] there are plenty of Indians now who are willing to sacrifice the unmanageable, chaotic, real-life Indians for the sake of the idea of India. (Nandy, 2002a: 79)

This ego ideal and its accompanying fantasy structure are further supported by the institutions of the state, and through the secular ethos and official ideology of the state. Further, concepts of national security and national integration are also defined in relation to this secular ideal. The real power of the ideology is actuated within processes of socialisation and, in Butler's terms, through processes of subjection where identities are formed and made over in accordance with this secular ideal. The concept of subjection denotes more than processes of social engineering though these processes are central to the *becoming* of a politically recognised subject. For Butler, 'subjection is the paradoxical effect of a regime of power in which the very 'conditions of existence', the possibility of continuing as a recognizable social [and political] being, requires the formation and maintenance of the subject in subordination' (Butler, 1997: 27). In Nandy's analysis this regime of power that establishes the 'conditions of existence' are evident in the ways in which a hierarchical ordering of the subject as citizen emerges within Indian public life. Within Indian political culture these processes of subjection produce a hierarchical ordering of the subject as politically recognised citizen. This typology is expressed in four subject types that have much to reveal about the inclusions and exclusions operating within Indian politics. Consistent with India's inheritance of a secular modernity, the ideal subject in public life (and the one validated within this political culture as the true secular citizen) is one who displays the characteristics of a non-believer in public and in private. Nandy cites Jawaharlal Nehru, the secular statesman, as the ideal and much idealised secular subject, and in doing so also emphasises the complexities of subjectivity. In Nandy's depiction, Nehru's public commitment to secularism, as is the case with all ideal types and idealised images, can never fully be realised. In addition, the boundaries between the pre-modern and modern self cannot always be necessarily resolved or so neatly cast within such fixed identity categories. Nehru, even with his Anglo-Saxon credentials and Western education, was unable to live up to this ego ideal in totality, especially in his private life. As a statesman within public life, Nehru came close to fulfilling this ideal in his unwavering commitment to the integrative features of secularism in establishing an independent postcolonial state. The concept of tolerance that accompanies this ideal political subject also takes on a specific meaning. As demonstrated by Nehru's credentials, 'tolerance is definitionally the prerogative of one who has some Western education, and some exposure to modernity, especially the modern idiom of politics' (Nandy, 2002a: 37). This establishes a distinct boundary point of identification, and differentiation between the ideal tolerant secular political citizen and those others who fall outside of it. Those left outside of these boundaries are afforded a very different level of recognition within political culture. They may even be abjected from view and cast away from politics, as disruptive and threatening reminders of a pre-modern or even non-modern India. The concept of the abject subject in political culture is an increasingly crucial issue and again has much to reveal about the processes of identification operating within a society.

Within this typology the least favoured subject and least recognised within Indian political culture is the non-modern figure that threatens these processes of identification. This subject type is, by definition, a believer in private and in public life. For Nandy, this deviation from the ideal secular subject is best exemplified by Mohandas Karamchand Gandhi. Gandhi's challenge to politics, his methods, political identity and self-representation were intimately tied to the cosmologies of faith, pre-modern traditions and cultural practices. Articulated within the vernacular of religiosity, Gandhi's politics and calls for *ahimsa* (non-violence) and *satyaghara* (non-violent resistance) do not comply with a secular political ontology. In Nandy's account, Gandhi's presence within Indian politics challenges the normative political subject, and brings with it the possibility of re-conceiving politics in very different terms. This deviation from the secular ideal, along with Gandhi's own critique of modernity, is significant in Nandy's own critique of secularism. However, Gandhi's disruptive anti-secular worldview was not without consequence as Nandy has detailed in his analysis of Gandhi's assassination,[6] and in a number of other places in his work. It is interesting to note that while Gandhi's politics were imperative to the anti-colonial movement, his place within a newly founded independent postcolonial Indian political culture was more ambivalent. Dipesh Chakrabarty argues, for example, that while Nehru was a supporter of satyaghara in theory, he did not support this as 'valid' political praxis within 'official' Indian political culture and statecraft. Nehru's Western education and belief in the Western secular axioms of politics overshadowed his alternative views. Chakrabarty argues that postcolonial politics needed to be distinguished from the political repertoire and techniques of anti-colonial movements. As he states, 'now that India was a postcolonial, independent state based on the democratic principle of representation through universal adult franchise, actions that called into question that sovereignty of the new state were necessarily illegitimate in the eyes of Nehru' (Chakrabarty, Dipesh, Majumdar, Rochona and Sartori 2007: 33). Within such a political schema Gandhi remains a threatening figure. In Nandy's analysis it is, however, precisely the alternatives that Gandhi offered, and his perceived 'illegitimacy' in the postcolonial political context that is significant. For if political consciousness is to retain its creative force (that is, both its disruptive and regenerative possibilities in postcolonial politics), then it would need to acknowledge these religious cosmologies, traditions and faiths of the least favoured Indian citizens. Gandhi's defiance of the Western secular axioms of politics is celebrated as disruptive and creative in equal measure. Consistent with the intellectual directives of Gandhi and Freud, Nandy warns that any mode of dissenting consciousness must retain a critical distance and not become another 'reformist sect within modernity' (Nandy, 2002a: 38).

There are two further typologies that Nandy identifies along with their inclusion into a secular public culture. Deviating from Nehru's archetypal image is the non-believer in public and believer in private. This subjectivity is relatively benign within Indian political culture as the secular ideal is maintained. It remains less threatening because consistent with secular norms, the divisions between public and private and secular and non-secular are reproduced. This divided public–private self is generally accepted as part of the contradictory features of being quintessentially Indian. Next in this typology of an ideal political citizen, but before Gandhi's disruptive position, is the subject who is a believer in public and non-believer in private. This is an altogether more threatening position, and Nandy explores this in a number of writings, particularly in his critique of Hindu Nationalism. This subject type proves a different threat to the secular ideal and confirms the ways that the ideal and these processes of subjection ultimately work against its own aims. What is problematic is not the issue of taking on religious identities, but the processes of re-making religious identities into political ones to accord with the visions of the rational political actor. Figures like V.D. Savarkar, the founding ideological father of Hindutva and pan-Hindu Nationalism, along with his reformist political agenda of making India Hindu, represent the dangers of this political identity. For Nandy, Savarkar's question of 'Who is a Hindu?' and who has claims over an Indian Hindu nation is less a metaphysical questioning, and more a politicisation of Hinduism—a re-making of Hinduism into a political identity category. This politicisation of Hinduism, or the re-making of Hinduism into a political identity, is evident in the ways in which the ideology of Hindutva has been imperative to the political claims and identity of the BJP.[7] What is interesting is that political identities like Savarkar's (a believer in public and non-believer in private) remain within this dominant political culture less threatening and closer to the ideal, than a figure like Gandhi. For it is Gandhi's commitment to a religious way of life in private and public, his resistance to processes of subjection, and his explicit transversal of the secular ideal that remain threatening and destabilising.

In identifying these four subject types operating in Indian politics he then confronts the effectiveness of the ideology of secularism in keeping religion out of politics. For religion does not necessarily disappear from political view. For religion now returns carrying the weight of these processes of subjection, as made over political identities. This, for Nandy, is where the pathologies of secularism reveal themselves, in these processes of re-making religious identities into political identities. These remade political identities foster the conditions for social and political discontent. The political theorist Saba Mahmood, writing in a different context, has taken this confrontation with the psychic life of secularism further. Mahmood, in her critique of secularism, notes that 'the political solution that secularism proffers lies not so much in tolerating differences and diversity but in remaking certain kinds of religious subjectivities (even if this requires the use of violence) so as to render them compliant with liberal political rule' (Mahmood, 2006: 328).

Nandy's own claims regarding the changing dynamics of social and political intolerance in India as evidenced in the last twenty years lead to a similar conclusion. However, the clues to these dynamics are also evident in this hierarchy of the subject and the political value afforded to these subjectivities. What is problematic is that the range of possible subjectivities and concepts of Indianness represented in public life and within politics are truncated. Equally, what is foreclosed from analysis is the complexity of human subjectivity. This complexity includes the ways in which contradictions, ambivalence and ambiguities within subjectivity can challenge the divisions between a public and private life. Official secularism of this kind, in which the ideal secular citizen is rewarded as a true Indian, compromise democratic processes by truncating the political personality of the citizen. As Nandy's analysis affirms, only a part of oneself is represented in politics. This representation of self in politics can be noted as the acceptable parts of self, while those other parts have to be carefully kept outside of it, and, in its ideal manifestation, are not even expressed in private life. These inherited and imported divisions of self-organisation and representation work to re-structure what he claims are the more porous boundaries of selfhood. For Nandy, these porous boundaries of selfhood are a crucial feature of human subjectivity. Consistent with this hierarchy and psychic organisation, the believer in public life is deemed as having an 'inferior political consciousness' (Nandy, 2002a: 37). The exceptions to this claim of an inferior political consciousness are movements like Hindu nationalism, which have succeeded in (re)creating themselves as a political identity, and not a religious identity. Hence, such movements, despite their appropriations of distinct religious motifs, myths and symbols, do so as reconstituted political identities. The processes of re-making religious identities into political ones, as evidenced in the case of the rise of Indian Hindu nationalism are explored in the following chapter. Nandy's objection is that this subject type is cast as inferior, and the effects of the ideology of secularism in processes of identification forecloses a particular internal dialogue from taking place. 'Instead of a dialogue between the public and private within a person and between politics and culture – the two spheres are rigidly separated and the latter is frozen in time' (Nandy, 2002a: 37). These divisions underpin the typology of political selfhood that operates in validating political culture and political identities.

There are two dominant secular modernist trends in Indian politics that continue today as effects and affects of this dominant and normative secular ideal. The first is a belief that with the growing secularization of society the irrationality of faith and pre-modern aspects of culture, even within the private spheres of life, will be eroded and supplanted by science, rationality and modern education. The second is that this will then pave the way for the efficient and effective running of the sanitised sphere of politics and public life already discussed. The indirect message carried forward within these processes and attitudes is the need to educate, modernise, civilise and secularise. In Nandy's analysis, 'the theory [of secularism] is an indirect plea to educate, guide and break in the citizenry into this secular sphere, the sphere of the raja dharma, with the help of a modern vanguard acting as a pace-setter in matters of social change' (Nandy, 2002a: 40). The role of the vanguard as the ideal political subject is by definition educated, Westernised and middle class, and performs a vital function in modelling and consolidating the identity of the rational secular political actor. The modus operandi of the vanguard is, therefore, to ensure that the irrational and now pathological expressions of religion and ethnicity (fundamentalism, fanaticism, xenophobia, ethnocentrism) remain at the borderlands of politics.

Although Nandy is critical of the role that the vanguard plays in preserving the secular ideal, he does acknowledge the role the vanguard can perform in preserving a sphere of collective sanity and/or social order. The vanguard can perform an integrative function in safeguarding the normative boundaries operating within political culture.

For Nandy, the value of the integrative function that the vanguard can perform becomes necessary within contexts of political crisis, and within isolated historical events, where social and political cohesion has been needed. For instance, he acknowledges that during the formation of the Independent Nation State in 1947, the vanguard had a distinctive role to play in instituting the ideology of secularism. Nandy acknowledges the consensus surrounding secularism, and its symbolic function as an ego-integrative ideal, during the establishment of nation. In this instance, the ideology of secularism is intimately tied to questions of national identity, and to consolidating the boundaries of the Indian nation state. The ideology proffered by the vanguard contributed to safeguarding national integration and unity following the violence and the mass displacement of peoples and fragmentation experienced during the Partition of India. Nandy concedes that this consensus was vital in 'that an area of sanity needed to be maintained in the polity' and that this sanity came in the form of the Nehruvian consensus (Nandy, 2002a: 40). The Nehruvian consensus has been described by Rajeev Dhavan as the 'the Great Discourse', and was founded on the holy trinity of science, secularism and socialism. This consensus dominated administrative and political society and the ideological apparatus of the Indian state during this time.[8] The point remains, though, that this kind of consensus, crucial as it was in establishing a political imaginary and in creating a collective political consciousness, has reached its limits. The limits of state secularism have now been reached in Nandy's depiction with detrimental consequences. The contemporary pursuit of national unity and an Indian national identity has homogenised and standardised concepts of tolerance. The pathologies of secularism that he warns against, and confronts in his critique of secularism, are evident in these processes.

Defending secularism and the secular ideal, including justifying the pursuit of the ideal, is becoming a more complex undertaking. In Nandy's account there are three changes within Indian political culture that have further complicated the viability of this ideal. First, political participation has expanded and it is no longer possible to screen those entering politics according to their subordination to the secular ideal, their secular morality or ideal citizen rating. This expanded participation has brought with it democratic representation from what was once considered the 'ethnic backwaters of India'. Nandy references these ordinary peripheral believers or non-modern peripherals as 'eking out their lives in the backwaters of South Asia in the ways in which such people eke out their lives throughout the

South' (Nandy 2002a: 46). For Nandy unequivocally, 'democratisation itself has set limits on the secularisation of Indian politics' (Nandy 2002a: 41). Indian democracy, along with concepts of democratic pluralism, has been strengthened, empowered and rejuvenated by these expansion processes. For Nandy, these expansion processes have proven resilient against the normative and homogenising features of statist secularism. This argument is consistent with his broader intellectual efforts to explore subjectivities and recover the critical features of ambivalence, diversity and pluralism within Indian democracy. The second and more destabilising change, following from this expanded political representation, is that these new voices and political identities entering public life create new conditions. This provides the conditions for the political use of religion and ethnicity in politics, 'turning it into an instrument of political mobilisation within a psephocratic model' (Nandy, 2002a: 41). An example of this process is the politicisation of Sri Rama by the forces of Hindutva as a truism in Indian politics. This is reiterated by the electoral strategy and slogan of the BJP of 'they know it we know it'.[9]

The danger for Nandy is that while religious traditions and ethnicity have found political currency in pathological form (as re-constituted homogenised political identities), this has not been accompanied by a greater tolerance of faiths. Further, these processes of expansion have not been accompanied with the checks needed against corruption and violence in public life. That which passes as faith in public life is not expressed in the language of the sacred, but as an impoverished version of itself, manipulated for political ends. Nandy further distinguishes the appropriation of religion for political ends by noting that these accounts of religion lack a theory of transcendence.

> By projecting into history the conceptual grid of the European Enlightenment and dishonestly claiming them as part of the secular worldview, Indian secularists have participated in an ethnocidal project, the direct results of which are the impoverished versions of faiths that have come to dominate Indian public life. (Nandy, 2002a: 50)

Nandy laments the ways in which religion returns and enters into political culture, by accepting what are the terms and conditions of subjection. The effect of this return is that it is a compromised return, as something is forsaken within this re-made concept of religion. For under the guises of both the zealot and the Western secularist, the return of religion is reduced to the 'status of handmaiden of politics' (Nandy, 2002a: 43). This comes with a third development within Indian political culture. Since the 1960s there has been an increasing disenchantment with secularism expressed in the growing frustrations and scepticism of the blind faith that it demands from its followers. Confronting what is assumed to be India's political destiny, Nandy cautions that 'Western style secularisation has shown incapacity to keep pace with politicisation in this part of the world, and it shows no sign of being able to do so in the future' (Nandy, 2002a: 43). This incapacity of secularism has ensured that 'ethnicity is refusing to obligingly sing its swan song' (Nandy, 2002a: 43). It is, through the pathologies of secularism, in fanaticism and extremism that ethnicity and religion have been made over, and re-cast as political identities, and are finding political expression and currency in detrimental ways.

THE BOUNDARIES OF SELFHOOD AND TOLERATING DIFFERENCE

A further consequence of the boundaries constituting politically recognised subjects is the way in which 'official' modes of tolerance emerge. Consistent with Nandy's confrontation with the positioning of boundaries of selfhood thus far, there do exist alternative modes of toleration outside the purview of the State. This concept of tolerance is already present for Nandy, notably as a latent presence, surviving as the underside of Indian political culture. This is secularism not defined in opposition to the sacred, but in opposition to the 'ethnocentrism, xenophobia and fanaticism' that is increasingly finding political currency and support (Nandy, 2002a: 43). Unlike the social basis of Western secularism linked to the statist model, a Gandhian approach to tolerance shifts the emphasis 'from outer to inner incentives' (Nandy, 2002a: 43). There is within Gandhi's critique of modes of toleration a questioning of the boundaries between public and private, external and internal. Official tolerance is the prerogative of the state, and implemented instrumentally through its workings as an external reference point for social and political cohesion. In contrast, the tolerance that Nandy advocates as latent within Indian political culture is disconnected from modern statecraft. In a similar vein to Gandhi's approach, Nandy locates the question of tolerance internally and externally, with an emphasis on the dialogue that needs to take place between these internal and external registers. For, as Nandy emphasises, the concept of tolerance that he is interested in working with is located as both internal to the self and to culture. The dangers are that these internal capacities, along with the capacity for dialogue between these internal and external registers, are being

foreclosed by the peripheral and fanatical voices now accepted *as* religion in politics. The effects of these processes are, then, that these
excluded and unofficial expressions of tolerance continue to be cast
from view despite their latent presence as a critical underside of
Indian political culture.

Nandy explains that 'the clash between modernity and religious
traditions in much of Asia and Africa elicits from each of the four
political responses to ethnicity' (Nandy, 2002a: 43). These four responses to ethnicity found in a number of postcolonial societies, are
described as 'half ideal-types and half mythic structures' (Nandy,
2002a: 43). An understanding of these responses provides further insight into these processes of subjection. The four subject types and
the responses available within Indian political culture for addressing
questions of ethnicity are the following: Western-man as the ideal political man, the Westernised native, the zealot, and the non-modern
peripheral ethnic. The analysis of the limited possibilities available
for addressing ethnicity in Indian secular political culture advances
Nandy's argument that secularism ultimately works against its own
aims. Moreover, the ideology of secularism provides the political conditions for the proliferation of intolerance and communal violence.

WESTERN MAN AS THE *IDEAL* POLITICAL MAN

The first of these responses, Nandy suggests, has little in common
with the other three responses but is noteworthy in its own right.
The Western man as the ideal political man is a familiar cultural archetype and central to the victory of Western colonialism. The imago of the Western man armed with a rational and secular mindset,
and modern and progressive ideals is central to the successes of the
West. According to these markers of modernity, he or she stands in
direct opposition to the non-Western man, and in this sense, is a
reminder of the non-West's failure to Westernise. To what extent is
this image psychically powerful and successful in structuring identities? Nandy suggests this ideal is an illusion or a shadow, given that
the non-Western man does not recognise himself and his identity
as positioned within this dyad. This imago of the Western man is
pivotal though to processes of identification, and moreover to the
range of possible political identities available in postcolonial societies. The Western man despite his mythical status remains the central reference point for all to aspire to the construction of successful
and progressive political identities. As Nandy explains, 'the shadowy

Western man, then, becomes a critic of the Indigenous personality as well as a projection of the ego-ideal of these sections of the indigenous population' (Nandy, 2002a: 44).

The projection of the ego ideal, part of the precarious process of psychic organization, both at the individual and collective levels, is not without repercussions. Nandy does not critique the function of an ego ideal here, but rather notes that the operation of this ego ideal is problematic. The ego ideal is, for Nandy, derived from an external cultural source and, as already detailed, has its historic foundations within the traditions of Western Enlightenment and modernity. This 'Enlightenment consciousness is [and remains] complicit with the violence, uprooting, and the de-culturation they have confronted in their lives or in their pasts of their communities' (Nandy and Deftereos, 2005b: 6). These aspirations to identify with this ego ideal within societies have often met with violent and tragic ends. Subjection to this ideal has repercussions beyond individual identity and political consciousness, and has a direct impact on shaping communities and societies in profound ways. 'If the sections are powerful, they may even manage to set up this sectorial ideal as *the* ideal for the entire society' (Nandy, 2002a: 44). In such cases, a new eupsychia emerges, a utopian personality that sets the benchmark for identity and identity politics (Nandy, 2002a: 44). Nandy makes use of the term 'eupshychia', a term coined by the psychologist Abraham H. Maslow to denote a utopian concept of personality. It is a concept that explores an ideal person or ideal psychological states. This too, though, can become a tool for homogenisation and compliance, as this eupsychia functions as a critique of the indigenous personality and is established in opposition to the traditional eupsychias surviving in these societies. The point of contention remains the ways in which this eupsychia affirms a dominant and homogenising imagining. While this eupsychia performs an integrative function, it also forecloses other possibilities, especially existing traditional or even non-modern eupsychias whose reference point is not Western man.

There are certain characteristic personality traits that accompany this subjectivity. These traits include a rational pragmatism in political matters and in affirming the rational political subject. These traits are also demonstrated in the managerial attitude adopted in response to ethnic and religious tensions in which the business of nation-building and national unity takes precedence, and involves hard decisions and realism in dealing with ethnic minorities. Such internal policies are also reflected in the realist and neo-realist policies adopted by nation states in relation to international relations, a reaction to ethnicity which in South Asia are over-determined by the colonial legacy that mark a number of postcolonial states in this region. For instance, in South Asia such managerial attitudes to ethnic minorities are reproduced by defending processes of nation-building and development in what are deemed to be under-developed parts of the world. Nandy questions whether these efforts to politically manage differences and diversity within a poly-ethnic and poly-religious Indian democracy ultimately differ from that model of governance it goes to such lengths to distance itself from—a theocratic state. Under either system, the status afforded diversity and the political status of minorities bear a striking family resemblance. In either scenario, 'minorities face the prospect of being Westernised—the usual euphemism is modernised—in a Western-style nation state' (Nandy, 2002a: 44). Nation-building (in conjunction with the modernising project) if it is to succeed requires the hard de-cisions, the *Realpolitik* and managerial style of this personality—the Western political man. However, the political status of ethnic minori-ties under the influence of the Western political man is no different to that of an ethnic majority. It entails compliance with these normative processes of subjection.

THE WESTERNISED NATIVE

The second possible response to ethnicity is from the Westernised na-tive. This is the subject who, in these processes of *becoming*, does so by successfully internalising the imago of Western man, thus accepting the conditions of subjection. The experiences of the Westernised na-tive, and the ambivalence that these processes of internalisation gen-erate, have been written about extensively by a number of theorists within postcolonial studies.[10] This is the story of the native or ethnic who has internalised the ideology of their oppressors and now car-ries the *intimate enemy* and the colonization of the mind that Nandy details in *The Intimate Enemy* as constitutive of selfhood. The psychic life of power or the colonisation of the mind, to adopt Frantz Fanon's axiom, however, brings with it distinct notions of a divided and alien-ated self. These internalised beliefs regarding the desire to modernise or universalise one's own culture by identifying with the coloniser take place alongside a number of inner contradictions, which are dif-ferent from a more generalised existential malaise that underpins all human subjectivity. The Westernised native differs, in that they are confronted with an additional ambivalence and contradiction. The disjuncture arises because the ego ideal of the Western man, that the Western native internalises, can never be fully realised within his or her society. The painful disjuncture between this internal (mis)recognition with an external experience, which mirrors a different reality back to the self, can become overwhelming and consuming. One possible defensive response to this potential loss of ontological security is in the over-determined desire to modernise and secularise one's own regressive native culture, including the regressive parts of one's self. This defensive response takes place as an attempt to counter this loss or a pending disaster of possible abjection, or the dissolution of the boundaries of selfhood.

The other tension within this subject position is whether the cultural self, already established in tension and contradiction with this political self, can be abjected and cast from view. In re-affirming the ambivalence, radical alterity and contradictions within all human subjectivity, Nandy points to the ways in which these tensions reveal themselves even within the seemingly fixed identity of the ideal Westernised native. As already discussed, this is demonstrated by the ideal political secular citizen, the non-believer in public and private, epitomised by Jawaharlal Nehru. However, within the imago of Nehru as the secular statesman, Nandy builds a secondary argument around the question of ambivalence, contradictions and conflicts of the Westernised native. Nandy captures this ambivalence within subjectivity when emphasising that Nehru, 'in his weaker moments, gave in to astrologers and tantrics of all hues' (Nandy, 2002a: 45). These are weaker moments because they represent a deviation from the established boundaries of a normative secular political subject. By turning to *tantrics*, Nehru is also turning to, or rather expressing, a part of his cultural self, and it is this aspect of self that threatens these processes of subjection. Further, these parts of a cultural self threaten and undermine the ontological security that the ideal political subject safeguards.

The point for Nandy is not to detract from the significance of Nehru as a secular political figure, but to highlight that the ego ideal does not allow for the interplay between these contradictions and ambiguities in representations of his political personality. A similar point can be made about the Indian religious, social and educational reformer Ram Mohan Roy who, as Nandy explains, was known to take a Brahmin cook with him to England to observe his personal food taboos after a life-long defiance of Hindu caste codes. Such contradictions within these political personalities become all the more arresting, given that parts of this cultural self are revealed only in the personal sphere. It is no coincidence that this unravelling is in the personal sphere, especially given that such figures in public have fought tirelessly for India's secular identity, a modern Indian secular state, and a secular political culture in public life. There is for Nandy, though, a distinctive turning against one's own cultural self in order to secure this idealised political identity and the boundaries of politics. The point remains that even in the making of successful and celebrated political identities, psychic life and the boundaries of self cannot always be so neatly defined. The certainty and security cannot even be secured by figures like Nehru, whose public image and personality was secured by his commitment to scientific rationality, reason and secular modernity. However, Nehru's subjectivity betrays this idealised image. Central to understanding Nandy's confrontation with the secular ideal is the exploration of the ways that contradictions and ambivalence within subjectivity find recourse in psychic life. The cultural self is not, and arguably cannot be, fully cast away or repressed from view. For as psychoanalysis affirms even in subtle ways, dismissed or repressed parts of the self always find recourse within the timelessness of psychic life.

Although the Westernised native and Western man may share the same ego ideal, they can differ politically in their approaches. This difference is discernable in the role that they may perform within their own societies and, therefore, they may also be political adversaries. Notwithstanding the overriding aim to modernise their own culture, they, however, share in the European vision of progress and concepts of a good society. Even as adversaries they agree that 'the fate of the tropics' to paraphrase the subtitle of Nandy's text *Romance of the State* (2002a) is on this pathway of modernisation, Westernisation, secularisation and universalisation. The external challenges the Westernised native faces, in addition to the internal ones discussed, are exemplified in the role that they perform in politics. This role performed in politics requires a particular attitude. Armed with a reformist attitude, these internal contradictory tensions must be repressed in order to deal with what are perceived to be 'the backward, religious masses' within their own cultures (Nandy, 2002a: 45). These challenges of backwardness and a constituency that is willing to take advantage of the irrationality of faith to mobilise people for political ends are significant for they can bring forward another disruptive element. More often than not, leading the masses is an 'unscrupulous leadership ever willing to take advantage of irrational, superstitious faiths' (Nandy, 2002a: 45). The responses to combat this are to be found in a return to the imago, the internal referent of Western political man. The Westernised native, thus, constantly invokes the established (Western) eupsychia as a yardstick, in order to compare and contrast the regressive realities of their own non-Western culture. Nandy claims that given these processes, and the tacit self-knowledge at play, the Westernised native will address religious and ethnic difference as a civilisational question. This approach sits alongside the knowledge that they will always fall short of achieving this ideal of civilising the natives into modern subjects. Irrespective of this failure, the Westernised native, having inscribed these ideals through self and within culture, is compelled by these processes to pursue these aspirations and ideals. Nandy concludes that while the Western native may on some level recognise the conflict and contradiction of their situation, they will continue to submit to these processes as part of an attempt to cast away ambivalence and contradiction. Thus ultimately, the Western native continues to work towards consolidating the ontological security derived from these processes of identification and subjection in service of self and for their culture.

THE ZEALOT

The third response to ethnicity is that of the zealot, that is, the Muslim or Sikh fundamentalist or, in the case of the Hindu, the Hindu Revivalist or Cultural Nationalist. The role of the Hindu nationalist is explored in greater detail in the following chapter as its growing political appeal in the 1990s worked to define concepts of Indianness, national identity and national unity in very specific ways. The point remains that for Nandy the rise of Hindu nationalism is intimately connected to the pathologies of secularism. It is important to note that for Nandy, it is the zealot, along with the Westernised native, who has had a strong political presence within contemporary Indian politics, particularly since the 1990s. The rise of Bharatiya Janata Party (BJP) during this period and its militant calls for a Hindu *rashtra* (nation) has a case to answer for the methods adopted to appropriate religion and ethnicity for political gains. It is also worth noting that the zealot, according to Nandy's earlier distinction, may coincide with the political citizen who is a believer in public and non-believer in private. Unlike the Westernised native, the internal psychic life of the zealot demonstrates a more overt expression of the inverted aggression found in the Westernised native. This aggression in the zealot is

expressed as fanaticism, xenophobia and ethnocentrism and is greatly feared by the Westernised native who, irrespective of the internal
conflict endured, seldom conveys and acts upon this divided subjectivity in public life. The zealot's impetus for expressing this aggression
is markedly different. The zealot's behaviour, unlike the Westernised
native, is fuelled by political motivations rather than from a civilisational one. In simple terms, for Nandy, the zealot has turned against
their cultural self. The defining characteristic of the zealot is the way
that traditions, religions and ethnicity are strategically appropriated
for political gains and ends. Religion, traditions, culture and ethnicity become tools for the zealot in a zero-sum game of electoral politics, within what J.P. Carse has noted is the 'finite game of politics'
(Carse, 1986). In contrast to the Westernised native, the zealot's aggressive tactics can mobilise people, particularly within urban areas
appealing to semi-modern constituencies 'suffering from an acute
case of false consciousness' in different ways (Nandy, 2002a: 45). For
Nandy, the great threat and danger of the zealot in Indian politics is
to be found in the deeply internalised repressions and defences that
propel the over-determined and extremist attitudes and responses
to religion and ethnicity. Nandy describes the zealot as 'reacting to
and yet internalising the humiliation inflicted on all faiths by a triumphant anti-faith called Western modernity, [he or she] has accepted
the Western Enlightenment's attitude to all faiths, including his own'
(Nandy, 2002a: 45).

In taking on the Western Enlightenment attitude and, despite the
claim to faith in public life, the religious beliefs of the masses are
an embarrassment to the zealot. The seeming paradox is explained
as 'no accident; [for] the one universal trait of an ideology is always
a certain contempt for the targeted beneficiaries of the ideology'
(Nandy, 2002a: 46). The ethnicity acquired by the zealot in politics is
an 'ethnicity [that] is skin deep and reactive', and is in this account
another variation of the secular political man of post-Enlightenment
Europe (Nandy, 2002a: 46). To some extent the zealot shares the
internal contradictions of the psychic life of the Westernised native,
though in an exaggerated and more complex way. The zealot
externalises this internalised aggression towards the self, projecting
this onto the other in ways that differ from the Westernised native.
What is problematic about this projection of aggression is that the
zealot carries an overwhelming level of hatred and disgust that is
a distinct feature of his political identity. Within these processes
of subjection operating to make the zealot into a political subject

there is a double level of loathing at play. The zealot demonstrates hatred for the Westernised ethnic as having proverbially sold out to Western man, and an even deeper hatred for the ordinary pedestrian ethnic and their embarrassing ways. Despite this hatred and embarrassment for the everyday ethnic, this is the constituency that the zealot represents in politics. The zealot and his appropriation of religion and ethnicity as a political identity affirm the pathologies of secularism and processes of subjection operating in Indian secular political culture. This explains the similar objectives and goals shared, at least politically, between the Westernised Hindu and Westernised Muslim. For Nandy, both are modern identity categories or typologies defined by one's modern credentials. In the case of the Westernised Hindu or the Westernised Muslim zealot, it is this modernity that determines political identity, and one's political status, thus overriding religious and ethnic differences.

THE NON-MODERN PERIPHERAL ETHNIC

The final response to ethnicity is provided by the non-modern peripheral ethnic. The work of the Subaltern Studies Collective has been invaluable in contributing to our understanding of the boundaries of exclusion in Indian politics and society, and in exploring these 'subaltern' voices. The non-modern peripheral ethnic is the most significant subject type in Nandy's analysis and confrontation with secularism. The ordinary or non-modern peripheral is so named by the zealots and secularists to reflect his political status within Indian political culture. There is, however, an advantage to this peripheral status; it demonstrates the subject's distinctive non-conformity and non-compliance with processes of subjection. Located by definition at the periphery or borderlands of political life, can the non-modern peripheral ethnic even be recognised as a subject? For Nandy the answer to this question is evidenced in the ways in which they are represented as both outside of and irrelevant to a dominant and normative political culture. The non-modern peripheral that is abjected from political view exists within what Kristeva notes are the borderlands of signification.

In Nandy's reading where this abjection has been challenged is through democratic processes and through expanded political representation. This expanded representation and presence within politics, particularly by people traditionally at the borders of society, has necessitated an acknowledgment of these subjectivities. To what extent, though, does this democratic right correlate with the non-modern peripheral's political status? The non-modern peripheral's presence in Indian democracy is de-valued and the backwardness of the peripheral ethnic, along with their lack of knowledge of democratic processes, overshadows their status as citizen. Nandy argues that these attitudes and processes of exclusion take place because the status of the non-modern peripheral ethnic remains at the borderlands of signification, or what can be described in Butler's work as 'the not yet subject'. There is a parallel to be drawn here between the intimate enemies, the non-modern self that is carried within the Indian subject and the voice of the critic. Gustavo Esteva and Madhu Suri Prakash emphasize that Nandy's analysis demonstrates the ways in which 'the non-subjects, who refuse to play the game, are disqualified or declared bad subjects' (Nandy, 2004a: 5). The 'bad subject' has a distinctive psychoanalytic meaning in Nandy's analysis. Given this abject status, the non-modern peripheral, cast in Butler's terms as the bad subject, becomes an important and controversial figure in Nandy's critique. Nandy works to reclaim the disruptive and creative possibilities that the bad subject carries forward. Despite the external condemnation of the bad subject, by both secularists and zealots, the ordinary peripheral has some internal advantages. In Nandy's reading, there are a number of internal resources that continue to distinguish this subject type from the others explored thus far. These resources include a defiance of norms, but also a very different understanding and representation of self and, by extension, self/other relations. This alternative modality of being is privileged in the following way, as he contends that,

> neither the modern secularist nor the crypto-modern zealot has the sensitivity to stand witness to this other battle of survival. Neither has the time to remember the experience of neighbourliness and co-survival, which characterises the relationship among the peripheral believers of different faiths. (Nandy, 2002a: 47)

It is in the non-modern peripheral's combination of sensitivity and memory of a cultural self that dissenting practices of religious and ethnic tolerance are to be found. There is a dynamic in operation that is internal to both the self and expressions of Indianness and Indian culture. This can also be expressed as an inner resource of survival and co-survival, which Nandy wants to retrieve back into political view. This can be described by the Hindi word *manta*. Importantly the internal referent for the peripheral ethnic is not Western man but an enduring ambivalent cultural self. Shifting the focus in this way enables Nandy to establish this subject position as outside of the other three already discussed. For the non-modern peripheral, tolerance (for self and of others) does not come from official doctrines instituted through modern secular statecraft but from these unofficial modes. This is an account of tolerance that, according to Nandy, has a long established presence and history in the Indic civilisation. Moreover, the non-modern peripheral, armed with these unofficial modes of tolerance, continues to threaten and challenge the boundaries between self and other, tolerance and intolerance, public and private, secular and non-secular. The subjectivity of the peripheral remains defiant against these processes of subjection because 'these grammars survive, in spite of the efforts of learned scholars to read them as folk theologies—as inferior, disposable versions of Hinduism and Islam' (Nandy, 2002a: 51).

The tolerance that Nandy is interested in exploring is conceptualised as an internal question, within subjectivity. This concept of tolerance is intimately connected to the concept of porous boundaries of self and lies within the pluralism of Indian culture and traditions, outside of the well-bounded subjectivity that the secular self ensures. Cleary, all subjectivity is well bounded but the fluidity in the construction of selfhood performs an important function. Consistent with the psychoanalytic focus of Nandy's critique, tolerance is located as an internal question, pertaining to the ways in which both individual and collective boundaries of selfhood are cast. In later work, and following the criticisms of a number of friends, he acknowledges the limitations of the term and suggests hospitality might take us further in capturing the inter-religious amity he has in mind.

Nandy adopts Ivan Illich's use of the concept—conviviality—established in his 1973 text, *Tools of Conviviality*, which, in a similar way, re-configures tolerance from within and in support of the practical knowledge of the average citizen. Nandy's appropriation of the term carries forward Illich's own use of the concept in his critique of the institutionalisation of specialised knowledge. For, like Illich, Nandy, too, is addressing the power of political myths or the processes through which specialised knowledge like official accounts of tolerance become dominant and foreclose other possible knowledge and experience, particularly the practical knowledge of the non-modern peripheral Indian. In either case, the emphasis is on a pluralisation of the experiences and possibilities of tolerance, derived through a reconstitution of self/other relations. Nandy states that 'hospitality is a recognition or an association, a coming together of an entirely different sort', for it implies that 'in being hospitable; you recognise the plurality of experience' (Nandy, 2004a: 14). Hospitality does not imply compliance to a normative view (secular or non-secular), belief or practice but, in broader terms, embraces the ambivalence and ambiguity of the inter-subjective realm. It reconfigures the positioning of the boundaries between self and other, because simply stated, 'hosting the others simply means opening one's arms and doors for them, to accept their existence in their own places...' (Nandy, 2004a: 14). This is an entirely different intellectual and psychological task, for opening one's self up to the possibilities of this hospitality creates a different encounter and even ethical moment in relation to the other. In a different context, Kristeva also takes up this question of ethics that may be possible in this moment of encountering the other, in her reading of cosmopolitanism. Tolerance, expressed as either hospitality or conviviality, radically challenges and displaces existing understandings of official tolerance. Nandy argues, 'It [conviviality] disconnects us as effectively as hospitality does from the baggage that the term secularism carries' (Nandy, 2002h: 1).

As has been argued, official accounts of secular tolerance can be compromised in times of expanding representation and participation in politics, especially by the zealot and the Westernised native. In contrast to this, the tolerance or hospitality expressed by the non-modern peripheral contributes to a broader understanding of the concept, while preserving a dynamism and pluralism within the self and within Indian democracy. Despite attempts to truncate political personality and differences, people do bring their own categories of understanding, self-understanding and representations into 'the fray of democratic politics'. Nandy states that,

> people always will bring it [their ideas and values] into the fray of democratic politics anyway. Once you give the vote to people, you are never sure on what criteria they are voting with, they can and do bring their private into the public. And all this talk about keeping religion and culture to private life, you know that is the basic assumption of secularism, and bringing only political choices into the public sphere, it is absolutely bogus. (Nandy and Defteros, 2005d: 3)

The implications are that this pluralism disrupts and ruptures the positioning of the boundaries of political culture. In Nandy's account, these processes of subjection operating in Indian secular political culture come face to face with democratic pluralism and, in doing so, the boundaries of political culture itself come under question. In emphasising these tensions, Nandy asks a series of confronting questions: 'In a democracy what kinds of rights do you grant to ordinary citizens? How do you de-expertise a democracy?' (Nandy and Deftereos, 2005b: 7). Underpinning this confrontation with secularism is the voice of the radical democrat defending democratic pluralism and democratic processes. As Nandy affirms, 'the democratic rights of citizens or democratic processes should not be limited to that kind of thought, that kind of emphasis on abstract virtues to which the Indian elite supposedly have a monopoly right' (Nandy and Deftereos, 2005b: 7).

The critical and analytic value that the non-modern peripheral, or the bad subject that Gandhi represents, is worth revisiting. In Nandy's account, the political identity worthy of further consideration is the non-modern peripheral best personified by Gandhi. According to Nandy, Gandhi as a political figure did not commit to 'the hopeless task of banishing religion while expanding democratic participation in politics but dared seek a politics which would be infused with the right kind of religion and be tolerant' (Nandy, 2002a: 50). This unapologetic non-compliance with the secular ideal does, however, cast Gandhi as the threatening and disruptive bad subject. Although a significant political figure in the formation of Independent India, Gandhi's subjectivity as a bad subject contributes to the ambivalent status he continues to receive today within an Indian political imaginary. This ambivalence is demonstrated in the ways that Gandhi remains both a celebrated and maligned political memory. For Nandy, this contradiction and ambivalence in the ways in which Gandhi is remembered and represented is worthy of analysis. Nandy works with this by reclaiming the ambivalence within Gandhi's subjectivity by acknowledging that there are a number of different representations and imaginings possible. In an article titled, 'Gandhi after Gandhi', Nandy explores this ambivalence by identifying four Gandhis that remain alive today, 'each with his own eccentricities, conveniences and place in the psyche of the society' (Nandy, 2000a: 38). There is the story of the Gandhi of the Indian state, the Gandhi of the Gandhians who follow his philosophies in daily life, there is the Gandhi influencing local voices of dissent in Indian public life today, a Gandhi who 'considers local versions of Coca-Cola more dangerous than imported ones', and finally the Gandhi who is the ideological force behind a number of environmental, nuclear and feminist movements. For Gandhi, as a figure that rejected and traversed the fantasy of the secular ideal and norm, is confronted with an interesting predicament. In not complying with these processes and in not reinstating the norm, Gandhi is cast as the bad subject, the less than ideal political subject, and ultimately as a non-subject. Nandy suggests that in response to Gandhi's defiance, there are a number of defensive attempts to cover over this aspect of Gandhi's selfhood. This is evident in the work of modernists and revisionists who have sought to re-claim Gandhi's identity and political significance as a modern figure.[11] In doing so, these modernists and revisionists have also defended and re-claimed their own existence, placed under threat by the bad subject. For Nandy, such revisionist efforts can be explained, at least in part, by the necessarily embarrassing anti-secular language of religiosity that Gandhi brought into public life. The other part can be explained by Gandhi's highly ambivalent presence within Indian political life. Such efforts to minimise Gandhi's ambivalence in favour of the certitude of his (re-claimed) modern guise are reinforced through the argument that he shares a number of similarities with Nehru. For example, commentators like Nauriya, in an effort to re-claim Gandhi's modernity, have argued that his use of the term 'secular' can be described as Nehruvian, thus remaking the image of the bad subject in the image of the ideal and idealised subject.[12] In contrast to such readings, Gandhi remains for Nandy a defiant figure worthy of celebration, for both his failure to reinstate the secular norm and his ultimate rejection of the secular ideal.

Gustavo Esteva and Madhu Suri Prakash affirm that a figure like Gandhi, as a non-modern peripheral ethnic, can only be recognised as the non-subject or the bad subject. As they state, 'Gandhi was classified as a "bad subject"—from the very beginning of his struggle until well after his assassination', and to this extent, 'the educated elite misunderstood him almost universally'. Despite being misunderstood, the authors argue that Gandhi's ambiguity locates him as the non-subject and bad subject.

> Once in a while someone like M. K. Gandhi demonstrates what it means to have the autonomy, dignity and freedom of the 'non-subject' to be neither the coloniser nor the colonised; neither the oppressor nor the oppressed; neither the hawk nor the dove; neither the terrorist nor the terrorised; neither the empowerer nor the empowered; neither the conscientiser nor the conscientised. (Gustavo and Prakash, Madhu Suri, in Nandy, Ashis. 2004: 5)

It is only by seeing Gandhi as a figure who endorsed Hinduism and Islam as a *culture* and not a *religion* that his position can be freed from its threatening and disruptive anti-modern foundations. The intensity of Gandhi's threat is evidenced in the extreme efforts to abject him from view. This is the Gandhi cast by Hindu militants as the bad subject or the non-subject, who in failing to reinforce and reiterate the norm endured three attempted assassinations. Gandhi paid the ultimate sanction in being assassinated by the Hindu militant Nathuram Godse (Nandy, S. Trivedy et al., 1995: 65). In his article titled 'The Fear of Gandhi: Nathuram Godse and His Successors', published in *The Times of India*, Nandy argues that it is no coincidence that Godse was a Hindu militant and that he used his political allegiance to a unified Hindu India in defending his actions. During his criminal trial, Godse drew on his passionate commitment to national unity and subjection to the secular ideal as his defence, to eliminate the great threat that Gandhi represented to political culture. Gandhi, thus, pays the ultimate cost for his defiance of the secular ideal in failing to reinstate the norm. Judith Butler suggests that in these processes of affirming identification,

> the subject is compelled to repeat the norms by which it is produced, but that repetition establishes a domain of risk, for if one fails to reinstate the norm "in the right way," one becomes subject to further sanction, one feels the prevailing conditions of existence threatened (Butler, 1997: 28).

In Nandy's analysis, this, however, does not detract from Gandhi's features, for it is his failure to reinstate the norm that is worthy of celebration. Moreover, it is the return of the possibility of non-compliance and defiance that is significant for the mode of criticism at work. There is in this moment a possibility to rupture and regenerate meanings, at, what Kristeva notes, are the borderlands of signification. In Nandy's account, Gandhi recognises this possibility, given that his 'creativity, after all, presumes a certain marginality and, in the matter of culture, a certain dialectic between the classical and the folk'. Nandy continues, 'It has to transcend the classicist—and elite—formulation that classicism is the centre of the culture, to protect the classicism itself from becoming a two-dimensional frozen instance of a culture museumised or shelved' (Nandy, 2002a: 51). The operation of the dialectic ensures that a key dynamic remains in place to safeguard against the stagnation and homogenisation of alternatives. Whether this mode of dissent generated by the bad subject can be accepted as a form of creative and meaningful critique is connected to whether these processes of subjection can be confronted, worked-through and traversed.

Secularism and the Dynamics of Political Intolerance

Nandy's reading of how processes of subjection create political identities and respond to ethnicity furthers his claim that the secular ideal in India is working against its own aims. The pathologies of secularism, including the making of religious identities into political ones, are detailed in his reading of the dynamics of intolerance. These are not random irrational outbreaks of communal tension, but can be explained through the dynamics already outlined. To this extent, his analysis written in the 1980s was a forewarning of 'the crisis of secularism' that was to be acknowledged at a later date. For instance, in a scenario involving two religious communities, Nandy claims that there would be an overt affinity between modern believers within these communities. Thus, a common dialogue may ensue between a Westernised Hindu and Westernised Muslim whose common enemy comes in the form of the zealot. There is, though, a 'less overt affinity between the de-cultured Westernised ethnic and the partly de-cultured zealot'.[13] At play in this scenario is the 'hostility of the Westernised ethnic towards the peripherals of his own, as well as other faiths, that the Westernised ethnic sees as passive or prospective zealots' (Nandy, 2002a: 49).

There is an accepted hostility between Hindu and Muslim zealots, who voice their respective fanaticisms, ethnocentrisms and xenophobias with equal vigour. The hatred of the Hindu and Muslim zealot towards the everyday practitioner of his faith 'is nearly total' (Nandy, 2002a: 49). What is difficult to confront is that there is a covert affinity between peripheral Hindus and peripheral Muslims in the roles they play in fostering intolerance of difference. Both the Hindu and Muslim peripheral remain limited in their capacity to recognise a plurality of experience, and in turn to recognise the possibilities for alternative modes of toleration and of hospitality. As Nandy points out, recognising this shared psychic space between the peripheral Hindu and Muslim is a radical confrontation for modern Indians to accept. In standard explanations, it is the historical, cultural, ideological and religious differences that exist between the two that are emphasised. In such accounts, it is often the anti-modern Indian communal self that is the breeding ground for intolerance.[14] Nandy's analysis, thus, also runs contrary to more conventional readings of communal strife in which ethnic and religious intolerance remains a symptom of regressive and backward communities who fail to identify with the secular ideal. The response to this view is that this intolerance can only be managed through the aggressive reiteration of official state secularism that can reinforce and strengthen concepts of secular tolerance.

For Nandy, as already detailed, there are distinct limits to secularism's ability to safeguard tolerance. It is also no coincidence that the Hindu zealot does not necessarily belong to a regressive and backward community. The Hindu zealot is an astute modern political player who contributes to the seeds of intolerance under the guise of tolerance, while seemingly defending national identity and cohesion. For Nandy, part of the mass appeal of Hindu nationalism is its success in mobilising people in this way, and the 'strong set of psychological defences within its popularity' (Nandy and Deftereos, 2005c: 17). This popularity is also not removed from Hindu nationalism's highly sophisticated modernist creed and political identity ends. The logic of Hindu nationalism as a political identity—and herein, lies its popularity—exploits and perpetuates a growing sense of insecurity surrounding concepts of Indianness, and can be understood as a defensive and reactionary movement.[15] At the heart of these assertions for a pan-Hindu nation, predicated on tolerance and social and political unity, is, however, a fundamental contradiction. As Nandy warns, the tolerance proffered by the Hindu nationalists is highly dubious. He states:

> If you claim that you are tolerant, then you cannot use that tolerance as a marker of your superiority and then try to impose that tolerance in most intolerant ways. You know that is what I was trying to drive at. And then claim that we have to do this because others were intolerant! Some others were intolerant in the name of intolerance and others in the name of tolerance. That is the difference. (Nandy and Deftereos, 2005c: 17)

In the final part of 'An Anti-Secularist Manifesto', Nandy addresses the question of the changing nature of riots in India. There are two further charges made against the ideology of secularism. First, the inability of the secular ideal to safeguard communal amity despite its hegemonic and official claims to tolerance; and second, that secularism has failed to accept responsibility for its (overt and covert) involvement in acts of political violence, including the proliferation of riots within public life. The ideology of secularism may be able to cope with religious riots, which grow out of faulty passions vis-à-vis the irrational definition of the sacred, but it is unable to cope with riots that grow out of rationally managed violence. So, too, the Indian state can, to some extent, accept the faulty passions of peoples from the periphery or the ethnic backwaters of India who remain on the borderlands of politics. However, it cannot acknowledge its own complicity in the re-making of modern political identities. It cannot concede its own complicity with modern forms of violence, including those actuated by the Hindu nationalist movement. Nandy's analysis, therefore, contests existing scholarship that continues to present riots and pogroms as products of insufficient modernisation and secularisation. Nandy continues that 'one is forced to admit that communal riots in India have a modern connection...while religious violence was certainly not unknown in pre-modern or non-modern India, the kind of "rational," "managerial," "inter-communal violence we often witness nowadays can only be a by-product of secularisation and modernisation"' (Nandy, 2002a: 54). The 'embarrassing fact' is that the major threats to religious tolerance come from a modernising India and not from India's ethnic peripherals. For Nandy, neither the mechanical re-assertion of the secular ideal nor the more formalised certifications of the ideology, such as amendments made to the Indian Constitution in the 1970s, has succeeded in safeguarding secular tolerance as the only possible solution to communal strife.[16] According to Nandy, it is no coincidence that since these changes to the Constitution have been made, official secularism has become increasingly ineffectual in addressing these seeds of intolerance.

'An Anti-Secularist Manifesto', where Nandy's confrontation with secularism is first developed, therefore, details his anti-secular position as a radical questioning of the ways political identities and political culture are formed and the inclusions and exclusions that follow. In Nandy's reading, the psychic life of power underpinning Indian secular political culture and the political identities within it, exemplify the psychoanalytic focus of his work. This takes place at the intersection between political theory and psychoanalysis where Nandy's starting point for confronting the ideology of secularism is through a questioning of the subjectivity that structures Indian secular political culture, and political identities. This psychoanalytic focus is a necessary undertaking in Nandy's critique, if the cultural and psychological viability of secularism is to be seriously addressed. In this respect, the essay, despite its scathing condemnation of state secularism and its limits, cannot be read as simply anti-secular, without qualifying the psychoanalytic focus through which Nandy's anti-secularism is advanced. This anti-secularism cannot also be dismissed as a simple return to an imagined or nostalgic vision of a pre-modern India (if such a task is even possible), without considering the ways in which the tensions between the modern and non-modern operate in individual and collective concepts of selfhood. Nandy's confrontation with the psychic life of secularism is part of a more multifaceted task, addressing internal and external dynamics and inclusions and exclusions within individual and collective processes of identification.

For, in confronting the normative boundaries defining Indian political culture, secular and non-secular, public and private, modern and non-modern, Nandy demonstrates an intellectual sensitivity for the positioning of boundaries. This confrontation can also be read as an appeal for a broader understanding of politics. It is also an appeal to acknowledge the ways that the secular ideal structures processes of identification and, moreover, works to contain concepts of Indianness. This is part of an ongoing and consistent critical and analytic commitment to be found across Nandy's work.

To this extent, ambivalence, contradictions and concepts of pluralism, including democratic pluralism, are all central to Nandy's conceptualisation of politics. Attempts to abject ambivalences and contradictions from view in favour of a strict political identity are also central to his critique of Hindu nationalism, including its political appeal and popularity. The following chapter continues to explore the ways in which this psychoanalytic focus structures Nandy's critique of Hindu nationalism, as an extension of his reading of the pathologies of secularism. Although psychoanalysis reminds us that the possibility of strict identity is not entirely possible, Nandy situates Hindu nationalism as a defensive, and ultimately, destructive ideology, motivated by such prospects of homogenisation and standardisation. In his depiction, the aim of Hindu nationalism is in the 'making over' of Indianness into highly exclusionary and fixed terms, according to the internal aims of Hindutva ideology, and in service of creating a Hindu India. Therefore, like the mono-cultural and homogenising effects of secularism, Hindu nationalism, as a profoundly modern creed, functions in similar ways. Nandy's confronting claim is that the two are intimately connected, that Indian secular political culture provides the political conditions for contemporary manifestations of Hindutva. If Nandy's directive is to defy and traverse secularism's damaging political, intellectual and psychological categories of identification, then the question of re-claiming alternatives—including alternative concepts of selfhood and of tolerance—remains a continuing challenge for Indian democracy. This challenge in fostering the diversity and pluralism of Indian democracy reached crisis point during the 1990s, and in early 2000, with the popularity of Hindu nationalism and the Ramjanmabhumi movement reflected in electoral politics. These strategic and highly political efforts to create a Hindu nation, instituted through the political voice of the BJP, radically tested the democratic pluralism of the world's largest democracy.

NOTES

1. For a discussion of Kristeva's intellectual contributions to psychoanalytic theory and contemporary cultural and political critique see Beardsworth (2004).

2. It is the reprint of 'An Anti-Secular Manifesto' in *The Romance of the State* that is referred. Refer to Nandy (2002a).

3. There is an extensive body of literature critiquing this secular ideal as an inherited ideal and as a product of Western modernity. It is argued that this is significant for understanding the complexities of Indian secularism and the application of the concept to Indian society, given that India has not been exposed to the kinds of debates about the Church and State divide in pre-modern Europe.
   See for instance Chakrabarty (2002); Madan (1997); Chatterjee (1994).

4. For a discussion on what is now widely accepted as the crisis of Indian secularism, see Needham and Rajan (2007).

5. Examples of this kind of intervention include arguments for a universal civil code and abolishing religion-based affirmative action. This view also has support from what are deemed hard-line or genuine secularists, who claim that secularism within India has appeased minorities at its own detriment. They argue that more hard-line support and implementation of the ideology of secularism is needed in order to address the current crisis of Indian secularism. For a discussion of these issues refer to Nandy (2002a: 36). See also Baxi (2007) and Agnes (2007).

6. Nandy argues that Gandhi paid the ultimate price for his highly disruptive and threatening anti-secular worldview, and critique of Western modernity with his assassination. For a discussion of the politics of Gandhi's assassination refer to Nandy 1980c. For a discussion of the threatening and disruptive features of Gandhi's critique of modernity refer to Nandy (1997c).

7. See Savarkar (2003[1923]). Malik and Singh (1994).

8. On this point, see Dhavan (1992).

9. For a discussion of this process refer to the chapter titled 'Mapping the Secular in Bharucha (1998).

10. Fanon, Frantz. (1967). *Black Skin, White Masks*. New York: Grove Press.

11. Nanda (2002); Nauriya (2003).

12. See Nauriya (2003).

13. For a more comprehensive analysis of these dynamics, see Nandy (2002a: 48–49).

14. See Engineer, Asghar Ali (1984). *Communal Riots in Post-Independence India*. Hyderabad: Sangam Books.

15. For further information regarding Nandy's critique of these processes, see for, example Nandy (1994a, 1991). See also Lal (2003).

16. These changes made by the Indira Gandhi government were introduced into the Preamble of the Indian Constitution in 1976 during the Emergency in India when civil rights were suspended. The government, then functioning as a dictatorship, in passing the forty-second amendment certified the principle of secularism into the Indian Constitution. The term 'secular'

instituted equality of all religions and religious tolerance and that the government must not favour or discriminate on the basis of religion. The legal precedent for the inclusion of the term was provided in the judgment of the Supreme Court case, *S. R. Bommai versus Union of India*, that upheld that secularism was a principle integral to the Indian Constitution. For a discussion of the late entry of the term 'secularism' into the Indian Constitution, refer to Caroll (2001).

2

Containing Indianness: Secularism versus Hindutva?

In Nandy's writings, if secularism and its viability are to be seriously engaged with, confronted and worked through, then the way in which the ideology structures processes of identification needs to be explored. This includes the way Indian political culture and political identities are formed in relation to a dominant secular ideal. Nandy's confrontation with the psychic life of secularism is, therefore, part of a more multifaceted task. This psychoanalytic approach allows for an analysis of the cultural and psychic distortions that the ideology of secularism produces. These distortions or, rather, the pathologies of secularism, are evident in the way that political identities are formed and made over in relation to a secular ideal. There are distinct processes of subjection at play as identities, including religious and ethnic identities, are made into political identities in accordance with this ideal. In emphasising these processes, his analysis also highlights aspects of selfhood that have been abjected from view. As Nandy explains, 'While the personality of those within the fully secular, modern sector is well-represented in the democratic order, those outside of the modern sector have only a part of themselves represented in politics' (Nandy, 2002a: 37). What Nandy laments are the homogenising and standardising features of these processes of subjection. Furthermore, he equally laments the way in which the ambivalence that marks subjectivity and concepts of Indianness is foreclosed by these processes of making political identities.

However, Nandy's analysis of secularism emphasises that ambivalence cannot entirely be cast from view. Ambivalence remains within his account, an essential feature of subjectivity, and an essential feature within concepts of Indianness. In 'An Anti-Secularist Manifesto'

Nandy's confrontation with the secular ideal affirms this point (Nandy, 1985a). For example, even in his depiction of Jawaharlal Nehru, validated within Indian political culture as the ideal secular citizen, Nandy emphasises the ambivalence and contradiction that accompanies all subjectivity, including Nehru's. This is explored through what he suggests is Nehru's latent self, his pre-modern or cultural self that survives as the underside of his modern secular self. Nandy explores this in terms of the ways that Nehru's pre-modern or cultural self reveals itself in practices, such as his reliance upon *tantric*s that are suggestive of ambivalence. For Nandy, the dynamic interplay between dominant and latent parts of self is essential to confronting and working through processes of homogenisation and standardisation. Recognising that ambivalence is a feature of all subjectivity, or rather a condition of subjectivity, is also consistent with Butler's argument about the psychic life of power. For, as Butler elaborates in her account of subjection,

> the power imposed on one is the power that animates one's emergence, and there appears to be no escaping this ambivalence. Indeed, there appears to be no 'one' without ambivalence, which is to say that the fictive redoubling necessary to become a self rules out the possibility of strict identity. (Butler, 1997: 198)

In Nandy's critique, the pathologies of secularism reveal themselves as attempts to impose a 'strict identity', as political identities that foreclose ambivalence.

These attempts to foreclose ambivalence, as an effect of the distortions of the dominant secular ideal, are also central to Nandy's critique of Hindu nationalism. During the 1990s, ambivalence and Indian pluralism were further threatened by a changing Indian political landscape. This threat came with the rising popularity of Hindu nationalism and Hindutva ideology with its increasingly militant, and at times violent, political demands to make over India as Hindu. The popularity of Hindutva ideology reached its peak in 1999 when the BJP became the leading party in the National Democratic Alliance coalition government, holding power until May 2004. For Nandy, the greatest threat that Hindu nationalism and the Hindu right posed, and which continues today, is that the ideology that proffers a very specific and exclusionary account of Indianness. This account of Indianness functions as a 'strict identity', as ambivalence, contradiction and pluralism are cast from view. The internal logic of Hindutva ideology, in effect, works to reconstitute the positioning of the boundaries of inclusion and exclusion, thus limiting claims to Indianness. This reconstituted concept of Indianness is then used to justify the rightful and entitled claims over nation, and is appropriated to appease and further exacerbate anxieties regarding national integration. The Hindu nationalist claim to make over and 'purify' Indianness and India as Hindu, thus, necessitates the abjection of ambivalence and plural accounts of selfhood in service of a 'strict identity'. These concepts of making over and purifying Bharat India are re-occurring themes in Hindu nationalism. *Mother India* is one such example.[1]

The full extent of Hindutva's exclusionary ideas and practices are demonstrated in the outbreaks of violence that have surfaced, notably in the 1990s. This violence includes the political events that led to the destruction of the Babri Mosque in Ayodhya, Uttar Pradesh, in 1992, an event in which thousands of people, mainly Muslims, lost their lives. This was followed by the aftermath of violence and revenge attacks that spread across northern India between Hindu and Muslim communities. Events such as the Bombay riots in December 1992 and January 1993 and the Gujarat riots in 2002, in which 2,000 people died and 200,000 were displaced from their homes and communities, dominated the political landscape.[2] For Nandy these events and the violence carried out in the name of Hindutva cannot be explained by what is perceived to be the communal politics threatening India's secularity, and advanced by a number of writers.[3] Nandy radically challenges this account and argues that these are thoroughly modern acts of violence connected to a secular political culture. Further, these acts of violence carried out in the 1990s cannot be dismissed as aberrations, but rather, are part of larger defensive forces operating in Indian politics around concepts of Indianness, national identity, national integration and democracy. These are effects of more complex long-term processes, dating back to the Emergency in India and the policies of the Indira Gandhi and Rajiv Gandhi governments in the 1980s. According to Nandy, Indira Gandhi psychologically represents important aspects of contemporary Indian consciousness (Nandy, 1980a: 112). For Nandy, the political seeds giving rise to these events had been planted earlier and need to be understood as continuing effects of the distortions of a dominant secular ideology, altering cultural, social and political priorities within Indian political culture. This altering of cultural, social and political priorities in Indian political culture can also be understood as part of processes that were taking place on a global level, since the 1980s, with the rise of neo-liberalism and a general ideological shift to the cultural politics of the Right in Western liberal democracies. India's secular slogan of 'Unity in Diversity' has and, more importantly, continues to be radically tested by these processes.

The anti-Sikh riots in Delhi in November 1984, the anti-Muslim riots in Ahmedabad in 1985 during the anti-reservation stir and the anti-Hindu riots in Bangalore in 1986 also need to be understood as part of these ongoing disputes over Indianness. For Nandy, it is the pathologies of secularism that are being expressed in the xenophobia and fanaticism underpinning the politics of contemporary violence in India today. What is problematic, and needs to be confronted and worked through, is that 'the modern state itself invites the formation of such adversarial nationalities by leaving that as the only effective way of making collective demands on the State and playing the game of numbers in competitive politics' (Nandy, Trivedy, Mayaram and Yagnik, 1995: vii). As Nandy's critique of secularism highlights, these issues necessitate an approach that accounts for the way in which Indian political culture and political identities are formed. Moreover, it calls for a psychoanalytic approach that can account for the psychic life of power and processes of subjection operating in adversarial nationalities.

In Nandy's critique of secularism the Hindu zealot is a product of the processes of subjection operating in Indian secular political culture. As detailed in 'An Anti-Secularist Manifesto' the Hindu zealot is 'reacting to and yet internalising the humiliation inflicted on all faiths by a triumphant anti-faith called Western modernity, [and] has accepted the Western Enlightenment's attitude to all faiths including his own' (Nandy, 2002a: 45). This is exemplified in the fact that most of the reformers within the Hindu nationalist movement were either agnostic or non-believers, some of them not even practising Hindus. In Nandy's analysis, being a believer in public and non-believer in private is a defining characteristic of the political identity of the Hindu zealot. This is also the case with V.D. Savarkar, the founding father of Hindutva. Nandy suggests that Savarkar's political identity illustrates the complicity between secularism, modernity and Hindu nationalism. Secularism may provide the conditions for the Hindu zealot's political voice, but both secularism and Hindutva share the objective of making over India into a homogenised mono-cultural society. Confronting and working through the way in which religious and ethnic identities are made into political identities is central to understanding these processes.

This chapter details Nandy's critique of Hindu nationalism and its relationship to the pathologies of secularism.[4] He contends that at the core of the Hindu nationalism is 'a secular ideology of the state and a modern rationality' (Nandy, Trivedy, Mayaram and Yagnik, 1995: vii). Such a confronting proposition beckons an analysis of how these processes of making over Hinduism into a political identity take place. Nandy's approach in understanding the positioning of the boundaries of inclusion and exclusion operating within Hindutva, in who can make claims to Indianness and claims over nation, is vital. The final part of the chapter addresses the way the 'Ayodhya issue' and the Ramjanmabhumi movement affirm Nandy's argument that Hindutva ideology is a thoroughly modern and defensive movement. It is the end product of efforts to make over or 'convert Hinduism' into a 'proper' modern nation and a conventional ethnic majority', articulated through a defensive set of beliefs and political identifications. Nandy and the other authors state that the title of their text *Creating a Nationality: The Ramjanmabhumi Movement and Fear of the Self* (1995):

> represents the awareness that the chain of events we describe is the end-product of a century of effort to convert the Hindus into a 'proper' modern nation and a conventional ethnic majority and it has as its underside the story, which we have told here, of corresponding efforts to turn the other faiths of the subcontinent into proper ethnic minorities and well-behaved nationalities. (Nandy et al., 1995: vi)

These defences for Nandy, expressed in the pathologies of xenophobia and fanaticism, attempt to cover up the insecurity and fear that accompanies the ambivalence of concepts of Indianness and of selfhood. As he suggests, these are defences against ambivalence, contradictions and pluralism, in favour of the certitudes of a 'strict identity'. They are, thus, also defences against latent and disavowed concepts of Indianness grounded in a fear of self (or latent parts of self) and a fear of difference and otherness. Nandy's critique of Hindu nationalism thus warns us against the way in which the ambivalence that marks subjectivity, and more plural accounts of Indianness, is foreclosed by these political processes. 'In this respect at least,' he argues, 'there [is] no difference whatsoever between Hindu nationalism and statist secularism' (Nandy et al., 1995: 60). In addition to advancing the need to reclaim ambivalence, his critique alerts us to the fact that these processes of 'making India Hindu' have much to reveal about the health of Indian democracy.

THE MAKING OF RELIGION AS IDEOLOGY

There is an extensive body of literature critiquing Hindu nationalism and the threat that it poses to Indian secularism.[5] This includes

critiquing the political conditions that have given rise to these processes of 'making India Hindu'. Further, to what extent have these
processes compromised India's secular political identity? Partha
Chatterjee has questioned whether Indian secularism can even meet
the challenge of Hindu nationalism and the processes of making over
Indian identity. He notes the complicity between Indian secularism
and the Hindu Right, and to this extent questions whether the ideology of secularism can challenge the political forces of Hindutva.
As Chatterjee emphasises, the Hindu nationalist movement is located 'within the domain of the modernising state and [uses] all the
ideological resources of that state' (Chatterjee 1994: 1768). To suggest that state secularism can respond to processes that have provided the political conditions for Hindu nationalist views to flourish is dubious. John Zavos suggests that the focus of debate should
be on the internal logic of Hindutva, in order to understand the
threat that it poses to secularism. Zavos claims there is a need to
identify the shapes of Hindu nationalism, the shadows it casts on
Indian politics, in order to understand the full extent of this threat.
The metaphor of shapes is appropriate, he argues, because 'so many
Hindu nationalist ideas are concerned with the issue of 'shaping'…
in particular shaping Hindu society into a form that reflects the perceived glory of the Hindu 'race' (Zavos in Adeney and Saez, 2005: 36).
While Zavos rightly comments upon the altering of cultural, social
and political priorities, Nandy's account extends on this further. It is
not only the process of shaping in Hindu Nationalism that needs to
be confronted, but also the aspects of self and of Indianness that are
being contained and foreclosed through these processes. For Nandy,
this necessitates a reading of the way in which these processes of 'creating a nationality' are intimately connected to a 'fear of self', and a
fear and disavowal of a particular kind of Hinduism. Hindu nationalism and the political identity of the Hindu zealot must be understood
as part of more complex historical, cultural and psychic processes to
make over and reconstitute Hinduism. The ambivalence and pluralism that mark Hinduism, Indian traditions, and culture for Nandy
are being hijacked and reconstituted within fixed identity categories.
These processes of subjection are complete for Nandy because
'Indianness is no longer defined in terms of what Indians are and the
ways they live; it is derived from ideal-typical definitions' (Nandy et al.,
1995: 78). The deferral to these ideal-type definitions is significant
because this provides the psychic and cultural impetus for these processes of making over Indianness. 'Hence,' he argues, 'the long and

abiding connection between Hindu nationalism and Hindu social reform movements of all hues.' As the authors state, 'such ideal-typical
definitions then become the staple of the formations which see the
majority itself as flawed in character and as a fit subject for large-scale
social engineering' (Nandy et al., 1995: 78). For Nandy, the ideal-type
definitions that are used to make over Hinduism are intimately connected to the secular ideal operating within Indian political culture
and within political identities. To this extent, affirming the position
that the ideology of secularism is capable of countering the political
challenge presented by Hindu nationalism, is itself an effect of the
distortions of this dominant ideology.

Nandy's essay, 'The Politics of Secularism and the Recovery of Religious Tolerance' (1990), offers an analysis of why these processes have
found political expression in violence.[6] The essay also offers a more
detailed account of the complicity between a modern Indian nation
state, modern intellectuals and the modernising middle classes of
South Asia with these forms of violence. Nandy argues that these constituencies, namely modern intellectuals and the modernising middle
classes, are complicit with these processes of subjection operating in
Indian political culture. It is no coincidence that these constituencies
are also the most vocal in their support for the secular ideal and their
defence of the ideal is almost complete. For they maintain that the
violence carried out in the name of Hindutva needs to be addressed
through the re-assertion of the secular ideal, to counter the current
pseudo-secularism that marks contemporary Indian politics. Hindu
nationalists, particularly the BJP, have accused the Congress Party of
proffering pseudo-secularism. Nandy's critique radically challenges
these views given that both secularism and Hindutva are examples of
'faulty ideologies and unrestrained instrumental rationality', facilitating these forms of violence. Nandy references the work of philoso-
phers Hannah Arendt and Herbert Marcuse in arguing that the most
extreme forms of violence in our times come not from faulty passions
or human irrationality but from faulty ideologies and unrestrained
instrumental rationality (Das, 1990: 85). The essay can be read as a
confrontation with the effects of the distortions of the dominant secular ideology, which has given rise to the fanaticism and xenophobia
of the Hindu nationalists. Further, it is an attempt to recover concepts
of religious tolerance that, for Nandy, survive, albeit latently and resist these processes of reconstituting religion into a political identity.

Nandy distinguishes between two different accounts of religion in
order to explore the way these processes of subjection take effect. He
suggests that the concept of religion has been split into two distinct

interpretations with very different internal configuring principles: 're-ligion as faith' and 'religion as ideology' (Das, 1990: 69). Nandy proposes that both concepts are configured within accounts of self very different-ly. 'Religion as faith' is characterised as a way of living, or a modality of being derived from within the pluralism and diversity of the cultural and religious practices of South Asian traditions. This account of 'religion as faith' recognises that the boundaries that define Hinduism and the Hin-du self are fluid and open, evidenced in the way that Hindus can follow and also identify as followers of other and many faiths. Hinduism char-acterised by its non-monotheistic basis does not demand, for Nandy, an allegiance to a singular identification or to a singular fixed identity.

In contrast to this, religion as ideology uses religion instrumen-tally as an ideological tool for political gain. This reconstituted ac-count of religion functions politically as a sub-national, national or cross-national identifier of populations contesting for or protecting non-religious, political or socio-economic interests. The differences between these are significant for understanding the argument Nandy makes about the internal logic of Hindu nationalism. As Nandy and the other authors of *Creating a Nationality* argue, 'in fact, Hindu Nationalism has to specifically reject a cultural-moral definition of Hinduism, the political possibilities of which were to be later devel-oped by M.K. Gandhi' (Nandy et al., 1995: 59). The authors emphasise that a cultural and moral definition of Hinduism must be rejected in favour of this reconstituted, revised and made-over Hinduism. This Hinduism, now made over as a political identity, must distinguish and differentiate itself from concepts of 'religion as faith' and from the worldview of the non-modern peripheral Indian. It distin-guishes itself on the basis that it is a political identity, afforded a political status and political voice within Indian political culture. It must, therefore, distinguish itself as opposite from Gandhi's bad subject, who fails to reinstate the secular norm and is abjected from political view. The authors contend that it is Gandhi's commitment to this cultural-moral Hinduism as the basis of politics that is threatening and disruptive to Indian secular culture, and even more threatening to these boundaries of differentiation is that Gandhi's account of 'religion as faith' functions as a political critique of these processes. For 'his Hin-duism brings to politics a cultural-moral critique of Hindutva from the point of view of Hinduism as the living faith of a majority of Indians'. The authors continue that what is problematic is when nationalism is

given a monocultural content and the definition of Indianness ceases to be a statistical artefact to become a reality on the ground, the minority cultures become easy and legitimate targets of criticism, social engineering and, as a leader of the erstwhile Jan Sangh once put it 'indianisation'. When such targeting takes place, Indianness is no longer defined in terms of what Indians are and the ways in which they live; it is derived from ideal-typical definitions. (Nandy in Das, 1990: 78)

Nandy develops this point in a number of places in his writings, and asserts that Gandhi's critique of Hindutva must be understood as a feature of his scathing critique of Western modernity.

'Religion as ideology' is a product of modern India and of a secular political culture. Nandy affirms that Hindu nationalism 'has always been an illegitimate child of modern India, not of Hindu traditions' (Nandy in Das, 1990: 78). Hindu nationalism as a modern and contemporary creed shifts political dynamics, as traditions and religion are appropriated instrumentally in service of justifying reconstituted political claims over nation. The dangers are not necessarily in the fact that political claims over nation are being made. What is problematic for Nandy is how these claims are made and the form that these claims take as pathology, in order to make political demands on the State. When plural Indian traditions and open religions like Hinduism are given a mono-cultural content, then this gives rise to a highly specific and politicised account of Indianness. Who then can make claims over Indianness and nation becomes over-determined by the internal logic of the ideology and instituted in a series of specific exclusionary practices. This account of Indianness is organised around a series of ideal types and not through the embedded experiences of how people live and express their subjectivity. For Nandy, this deviation from an alternative account of 'religion as faith' forecloses openness, pluralism and ambivalence in favour of a strict identity. It equally truncates an engagement with different expressions of religion in contemporary India. The dominant form that religion now takes and in which it finds its political voice is in a de-sacralised account of religion.[7] As Nandy affirms, politics 'has become a site of contention between the modern that attacks or bypasses traditions and the modern that employs traditions instrumentally' (Nandy in Das, 1990: 78). Within this political culture traditions become a resource for these processes of subjection, as the modern Hindu zealot draws upon traditions, culture, myths and religious symbols to articulate its demands in the vernacular of the state.

In 'The Politics of Secularism and the Recovery of Religious Tolerance' Nandy re-affirms his argument that the pathologies of secularism work to foreclose fluid accounts of the self and of Indianness. Moreover, these pathologies foreclose the possibility of there being ambivalent expressions of subjectivity, even as latent features of the underside of culture. The recovery that is needed for Nandy is in the reclaiming of religious tolerance and the recovery of ambivalence inherent within a latent account of Hinduism. As detailed in 'An Anti-Secularist Manifesto' these fluid accounts of self, of Indianness, of Hinduism and of tolerance are already present in the non-modern peripheral subject. There is an emphasis placed by Nandy on the way that 'religion as faith' denotes a different account of self and through which a different account of tolerance is advanced. For it demonstrates the way in which the non-modern, and to this extent apolitical practices of toleration and hospitality, can resist processes of subjection. There is a resistance within these everyday expressions of Hinduism and Islam that reinforces ambivalence in the way in which the boundaries within religious identity are cast. Nandy concedes though that this resistance has to contend with another kind of resistance—the denial of the importance of one's own categories of identification in relation to these political processes. Nandy describes this resistance or denial of ambivalence that the non-modern peripheral represents, as a 'principled forgetfulness'. He continues, 'That resistance [the non-modern peripheral's resistance] is not noticed because another kind of principled forgetfulness comes into play when modern, secular scholars study religious or ethnic violence' (Nandy, Trivedy, Mayaram and Yagnik, 1995: viii).

In contrast to this, 'religion as ideology' or Hindu nationalism advances an account of self, through the disavowal and abjection of parts of one's self, in service of a 'fixed identity'. What must, therefore, be disavowed and abjected from view are parts of self, a premodern or cultural self, that remains peripheral, if not outside of politics. What is also abjected from view are ambivalence, contradictions and concepts of pluralism, all central to the non-modern peripheral account of Indianness. These more fluid accounts of selfhood are, thus, disavowed through processes of subjection in service of a well-bounded self or fixed identity. As Shrinivas Tilak argues, using the metaphor of illness and perversion to the relationship of Hindutva and the Indian Secularists, 'the Hindu tradition, religion, culture and literature today are victims of the modern ego' (Tilak in Sharma, 2001: 132). In Nandy's analysis this is an important association to establish and one that needs to be confronted, if secularism and Hindu nationalism are to be seriously questioned. For Nandy, the psychoanalytic argument is useful because it draws attention to the complexities of these processes of identification. Nandy draws on Tariq Banuri's comparison of the dominant position of the ego in Freudian psychology with the dominant position of the nation-state in contemporary ideas of political development. From a psychoanalytic reading such efforts of becoming the sovereign nation-state parallel the *becoming* the entitled sovereign subject. As Nandy suggests, 'to complete [Banuri's] evocative metaphor, one must view secularism as a crucial defence of the ego' (Nandy, 2004a: 119). If secularism can be understood as a defence of the ego, then Hinduism expressed in its pathological form as a reconstituted political identity, becomes a victim of these processes of identification.

However, the reconstituted Hindu self ('religion as ideology') projects that abjection of disavowed parts of self onto India's 'alien others' and this is where the dangers of Hindutva are to be found. Noelle McAfee has argued that these political conditions lead to 'national(istic) abjection', and that this 'breeds the worst kind of violence and inhumanity' (McAfee, 2000: 124). For Nandy, the dangers of this abjection (at the level of self and society) are in the way that these manifest and find recourse in psychic life, as isolation, denial and self-hatred. These deeply internalised defences in service of protecting the ego (and the ego ideal of Western man) characterise the psychic life of the Hindu zealot and the psychic life of Hindutva. Articulated in the exclusionary beliefs of its followers, these defences remain in Nandy's analysis unchallenged by an Indian secular political culture.

WHO CLAIMS INDIANNESS? THE POLITICS OF INCLUSION AND EXCLUSION

In contemporary Indian politics the remaking of religious and ethnic identities into political identities have complicated the claims made over Indianness. In Nandy's analysis, concepts of Indianness have been co-opted by the strong set of defences that are the features of a remade Hinduism. The positioning of the boundaries of inclusion and exclusion and who can claim Indianness plays out in specific terms. The obvious exclusions of the ideology are in the way minority cultures such as Muslims become the legitimate targets for hostility, threat and fear within reconstituted concepts of Indianness. On what grounds, though, do these claims of Indianness take form? How do these processes of 'making India Hindu', these processes of subjection, take place to affirm Hindu India and exclude its others?

There are a number of texts that have been central to the internal logic of Hindutva. These include V.D. Savarkar's text, *Who is a Hindu?* (1923), attributed as the foundational text of Hindutva ideology and Savarkar its ideological father. Other important texts include the writings of Madhav Sadashiv Golwalkar, especially *Bunch of Thoughts* (1966) and *We, or Our Nation Defined* (1944), and to a lesser extent Deendayal Upadhyaya. Nandy has argued that Golwalkar and Upadhyaya were important figures in the Hindu nationalist movement in the ways in which they broadened the ideological platform of Hindutva through their involvement in the Rashtriya Swayamsevak Sangh (RSS).[8] There is debate in critiques of Hindu nationalism regarding what role these texts have played in reconstituting Hinduism into a political identity. For example, theorists like Zavos have emphasised that these texts do not form a coherent body of work or advance a coherent ideological position. Zavos reiterates the fractured quality of these ideas, suggesting that it represents a broad field of thought. For instance, Zavos notes that although Savarkar is bestowed with the title of the ideological father of Hindu nationalism and his text the 'classic' text of Hindu nationalism, he was not a member of the RSS and, therefore, cannot in the organisation's version of history be portrayed as central in the development of Hindu nationalism (Zavos in Adeney and Saez, 2005: 36). In Nandy's account, while these texts may constitute a fractured set of ideas, the political processes of remaking the Indian self as exclusively Hindu are anything but fractured. For Nandy, V.D. Savarkar epitomises the subjectivity of the zealot and his questioning of 'who is a Hindu?' is asked in the spirit of the non-believer in private, and as a believer in public. While Savarkar begins with a seemingly broad construction of Hindu nationality, described by Zavos as 'catholic', embracing a broad range of religious and cultural systems, this approach to Hinduism and Hindu culture is ultimately made over (Zavos in Adeney and Saez, 2005: 40). Savarkar re-constitutes this depiction by questioning, and, in Nandy's depiction, by obsessively working on the boundaries of this range. Thus, Savarkar advances a series of tropes that position the boundaries of inclusion and exclusion defining Indianness and claims over nation in fixed terms. For example, this is demonstrated in Savarkar's formula of *pitribhum-punyabhum* (fatherland-holy land). According to this trope whoever can identify India as both their fatherland and holy land may then be considered a Hindu. For Nandy, the most crucial political exclusion and abjection that takes place is through Savarkar's trope of the *rashtra-jati-sanskriti* (nation-race-culture) that is seen as components of Hinduness. However, identification with the Hindu race and nation can only take place through *punyabhum*, for those who also identify India as a holy land. For Nandy, this is where religion operates instrumentally, now reconstituted as ideology, as concepts of nation, race and culture are defined by these overriding rightful claims to holy land. Based on Savarkar's account, those excluded and abjected from making claims to India and in turn, Indianness, are Muslims and Christians in that they locate their holy land and their cultural identity outside of India.

Despite writing about these processes in 1923, Savakar's questioning of 'who is a Hindu?' proves for Nandy to be enduring and resilient in its exclusions and abjections. The intensity of these boundaries of exclusion operating in the Hindu political identity is demonstrated in the key tenant of the ideology: resisting religious conversion. Consistent with the exclusions actuated through *pitribhum-punyabhum*, conversion to Islam or Christianity, therefore, amounts to a process of de-nationalisation. For Nandy this exemplifies Savakar's political identity as a zealot and his appropriation of identity politics for political ends. Savarkar's contributions can, thus, be measured alongside his political project of creating a distinct nationality. As a number of commentators point out, Savarkar admitted he was willing the nation into being with his mantra of 'we Hindus will to be a Nation, and therefore, we are a Nation' (Adeney and Saez, 2005: 36). David Smith also comments on these processes of making over Hinduism by noting that Savarkar himself referred 'to Hinduism as a creature from the deep. From what can be seen as the primordial depth of the imagination' (Smith, 2003: 187).

Who can claim Indianness is also established through history and geography. For Savarkar, the history unfolds, at least in broad terms, in the following way. Hinduness and, in turn, Indianness is rooted in the Aryan civilisation and the establishment of the Vedic tradition. It is important to note that there are variations in the way that Vedic traditions have been interpreted. For instance, Nandy and the other authors of *Creating a Nationality* explore the ways in which these variations have been taken up in different ways in the umbrella groups comprising the contemporary Hindu Nationalist movement. Their analysis includes a comparative discussion of these traditions within the RSS, the Vishwa Hindu Parishad (VHP) and the youth wing of the VHP, the Bajrang Dal. As they outline:

> Deviating from RSS orthodoxy, which permits only Mother India or Bharat Mata as a theistic presence, the VHP leadership, mostly Hindi-speaking north Indians, admit the greater power of theistic Hinduism as compared

to that of the Neo-Vedantic Arya Samaj. This thesis, though, is given a monotheistic slant, as an antidote to Hinduism's 'embarrassingly' non-revelatory, pagan character. (Nandy, Trivedy, Mayaram and Yagnik, 1995: 87)[9]

According to his account there was a gradual expansion of Aryan influence, leading eventually to the religious, cultural, and political unification of the subcontinent under Lord Ram. This was followed by periods of Hindu and Buddhist ascendancy, which, in turn, were superseded by the Muslim incursion and the beginning of a long period of struggle to maintain Hindu identity in the face of foreign invasions. Despite the Vedic civilisation of the Aryans being used as a reference point by a number of groups, it is claimed that Muslim rule created a decisive break in Indian history. Nandy argues that current grievances against Muslim minorities can thus be located and referenced back to these past, primordial grievances. These ideas have served to emphasise the embeddedness of the Hindu nationalist identity, in part because of its definable and uninterrupted historical lineage. This further works to entrench the Bharat nation as divine because of its sacred geography, which too has a historical lineage established through sacred Hindu texts, like the *Ramayana*. These processes have an important role to play in the positioning of the boundaries of inclusion and exclusion, by invoking what Sankaran Krishna has described as 'cartographic anxieties' (Shapiro and Alker, 1995).

These 'cartographic anxieties', particularly the fear of a loss of national identity, and national integration rely upon the appropriation of Hinduism, religious texts, and symbols to perpetuate exclusive and entitled rights over Indianness. This is evidenced, for instance, in the way that the Hindu gods Ram and Sita—the heroes of the myths of the *Ramayana*—become (re)instituted as archetypal Indians.[10] For Hindu nationalists, Ram and Sita are national heroes and not only religious figures. For Nandy this nationalist and exclusive claim must be confronted and challenged. He asks: 'Why does the VHP, like a greedy street peddler, sell Ram as a secular national hero, and not as a religious figure?' (Nandy, 2002h: 3). This archetype of Ram as a national hero is not only privileged but also then celebrated for political ends. For instance, as Chakravarti has argued in her critique of the 'saffronization of India', the Rajiv Gandhi government directly participated in celebrating and disseminating the myth of the *Ramayana*.[11] Chakravarti explores the Rajiv Gandhi government's decision during the 1980s to televise the serialisation of this myth, which went on to become one of the most popular TV serials in Indian history. The myth of *Ramayana*, in which Ram is represented as a martial hero defending the honour of Hinduism armed with his mighty bow, defending the honour of his wife, Sita, becomes one of the most popular images. This image is noteworthy not only because of the re-claiming of a masculine potency central to the affirmation and assertion of a masculine Hindu self, but because it is an image that played a central role in the dispute over the birthplace of Lord Rama at Ayodhya in the early 1990s. The act of defending Sita functions as a metaphor for the defence of the honour of Bharat Mata, Mother India. Although this is not explored at length in the discussion here, the role of gender in Hindutva ideology and in the development of Hindu nationalist movement is an important feature. For example, Nandy has argued that this reconstituted concept of Hinduism proffered by the Hindu nationalists is part of an attempt to masculinise the self-definition of Hindus. It is also an attempt to counter the colonialist view of Hinduism and the Hindu man as effeminate.[12] As Chakravarti points out, the dissemination of such myths through the media has been central to the growing political popularity of Hindu nationalist views during the 1980s and 1990s. Moreover, these myths have been fundamental to propagating the psychic life of Hindutva and in instituting its political demands within contemporary India. Runa Das comments on the relationship between gender and concepts of nation at play here. Das explores how 'the postcolonial India's states project of nation-building—reflective of a Western secular-modernity identity (under the Congress Party) and a Hindutva-dominated identity (under the BJP)—incorporates gender with continuities and discontinuities to articulate divergent forms of nationalist communalist identities, "cartographic anxieties" and nuclear (in)securities' (Das, 2008: 206).

The appropriation of Ram and Sita as identifiable national heroes thus serves to re-enforce the exclusions over who has claims to Indianness and nation. This is exemplified most recently in the way in which the plans to (re)build a Hindu temple in the wake of the destruction of the Babri Mosque at the proclaimed birthplace of Ram in Ayodhya are defended as a national project.[13] As Nandy argues in his comment on the Allahabad High Court's verdict in 2010, 'using religion to mobilise an apolitical citizenry is not the same as faith' (Nandy, 2010: 1). Within this climate any resistance to the (re)building of the temple, especially from Muslims, is deemed anti-national. The Muslim devotee protecting Muslim claims to the sacred site of the Babri Mosque is reconstituted in threatening terms and made over as the anti-national and anti-Indian subject. This recent example of rebuilding in Ayodhya demonstrates the way in which Hindutva has altered cultural, social and political priorities within Indian political culture. These exclusions were formalised even further when the BJP formed government and the Sangh took control of the national agencies in 1999–2004, including the Indian Council of Historical Research and the Ministry of Education. These processes of making India Hindu were instituted in pedagogical practices and in the revisionist history in public school curriculum, documented at length by the historian Romilla Thapar.[14] The education reforms were primarily organised around accounts of history that characterised Hinduism as indigenously Indian, and Islam and Christianity as alien invaders in India. The periods of Islamic rule in Indian history, such as the Mughal Empire, are constructed as Muslim attempts to conquer and exploit an indigenously authentic Hindu India. These pedagogical practices are significant in consolidating and perpetuating Hindutva's defensive beliefs within individual and collective life. The defence reaches its logical conclusion in the argument that Hindu violence against Muslims, like the violence witnessed at Ayodhya, is a natural manifestation of a historically constituted Hindu rage. Equally revealing are the responses to the 2010 verdict, which as Nandy emphasises has not pleased the VHP and the Hindu Mahasabha, 'which were seeking neither justice not a reaffirmation of ethics, but a clear-cut triumph. The other indication is that the judgement has antagonised many secular extremists, seeking another kind of triumph and vengeance' (Nandy, 2010: 1).

In Nandy's analysis these defences demonstrate the political victory of the Hindu zealot, of 'religion as ideology' over the everyday follower of Hinduism, of 'religion as faith'. He notes that 'this re-engineered, culturally bipedal Hindu is to be backed by an ideology that is a pasteurised Brahmanic version of the dominant public ideology of the modern West' (Nandy et al., 1995: 49). What is discernable about the ideology is the positioning of distinct boundaries of inclusion and exclusion. While Nandy acknowledges that these boundaries are inescapable, he objects to the reconstitution of these boundaries in service of the ideology. As he explains, 'the ideology works on the basis of a number of obvious polarities: genuine secularism as opposed to pseudo-secularism, genuine history as opposed to false history, true nationalism as opposed to false or effete patriotism' (Nandy et al., 1995: 49). It is, however, through the politicisation of these polarities, the re-assertion of these boundaries as 'fixed' and without ambivalence, which enables the defensive logic of the ideology to reproduce itself as a feature of contemporary Indian political culture.

THE IDEA OF INDIA: HINDUTVA'S TESTING GROUND

The late Indian philosopher Ramachandra Gandhi had suggested that Ayodhya functions as a site 'where the honour of India's spiritual traditions [is] being severely tested' (Gandhi, 1992: ix). The Ayodhya dispute is a reminder of other disavowed selves and other accounts of Hinduism that are deemed to have no place in contemporary politics. In Nandy's analysis, Ayodhya is a testing ground for these reconstituted dominant political selves and their accompanying exclusionary demands. Moreover, these demands are articulated in the vernacular of the modern secular state, and appropriated for political ends. Nandy argues that 'the destruction of the Babri Mosque, began the day Prime Minister Rajiv Gandhi unlocked the gates of the temple within the mosque to gain an electoral advantage' (Nandy and Jahanbegloo, 2006: 72). It did not begin on 6 December 1992, when the supporters of the VHP, the Shiv Sena Party together with the then opposition party, the BJP, led the destruction of the mosque. Nandy states that,

> it is no accident that, despite the claim of some Hindu nationalists that more than 350,000 Hindus had already died fighting for the liberation of the birthplace of Rama, Ramjanmabhumi, during the previous 400 years, the residents of Ayodhya themselves lived in reasonable amity till the late 1980s. (Nandy, 2004a: 114)

The role of the Sangh Parivar and the BJP is significant here, because for Nandy the case for the destruction of the Babri Mosque was not taken up until after the mid 1980s. As he emphasises, 'the Babri mosque was turned into a political issue only after India's urban middle class attained a certain size and India's modernization reached a certain stage' (Nandy, 2004a: 114). With respect to the role of the BJP in these processes Crossman and Kapur argue that 'the BJP represents the force of the Hindu Right that must be met and challenged at the level of ideology, at the level of discursive struggle over the content and meaning of secularism' (Crossman and Kapur, 1999: xvii).

The destruction of the mosque is representative of Hindutva's political victory, because 'religion as ideology' has succeeded in its aims. Furthermore, 'the arguments justifying the destruction of the mosque were premised on the concept of secularism and tolera-tion based on religious identity' (Crossman and Kapur, 1999: xvii). Crossman and Kapur suggest that, in this instance, the Muslims were accused of demonstrating their intolerance by eradicating the *janambhoomi* (birth place) of Hindu belief and religious practice

(Crossman and Kapur, 1999: xvii). Nandy adds to this by noting that such attitudes justified further the actions of the Hindus in defending against and, hence, avenging these contested claims. Tensions escalated again in February 2002 when more than 50 people died when a train carrying Hindu activists returning to Gujarat from Ayodhya was set alight, allegedly by a group of Muslims. This again sparked off unprecedented communal terror in the state of Gujarat and across northern India reaching as far as Mumbai, which led to the bloody death of mainly Muslims. The bloodshed at Gujarat was viewed as the most serious threat to India's secular identity since 1947. Nandy reinforces the point that these acts of violence must be understood as political processes that were equally motivated by electoral politics. He states that 'in Gujarat, the riots took place not in Saurashtra and South Gujarat where the BJP was well placed electorally, but in central and north Gujarat where the party was unsure of its performance' (Nandy and Jahanbegloo, 2006: 72). The issue for Nandy is a political one, located within an Indian secular culture and not outside of it; and not a question of communal politics as supporters of secularism want to believe. The authors of *Making Indian Hindu: Religion, Community and the Politics of Democracy in India (2005)* also note that,

> when local conflicts of any kind become communal, they [the middle classes] advertise the RSS [Rashtriya Swayamsevak Sangh] idea that India is still wracked by Hindu failure to purify Bharat as a Hindu homeland. Metaphorically, communal conflict anywhere affirms that Hindu India lives at odds with its alien others. (Ludden, 2005: xvii)

In an article dated 18 February 1991 that appeared in *The Times of India*, Nandy suggests that the battle between Hinduism ('religion as faith') and Hindutva ('religion as ideology') is inevitable. 'Hinduism versus Hindutva: The Inevitability of a Confrontation' critiques the direct assault that Hindutva makes on Hinduism. Nandy adds by noting that this occurs at a pivotal historical moment when 'secularist dogmas have broken out in many forms and in many places in the world' (Nandy, 1991: 1). For Nandy, Hindutva as an ethno-nationalist revivalist movement represents the political anger of upper-caste, lower-middle class Indians, 'who have uprooted themselves and their traditions, seduced by the promises offered by the modernisation of indict, and who now feel abandoned' (Nandy, 1991: 1). This disenchantment has its foundations in the demise of imperialism, modernisation and secularisation in India and with the failure of development. For Nandy, 'Hindutva at this plane is Western imperialism's last frenzied kick at Hinduism'. He continues, as one of those pathologies, which periodically afflict a faith or way of life, the inner workings of the ideology can be explained by a series of psychological defences already discussed. To this extent the ideology and horrific violence which erupted in Ayodhya cannot be understood as separate from the 'social forces and the ideologies of dominance that have spawned'. (Nandy, 1991: 2)

This is the end of long and complex processes that culminate in attempts to create a nationality under a reconstituted Hinduism. It is for Nandy the end product of a century's efforts to convert Hindus into a proper modern nation and ethnic majority: 'Where the identity of the Hindus [a religious identity] is re-formulated and re-imagined through the *ideology* of Hindutva, as a monotheistic religion located in the *shilyanya* bricks that would be used to build the temple, the undisputed home of the solo-Hindu deity Ram' (Crossman and Kapur, 1999: xvi).

Why then, Nandy challenges, 'does the BJP talk of genuine as opposed to pseudo-secularism, and not religion?' (Nandy, 1991: 2). In his writings on the modern and secular seeds of discontent, he depicts a modern Indian secular state that draws on the ideology of secularism, not as a means for controlling religious strife through secular tolerance, but rather as a way to promote its inverted psychoanalytic double: xenophobia and fanaticism in the form of modern super-religious political allegiances with access to instrumental forms of violence. In working against minorities, attacking the inherent diversity and pluralism of the Indic Civilization, and belittling Indian national democratic slogans of Unity in Diversity, secularism of this kind can only represent 'the blood-thirstiness of the Indian statists' (Nandy, 1991: 2).

The effects of the distortions of Hindutva ideology in making over India in mono-cultural terms are evident in the way in which Indian culture has been altered. In 'A Report on the Present State of Health of the Gods and Goddesses in South Asia' Nandy argues that these processes of subjection in Indian secular political culture and within Hindu nationalism have led to a culture of containing ambivalence. This is evident in the specific public culture that forms around these reconstituted political identities. Nandy focuses on a contemporary example to demonstrate the consequences of this culture of containing ambivalence. He refers to an incident in Mumbai where a Muslim playwright wrote and staged a play. The narrative of the play included Hindu gods and goddesses as characters in the drama. According to Nandy, the actions of the playwright in using Hindu gods and goddesses as characters provoked a highly political and defensive response. As he explains, 'it provoked not the audience but a formation of Hindu nationalists, particularly the Hindu Mahasabha which had for long been a spent political force in Bombay, the city being dominated by another more powerful Hindu nationalist formation, the Shiv Sena' (Nandy, 2004a: 130).

In particular, it provoked Vikram Savarkar of the Hindu Mahasabha, the grandson of the non-Hindu believing father of Hindutva, V.D. Savarkar. Vikram Savarkar continued the 'family business' and family traditions by staging a demonstration as an act of protest, in front of the theatre where the play was being shown. The demonstration was less than peaceful and attracted large numbers and widespread media coverage. It culminated in a dramatic publicly staged apology when the playwright bowed down and touched Savarkar's feet. The apology was provided for allegedly disrespecting the sanctity of Hindu symbols and Hindu faith, in representing them as characters in the play. Savarkar and his supporters asserted that the playwright had no right to communicate in the language of Hinduism, even if this was a case of poetic licence, because he was not a Hindu. These images of the playwright's apology to Savarkar by bowing down in front of him were widely disseminated in the media and printed in leading newspapers, thus consolidating the humiliation of the playwright. This point about making an *apology to* Savarkar is interesting, especially when contrasted with the fact that two key political figures involved in the Ramjanmabhumi movement and responsible for the horrific violence carried out at Ayodhya refuse to offer a public apology for their complicity in these events. Both L.K. Advani, the then Deputy Prime Minister, and Narendra Modi, the Chief Minister of Gujarat, have refused to offer an apology for the crimes carried out at Ayodhya and Gujarat. The concept of humiliation performs an interesting symbolic political function within this example, one that supersedes the personal moment of humiliation experienced by the playwright. For Nandy, the humiliation was complete because the apology functioned as a means of re-instating a boundary that had been transgressed, in allegedly disrespecting Hinduism. It was also complete because it re-instated a dominant social, cultural, political and psychic order predicated on the exclusion of the Muslim playwright from accessing religious Hindu symbols.

Nandy comments on the political significance of humiliation in the following way. He notes that 'no humiliation is complete unless the humiliated feel humiliated and the creation of that feeling can be part of a political programme'. In this article, Nandy argues that the political value of humiliation is recognised by ethno-nationalists, particularly by Hindu Nationalists, although he distinguishes between the perceived experience of humiliation and the historical trajectory of this humiliation, for while 'the sense of humiliation and feelings of inferiority in recent times is real, history serves as a projective test, and political propaganda works' (Nandy, 2002f: 12).

The humiliation of the playwright, through the political spectacle of apology, is complete because it was constituted and staged within the political programme of the Hindu Mahasabha. However, it is from the perspective of the playwright that this outcome is achieved in Nandy's analysis and not from Savarkar's own public vocal declarations of a political victory. Nandy's reading of these processes is a more ambivalent one, as he radically confronts and questions the conditions of this victory. This is a victory that is declared through the containment of the ambivalence of the subjectivity of the playwright and through the containment of a more open and plural account of Indianness. What, he critiques, is the way that the ambivalence within Indian traditions grounded in concepts of porous boundaries of self (including the Muslim self of the playwright) has been contained. This has been contained at the hands of the Hindu nationalists whose response to the playwright was deemed a political victory. Such a victory, for Nandy, can only be mourned, as '[Hinduism] had lost because a tradition at least fifteen hundred years old was sought to be dismantled' (Nandy, 2004a: 131). In the essay, Nandy draws on the Hindu motif of there being many 'Gods and Goddesses,' to suggest that this performs an important symbolic function within the psychic life of the individual, and collectively within India. He suggests that for the majority of Indians these images and symbolic attachments perform a vital cultural and psychic function, although this pluralism is being threatened by the homogenising claims of the Hindu nationalists. The pluralism of the 'Gods and Goddesses' acknowledges the myriad ways everyday life is lived and can be experienced as ambivalent and contradictory.

In the example of the playwright, Hindu nationalists affirmed their commitment to containing and abjecting pluralism and ambivalence from public view. In asserting a prohibition, barring access to that which is identified as pertaining exclusively to Hinduism, the boundaries between the playwright's clearly demarcated Muslim identity, and what he is not—a Hindu—is asserted in the public sphere. In this case the boundaries of politics are also affirmed and consolidated through a distinctive repudiation of the other. What is problematic, for Nandy, is precisely the ways that these boundaries of identification dominate public space. As Sandria B. Freitag argues, 'the real outcome of the Ayodhya story that must be measured with care is the extent to which negotiating space in India's distinct civil society has disappeared' (Freitag in Ludden, 2005: 234). For Freitag, only by understanding the extent of these changes can the consequences of making India Hindu be theorised. In Nandy's account he, too, acknowledges that there is a loss of public space and of public dialogue to negotiate identities, especially the boundaries of Indianness. Consistent with his psycho-analytic approach though, this is expressed as both a loss of external public space and a loss of internal psychic space. The way in which identities are, therefore, imagined, performed, experienced and lived becomes truncated by processes of homogenisation, standardisation and deculturalisation.

The ambivalence that Nandy is interested in preserving is located in the dialectical interplay between external and internal processes. In his writings, it is notably the ambivalent non-modern peripheral figure that carries forward this possibility and not a secular self or the Hindu zealot. The non-modern peripheral is privileged because as he explains, for those outside of politics, 'their [the Gods and God-desses] presence is telescoped not only into one's transcendental self but, to use Alan Roland's tripartite division, also into one's familial and individualised selves and even into one's most flippant, comic, naughty, moments' (Nandy, 2004a: 131). The dialogue that the gods and goddesses invite provides access to a number of parts of one's self without giving primacy to one aspect. Captured in the example of the Hindu Mahasabha and the playwright, 'religion as ideology' casts away from view the everyday plural and ambivalent ways of being, ways of living, and the porous boundaries that demarcate self and other. He develops this claim further by suggesting that living with competing ethical systems, such as those represented in the different images of the gods and goddesses, is a characteristic feature of Indian life. In doing so, he emphasises the range of possibilities available within broader imaginings of 'other' configurations of selfhood; though con-sistent with his approach he resists defining them too closely. Rather, he reinforces the point by noting the ambivalence and contradiction within every day accounts and experiences of Indianness, despite at-tempts to contain these features. As he reiterates, 'I have seen Indians live with enormous contradictions without batting an eyelid' (Nandy and Deftereos, 2005c: 13).

Nandy demonstrates that contradiction is a feature of subjectivity, of an Indian self and a feature of Indian culture by retelling a story (Nandy and Deftereos, 2005c: 13). The story is that when doing fieldwork for a book that the distinguished Indian Sociologist M.K. Srinivas was writing, he asked an Indian:

> You are Brahmin and you are not supposed to work with leather, so why do you? He said to him that when I go out of my house I put on a shirt to go to the office and I become a different person. I leave my caste behind by putting on my office shirt and when I come back and I take my shirt off then my caste comes back to me, or something of this kind.

Nandy continues, 'Now this would be unthinkable, this kind of ethical system would be quite unthinkable in many other cultures and communities…you know they are contradictory… [But] contradiction does not bother you. You are willing to live with that contradiction' (Nandy and Deftereos, 2005c: 13). The ability to live with contradictions and ambivalence facilitates tolerance for a certain kind of pluralism within self–other relations, where he challenges, 'It is presumed you will be able to do that' (Nandy and Deftereos, 2005c: 12). This tolerance for pluralism is not a product of modern secular identity, but reflected in experiences and practices of a different kind, in people's ability to negotiate contradictions within self, as a dialectic between inner and outer incentives. For Nandy, this capacity also reaffirms the possibility of 'a different kind of [Indian] modernity, where you can stand [this] you can live with enormous diversities and do not have to reconcile them constantly' (Nandy and Deftereos, 2005c: 13). As he describes, 'this concept [of tolerance] does not have the concreteness and definitive boundaries as it has in the European Judeo-Christian world. It is a bit more pagan!' (Nandy and Deftereos, 2005c: 12). The internal tolerance for pluralism and competing ethical systems can be contrasted with a modern secular self or reconstituted political identity, where contradiction and ambivalence are contained by a 'fixed identity'. Despite these processes of subjection operating in political identities, contradictions, ambivalence and pluralism are for Nandy important features of Indianness, including latent parts of self. What he concedes is that confronting about this latent self is that it is derived from an 'inner power, [and] has social-critical functions unacknowledged in most modern theories of legitimation' (Nandy, 1987a: xviii). In Nandy's analysis ambivalence and pluralism have the potential to confront and work through the positioning of the boundaries of the external (public) and inner (private). For 'it denies absolute value to any secular theory of society and it allows some knowledge to be subversive by allowing the users or producers of knowledge to take advantage of the contradiction between the outer and the inner powers' (Nandy, 1987a: xviii).

Nandy's critique of Hindu nationalism is an extension of his confrontation with the cultural and psychological viability of secularism in India. In his writings it is the pathologies of secularism that provide the political conditions for the rise of adversarial national identities which perpetuate the use of religion instrumentally for political gains. Hindu nationalism is for Nandy a profoundly defensive movement that must be understood as part of a complex historical, social, cultural, political and psychic process to make India Hindu. The internal logic of Hindutva ideology needs to be understood alongside these efforts to contain ambivalence within concepts of Indianness, and defends against a fear of self. This is achieved by re-positioning the boundaries of inclusion and exclusion in very distinct ways, thus affirming an exclusive authoritarian definition of 'Indianness'. Nandy's argument that the political voice of the Hindu zealot or Hindu nationalist is an effect of the distortions of a dominant secular ideology is a confronting proposition. Yet, as suggested, this willing confrontation is an important feature of his psychoanalytic reading of the way political identities in Indian political culture are formed.

The following chapter explores the way Nandy's confrontational arguments and approach inform the reception and representations of his work and identity as a critic of the state. A reading of the discursive field in which the debates of secularism are carried out, with an emphasis on the debates in the 1990s when Indian secularism was radically tested, is revealing of the threat that Nandy's anti-secularism presents. Nandy's critique of secularism and his critique of Hindutva ideology have more recently led to his being a 'test case' for his arguments, as he continues to receive a mixed reception from critics. The location of this mixed agitation and fascination for critics is in Nandy's *willingness* to confront accepted identities, meanings, fantasies, projections and ideals operating in politics. This willingness to work through the complexities of subjectivity and at the borders between cultural and psychic processes produces a confronting self-reflexivity that can disarm critics. How though does Nandy become a 'test case' for his arguments, or rather, how is Nandy's identity as critic of the state, as 'intimate enemy', made over in and through this discursive field? Further, what do these representations tell us about the limits and limitations of academic and public debates over the 'crisis' of Indian secularism?

Notes

1. These concepts of making over and purifying Bharat India are re-occurring themes in Hindu nationalism. See Jaffrelot (2007); Nandy et al. (1995); Ludden (2005); Ramaswamy (2010).

2. These figures do not capture the full extent of violence, or the systematic practices of rape and the burning alive of children that took place in the violence of Ayodhya and Gujarat. See BBC News, 'Arrests over Gujarat Riots Case', 22nd January, http://news.bbc.co.uk/1/hi/world/south_asia/3419695.stm. See also McGuire, Reeves and Brasted (1996).

3. This argument that Hindu Nationalism and the regressive communal politics of India are threatening the secularity of the modern Indian state is made in a number of places. See Engineer (1984); Nanda (2004a); Nanda (2006); Vanaik (1997); Bhargava (1998); Desai (2004).

4. Some examples of Nandy's writings on Hindu Nationalism include: Nandy (1991); Nandy (1994d). 'Fear in the Air: The Inner Demons of Society,'; Nandy (1994i). 'Violence in Our Times: In Search of Total Control,'; Nandy (2004a). 'The Twilight of Certitudes: Secularism, Hindu Nationalism, and Other Masks of Deculturation,'; Nandy (1997a). 'A Report on the Present State of Health of the Gods and Goddesses in South Asia,'; Nandy (2002c). 'Obituary of a Culture,'; Nandy (2002e). 'Telling the Story of Communal Conflicts in South Asia: Interim Report on a Personal Search for Defining Myths'.

5. Adeney, K. and L. Saez (2005); Crossman, B. and R. Kapur (1999); Ludden (2005); Desai (2004); Madan (1997); Malik and Singh (1994); Nanda (2004a); Smith (2003); Sarkar (2002); Sharma, A. (2001); Vanaik (1997).

   See for example Ludden, D. (2005); Desai (2004); Malik, Y. K. and V. B. Singh (1994); McGuire, J. and P. Reeves, et al. (1996); Nanda (2004a);

   Vanaik, A. 1997; Adeney, K. and L. Saez (2005); Crossman, B. and R. Kapur (1999); Madan, T.N. (1997); Sarkar, S. (2002); Sharma, A. (2001). Smith, D. (2003).

6. Nandy's essay 'The Politics of Secularism and the Recovery of Religious Tolerance' is published in Das, V. (1990).

7. The philosopher Raimundo Panikkar has commented upon this de-sacralised appropriation of religion operating in politics. Panikar argues against these instrumental accounts of religion. As he says, 'although the etymology of the word religion is closer to the meaning of dharma than it sounds to modern westernised ears, the prevalent political use of the word in the West today (spreading also over the planet) has restricted the meaning of religion to a very narrow sense, which has led many countries of the world to defend the privatisation of religion as something appertaining to the individual in his private conscience.' Raimundo, P. (2005). 'Presidential Address,' *Second International Conference on Religions and Cultures in the Indic Civilization*, New Delhi: 3. More importantly, these categories are neither synonymous nor mutually exclusive. See Bharucha, R. (1998).

8. Refer to 'Chapter VI. Family Business', in A. Nandy et al. (1995). *Creating a Nationality*: 81–99. For a more lengthy discussion of these figures and their involvement in the RSS see Basu, T. et. al. (1993).

9. For a discussion of the RSS refer to Anderson W.K. and S.D. Damle (1987).
10. Runa Das offers a brief summary of the *Ramayana* the story of Sita's abduction and its importance for Hindu nationalism. Das states that,

> In the Indian epic Ramayana, the story of Sita's abduction goes as follows: Sita (the princess-queen of Ayodhya and wife of Lord Ram) while in exile with her husband was abducted by the demon king Ravana. Following this abduction, a war ensued between Ram and Ravana, as a result of which Sita was rescued. What becomes glorified in this legend by the Hindu nationalists, is the focus on Sita's chastity, to prove which (since imprisoned by another male) she had to go through fire (fire represents the Hindu god of purity.)
>
> See R. Das (2008).

11. For an extended discussion of these processes, see Chakravarti, U. (1998); Hansen, T.B. (1999).
12. On this issue refer to Nandy (1983a); Nandy et al. (1995); See R. Das (2008).
13. For a discussion of the debate over the construction of the Hindu Temple dedicated to Lord Rama, at Ayodhya refer to Ellen Christensen (2003). 'Chapter 9: Reclaiming Sacred Hindu Space at Ayodhya: The Hindu Right and the Politics of Cultural Symbolism in Contemporary India'.
14. On this issue of the teaching history in India see R. Thapar (2009); N. Bhattacharya (2009).

PART B

Symptomatic Responses:
Reading the Politics of Blame

3

The Conceptual Battleground of Anti-Secularism and Culturalism

Nandy's scandalous critique of the ideology of secularism in India, even thirty years on, continues to generate intense debate. The post-Ayodhya climate of what is widely accepted as a 'crisis' in Indian secularism has reignited the focus on the political consequences of Nandy's anti-secularism and how this too contributes to an understanding of that crisis. Within a collection of essays titled, *The Crisis of Secularism* (2007) the editors note how this 'crisis of secularism' is to be interpreted and what solutions can be advanced that are central to how the debates on secularism unfold. This includes accounting for 'a mainstream national culture that is fearful of diversities, intolerant of dissent unless it is cast in the language of the mainstream and panicky about any self-assertion or search for autonomy by ethnic groups' (Needham Rajan, 2007: 9). It is also within this context that the representations of Nandy's critique and the significance attached to his identity, as a profoundly confronting anti-secular thinker, need to be considered.

This chapter offers a reading of the discursive field of academic and public debates and Nandy's contested location within them. Nandy's confrontations with the constitutive features of the modern secular Indian self, and the questioning of the secularity of Indian political culture are a source of both horror and fascination. In attempting to marginalise, de-authorise and even attempting to criminalise Nandy as a critic, it is his overwhelming disruption to the secular norm and logic of argumentation that is defended against. Typically Nandy's arguments, ideas and methods are overshadowed and over-determined by the threat and disruption both he and his anti-secularism carry forward. These symptomatic responses take form, as Freud argues, as a protective and defensive covering over, 'in order to remove or rescue the ego from the situation of danger' (Freud, 1936: 86). The danger, and the affective state of anxiety that Nandy's anti-secularism provokes, can be understood as a threat to the function of the secular ideal in individual and collective processes of national identification.

Within this discursive field, Nandy functions as a point of condensation for these anxieties, as he takes on the features of threat and disruption. In turn, he is repeatedly represented as an object of derision, taking on the discursive features akin to a Freudian phobic object. Nandy's identity and his mode of address are to be feared as his confrontation threatens the positioning of the boundaries of debate. Nandy also acquires the status of the abject figure in these debates, as someone who carries forward the real and potential threat to disrupt established meanings, the boundaries of debate, and moreover the boundaries that secure the modern secular subject with his readings of those 'other selves'. Nandy's anti-secularism becomes that which 'disturbs identity, system and order: it is the in between, the ambiguous, the composite...the symptom of disintegrating boundaries' (Fletcher and Benjamin, 1990: 181). These representations inform the critical readings offered by two critics of Nandy's work. Achin Vanaik and Radhika Desai radically question the intellectual and political value of Nandy's contributions to these debates. The anxiety and threat that Nandy's position provokes as one of India's leading anti-secular figures, also characterises the public exchange that took place in 2004 in Indian newspapers and journals. What is notable in this public exchange is Nandy's participation, and the brief reply offered to critics, though to what extent his dissenting voice as an abject figure can be heard is questionable. The attempts in 2008 to criminalise the voice of the critic represent the ultimate conclusion in this defence against the phobic object, in attempting to silence and cast him away from public view. The symptom, including symptomatic responses to an anti-secular position, may function as a defence mechanism, but in the process it both overshadows the argument used to arrive at such a destination while also radically reconfiguring Nandy's identity as critic, and the significance that can be afforded him and dissent more broadly.

DEBATING THE POSITIONING OF THE BOUNDARIES OF DEBATE

A survey of the literature debating Indian secularism reveals the full extent of the contestation that surrounds the concept.[1] This contestation includes debating whether the ideology of secularism, as an inherited Western political ideal, is suitable to India and more importantly, how this informs the current state of 'crisis' of Indian secularism. A number of theorists enter into the debates by situating their position in relation to this inheritance. For example, Partha Chatterjee argues that this inheritance imbues postcolonial India with a shared vocabulary with Western political theory that has at best an ambiguous legacy within India. This ambiguous legacy is also reflected in these debates and, for Chatterjee, is central to understanding the ways these debates unfold (Chatterjee, 1994).

Nasir Tyabji extends on this further by noting that qualifying one's position in relation to this inheritance is central to the debates. Tyabji suggests in the 'Political Economy of Secularism: Rediscovery of India' (1994) that this is now also a distinct feature of the debates. He states that 'it is standard procedure in discussions of Indian secularism to make an initial proviso: while in Europe the process of secularisation incorporated the process of the separation of the state from the church, this has not been so in India' (Tyabji, 1994: 1798). This proviso becomes a normative feature of the debates. It establishes an ideological boundary between those who claim this inheritance as central to the current crisis of Indian secularism and those who argue that this inheritance is a secondary concern to the secular pathways that India has taken of its own accord. The political theorist Rajeev Bhargava details at length the characteristics of the Indian variant of secularism. While accepting that an alternative conception of secularism is needed to counter the current crisis, he vehemently objects to an undifferentiated reading of the cultural and political context through which Indian secularism has developed.

The work of the anthropologist T.N. Madan in differentiating Indian secularism from its Western foundations though is not entirely possible. Conceptualising Indian secularism brings us back to the problematic question of inheritance and the postcolonial lag effects. Madan maintains that the ideology is 'a gift of Christianity', and sits uncomfortably with Indian home-grown categories of identification and social cohesion and the toleration of difference (Madan, 1997). In Nandy's psychoanalytic reading this disjunction reveals itself in the way the secular ideal structures processes of identification within Indian political culture and political identities. The secular ideal operates to make over religious and ethnic identities into political identities. Nandy consistently maintains that this inherited Western ideal must be confronted and rejected because these processes give rise to the pathologies of secularism. For Madan and Nandy challenging and rejecting secularism based on this inheritance leaves them open to a number of criticisms.

Joseph Tharamangalam's analysis of the debates of secularism conceptualises the debates and situates Madan and Nandy's contentious interventions further. Tharamangalam points out that critical social science (in India) became inextricably bound with the project of the enlightenment (Tharamangalam, 1995). Madan and Nandy's critique of secularism, both considered critiques of modernity, must also be understood as part of this. Tharamangalam sees little alternative to India's inheritance, dismissing the voices of Nandy and Madan as profoundly anti-secular and anti-modern. As he argues,

> critics such as Ashis Nandy and T.N. Madan reject secularism as radically alien to Indian culture and tradition and advocate a return to genuine religion and the indigenous traditions of religious tolerance as the best means to preserve and maintain a pluralist and multi-religious Indian society. (Tharamangalam, 1995: 457)

Tharamangalam casts Nandy and Madan as advocating a return to genuine religion and an indigenous culturalism: and it is here Tharamangalam suggests that their anti-secularism is to be found. What is interesting about this representation of Nandy and Madan is that their position is radically questioned and attributed to disruptive anti-modern features. Tharamangalam states: 'I am unable to see what kind of a social and political order can replace India's secularism without causing serious rupture to those social arrangements, values and ideals in the country that most of us deeply cherish' (Tharamangalam, 1995: 461). Tharamangalam cannot imagine an alternative to this secular ideal and, in affirming this, casts doubt on the validity of any alternative claims, or as the case may be even claims that question the sanctity of this secular ideal. Nandy as a figure who confronts and disrupts the national norms or these 'arrangements, values and ideals' becomes made over as 'intimate enemy'. To this list of potentially threatening critical voices Tharamangalam also adds the sociologist M.S. Srinivas whose calls for a renewal of faith can offer a solution to India's cultural crisis (Tharamangalam, 1995: 457).

Gyanendra Pandey has argued in a number of places in his writings that colonial bureaucratic rationality was responsible for the creation of religious and caste identities as political categories (Pandey, 1992; 1993). These complex historical processes have consequences for understanding the current 'crisis' of Indian secularism. For Pandey, this rationality informs the current proto-secular and anti-secular or communalist divide, and its accompanying politics of blame, structuring these debates. This divide takes form irrespective of Dipesh Chakrabarty's claim that modernist rationalism can never comprehend the character of religion in India (Chakrabarty, 2002). While the debate over the inheritance of these concepts remains, the divide and the boundary that emerges around these issues is itself highly contested. Shrinivas Tilak adds to a reading of the boundary that forms around these issues and through which the debates of Indian secularism are carried out. In Tilak's account the debates unfold with 'idealizing on the one hand, and scapegoating and persecuting on the other' (Tilak in Sharma, 2001: 126). To follow through on Tilak's account, those who demonstrate their commitment to the secular ideal, particularly as proto-secularists, are rewarded and idealised, while those like Nandy, who confront this ideal and work through its idealised features, are persecuted and dismissed. Therefore, according to this persecutory logic those who confront and, in Nandy's case, reject the secular ideal, even if this is a result of having explored its cultural and psychological viability, are cast as intolerant, as outsiders and as 'arch tyrants' (Tilak in Sharma, 2001: 126). A chain of association emerges as Nandy is cast as the arch tyrant, anti-modern, bad subject, and intimate enemy and even as anti-Indian.

The proto-secular and anti-secular divide informs the claims made by Sarah Joseph in the 'Politics of Contemporary Indian Communitarianism'. Joseph identifies a number of contributors to the debates who do so as Indian Communitarians, emphasising the regressive and disruptive features of these voices. These communitarians include Ashis Nandy, Partha Chatterjee, Sudipto Kaviraj and T.N. Madan. Joseph argues that what unites these theorists is that they 'have made a link between community consciousness and indigenous culture and this has supported their political project of reviving communities political actors today' (Joseph, 1997: 2517). Joseph connects this intellectual argument with a distinctive political project. In doing so, she politicises the identities of these critics. According to Joseph, Nandy's contributions to debating secularism need to be exposed for its communalist foundations, and its complicity with the contemporary political project of the Hindu Right. For Chatterjee, these very demarcations, including identifying anti-secular voices as communitarian, brings us back to the problematic question of the inheritance of these categories. Chatterjee emphasises that even when declaring the 'well-defined Indian referents, the loud and often acrimonious Indian debate on secularism is never entirely innocent of its western genealogies (Chatterjee, 1994: 1769). This is also evident in the way in which European or even American definitions of secularism continue to inform the boundaries of debate, in order to emphasise the inevitable shortcomings of the postcolonial Indian state.

Meera Nanda invokes these shortcomings in her analysis of the rise of communalism, or as she prefers, the wrongs of the religious right in India. In her text *The Wrongs of the Religious Right: Reflections on Science, Secularism and Hindutva* (2005), Nanda offers an assessment of the crisis of Indian secularism by comparing the secularity of the Indian state to American secularism. This comparative analysis highlights how Indians have a distinctively incorrect concept of secularism compared to their American counterparts, despite the growing body of literature questioning the secularity of American politics.[2] This deviation from the secular ideal though remains a marker of the failure of the secularity of the Indian state. For Nanda it also explains, '…why modernity in India has this feel of incompleteness, superficiality and even schizophrenia' (Nanda, 2006). Indian secularism thus fails because it has not been 'conscientiously' applied, but sacrificed instead for political convenience and electoral advantage. Nanda argues that it is only through the reaffirmation of a strengthened Indian secular state that the crisis can be addressed.

For the political scientist Rajeev Bhargava neither is the idealisation of secularism suitable for India, nor is its rejection feasible. Bhargava challenges the proto-secular and anti-secular logic operating in the debates by suggesting that an alternative concept and intellectual space is needed (Bhargava, 1998; 1994). Theorists like Chatterjee are more sceptical, maintaining that these attempts to situate new meanings as 'a matter of family resemblances' only work to strengthen the existing Western political discourse about the modern state. Whereby 'the resort to "new meanings" [*including alternative conceptions*] is [*again*] to invoke…a mark of the failure of this attempt' (Chatterjee, 1994: 1769).

John J. Caroll suggests that the late entry of secularism into the Indian Constitution needs to be taken into account. As Caroll points out, the term secularism is a late addition to the Indian Constitution, being formally incorporated in the preamble in 1976 through an amendment made by the Indira Gandhi Government. While the amendment codifies the general understanding of the nature of the Indian State, it has been argued that the original document contains a number of provisions that in totality lack conceptual clarity. For Dharma Kumar, the corrective is to be found in the legislative function of the Indian state that can clarify and institute the effective implementation of the secular ideal through legal processes and state apparatuses. Deviations from this goal, and the positioning of this boundary, are for Kumar to side with the Left Secularists, who like the Communalists, bear 'several marks of politically motivated scholarship' (Kumar, 1994: 1804). Whether or not these charges are substantiated, Kumar's association reinforces an established boundary operating within the debates. Theorists like Tejani conclude that there is now a characteristic impasse within these debates. Tejani describes this in the following way:

> those accused of bringing religion into politics are called communalists, those seen as pandering to religious minorities are branded as pseudo-secularists, and those charged with wanting to introduce Western (secular) modes of governance and ethics are pilloried as Macaulayites. The debate has been circumscribed by its own categories. (Tejani in Needham and Rajan, 2007: 45)

This is a useful assessment about how these boundaries of debate are positioned and are now working against their own interests to foreclose debate. The positioning of the boundaries in this way, as circumscribed by their own categories, perpetuates a series of defensive and counter-defensive responses that are reproduced as a distinctive feature of these debates. These responses ultimately create an impasse and do little to expand the boundaries of debate and the possibility for reinvigorating debate, by placing distinct limits on what can and cannot be debated and even heard. Further, it places distinct limits on what constitutes meaningful and audible critique and dissent within this discursive field. Characterising these responses as symptomatic captures the intensity of the protective defence mechanism operating within these debates, and the horror and fascination that accompanies Nandy's threatening and disruptive anti-secularism.

Symptomatic Responses: The Horror of Nandy's Interventions

In 1992, the editors of a special edition of the journal *Seminar* titled 'The Problem,' pointed to the stalemate characteristic of the debates. They argue that 'what was a vision, a living language, froze into a dead grammar' (Visvanathan, and Visvanathan, 1992: 14). For these authors, the problem with secularism or rather the crisis of secularism needs to be understood in terms of a loss of a vision, and loss of dialogue and debate. In confronting this impasse they ask 'what kind of dialogue, concrete and practical, has Indian culture showed evidence of?' they ask (Visvanathan, and Visvanathan, 1992: 15). Dialogue and debate has been foreclosed, circumscribed by its own categories, and consequently, the concept of secularism has become a symptom of this stagnation. The symptomatic takes form as a defence mechanism against threats, disruptions and insecurity, to an ego (or a national identity) in crisis. While the symptom is a protective defence mechanism what is problematic is that this carries forward its own internal logic. For 'the symptom is entrusted with the representing of important interests [and in doing so] it acquires a value for self-assertion; it becomes intertwined more and more intimately with the ego, becoming even more indispensable to the later' (Freud, 1936: 27). Freud's comments in this passage provide a deeper understanding as to why the symptomatic acquires a value for self-assertion. Within these responses to the debates on secularism this is evident in the over-determined representations of Nandy, as the symptom acquires 'a value for self-assertion.' Deauthorising and dismissing Nandy and his anti-secular position in this way affirms a persecutory logic that forecloses an engagement with the complexity of Nandy's ideas and approach.

Zaheer Baber argues that Nandy has 'been quite prolific in issuing 'anti-secular manifestos' (Baber, 1996). Nandy's distinctive anti-secularism precedes a consideration of how the Modern Secular critic arrives at the destination of 'spearheading the emerging culture of academic anti-secularism in India' (Baber, 1996: 317). Within such accounts, Nandy becomes the focal point, functioning like a point of condensation, as he is made over as the figure primarily responsible for continuing disruption. For Baber, Nandy's prolific anti-secular voice is to be feared because, both intellectually and politically, it is complicit with the politics of the Hindu Right in India. Nandy becomes the point of condensation for the affective states of disruption, fear, threat and anxiety. Consistent with the role of the phobic object in psychoanalytic theory, it 'assumes all the mishaps of drive as disappointed desires or as desires diverted from their objects' (Kristeva, 1982: 35).[3]

In Kristeva's reading, the object of fear, the Freudian phobic object, becomes a substitute formation, a projection carrying the weight of disappointed desires caused by a breakdown in the boundaries distinguishing subject and object, self and other. What is threatening about the phobic object is its disruptive potential as Nandy, along with his anti-secularism, also carries forward the capacity to breakdown established meanings and signification. This moment is radically threatening because the breakdown in meaning and signification is experienced as an assault to one's own constitutive values. This is an assault to established arrangements, values and ideals that the majority of Indians deeply cherish. The defensive structure of such symptomatic responses is repeated in Akeel Bilgrami's work. According to Bilgrami, the threat of the phobic object personified by Nandy is that he harks back 'nostalgically [and dangerously] to the idea of a pre-modern India' (Bilgrami, 1994: 1749). Bilgrami distinguishes Nandy from other anti-secularists like Partha Chatterjee whose contributions to the debates are marked by inconsistency. In contrast Nandy's threat is exacerbated and over-determined by his consistent commitment to religious communities. This consistency distinguishes Nandy from other critics of secularism even within the Left and determines his influence amongst the general intelligentsia. Evident in 'the words of his pages [which] leave nothing undetermined; there are no elements in his work running counter to his undistracted animus toward modernity' (Bilgrami, 1994: 1750).

CRITICAL READINGS: ACHIN VANAIK AND RADHIKA DESAI

Achin Vanaik's text *Communalism Contested: Religion, Modernity and Secularism* (1997) and Radhika Desai's article titled 'Culturalism and Contemporary Right: Indian Bourgeoisie and Political Hindutva' (1999) offer two different critical readings of the significance of Nandy's anti-secularism and anti-modernism. For Desai 'the significance of Ashis Nandy is not intellectual' as she explores the political consequences of his anti-secularism in relation to the cultural conditions giving rise to the Hindu Right (Desai, 1999: 702). As a political commentator and activist in India Vanaik's criticisms of Nandy can be located in his 'form of big thinking which abjures the scholarly prerequisites of developing substantial expertise across disciplines' (Vanaik, 1997: 64).

In the text *Communalism Contested* Vanaik defends the secular ideal within Indian history against a growing intellectual trend of anti-secularism, or 'subaltern indigenisms.' The chapter titled 'Communalism, Hindutva, Anti-Secularists: The Conceptual Battleground,' covers the terrain of this intellectual culture. The debates on Indian secularism can be defined as a conceptual battleground, shifting between the boundaries that mark secularism, anti-Secularism, and Hindutva, or communalism. For Vanaik, these concepts and the dynamics that they generate are central to understanding the precariousness of Indian politics. The conceptual differences and hence, the boundary that

distinguishes these positions are explained by the varying emphasis each ideology places on culture, civilisation, Hinduism and caste.
However, for Vanaik the boundary between anti-secularism and
Hindutva has increasingly been threatened. In Vanaik's reading, anti-
secularism cannot be so easily distinguished from Hindutva, even as
an intellectual position, as both increasingly share a dangerous conceptual and political space. There is a distinct threatening association
established between Hindutva and anti-secularism, the latter of which
can be seen 'as legitimising implicitly when not explicitly the assault
by communal forces (above all political Hindutva) against the current
level of secularity of the state' (Vanaik, 1997: 152).

According to Vanaik the three most important spokespersons for
this anti-secularism in India are Bhinku T. Parekh, T.N. Madan and
Ashis Nandy. It is however, Nandy who occupies a privileged position
within Vanaik's critique and is cast as 'the most intransigent of these
anti-secularists' (Vanaik, 1997: 153). The extent of Nandy's disruption
and threat to the positioning of the boundaries of these debates does
not end there as a number of additional phobic traits are identified.
Namely that, 'he is also the most uncompromising in his hostility to history, to the project of modernity, and the one most determined to read
Gandhi as an anti-modernist' (Vanaik, 1997: 154). Vanaik does concede that the anti-modernism advocated by Nandy may be a meaningful political choice, but is less forgiving of his reading of culture and
civilisation. Vanaik acknowledges that anti-modernism is a meaningful political choice today, because despite the power of modernising
processes, it still represents a powerful constituency, 'the authentic
Indian masses for whom culture and therefore tradition remains paramount' (Vanaik, 1997: 162). The problem is not with this position per
se but that in the hands of an intellectual like Nandy his 'understandings of religion, culture, society, civilization are not markedly different from many a culturalist or immortaliser of religion' (Vanaik, 1997:
162). Vanaik does not detail Nandy's argument regarding religion and
culture other than to align his voice with this culturalism.

Vanaik ultimately raises objections to Nandy's reading of culture
and civilisation, because it is laced with the culturalism he is warning
us against. Nandy's anti-modernism represents a conceptually flawed
distinction between the incompatibility of modernity with tradition
and culture, and it is this distinction which Vanaik also takes issue
with: to accept the conditions of modernity is deemed to be anti-
culture and to be an anti-modernist is to be profoundly concerned
with culture. The simplicity of the distinction is a reductionist one,

but the illusion of the boundaries at play prevents a deeper engagement and more thorough critical analysis of these accepted distinctions. From this point, he then enters into a series of generalisations and associations of Nandy's formulation and understanding of culture, civilisation and religion, where culture is understood as a way of life firmly implanted within indigenous knowledge systems, traditions and forms of subjectivity. Vanaik assures us that for Nandy, 'it means a culture dominated by religious consciousness that has not competed for the minds of men but offered itself as a lifestyle within which other lifestyles can be accommodated' (Vanaik, 1997: 163).

Vanaik deauthorises Nandy's voice as critic by asking, '… could it be that becoming a serious social thinker might require strenuous efforts to develop other disciplinary skills including those of history?' (Vanaik, 1997: 163). Representing Nandy as an inaccurate and unreliable thinker Vanaik further argues that, 'critical modernists are therefore feeble counter players or ornamental dissenters who should not ever be mistaken for serious critics' (Vanaik, 1997: 164). This provides Vanaik with the impetus to further question Nandy's methods, particularly his reading of culture and modernity, which are broadly described as possessing typical mentalities. One such example of this is Nandy's appropriation of critical traditionalism, used as a counter position to the dominant and homogenising features of modernity. Nandy's use of critical traditionalism is, as Vanaik highlights, drawn from Gandhi. This technique of making an individual personality or a personality type 'stand in' as an expression of larger social processes is, we are told, 'his favoured taxonomies of culture and society' (Vanaik, 1997: 164). The reader is left feeling that Nandy's intellectual integrity falls short here and that intellectual argumentation is fostered more by the whimsical techniques described by Vanaik, who remains dubious and fearful of these methods. He states that, 'this has not fazed Nandy, whose project is avowedly to 'recover' an indigenous social science' (Vanaik: 164). Nandy's anti-modernism, alongside his commitment to indigeneity, already established as disruptive threats within this intellectual culture and now extends to a responsibility for an indigenous social science.

Even Nandy, as the voice of a political psychologist with an interest in the cultural psychology is met with irreverence by Vanaik who would acknowledge the merits of such a task but that, 'it leads in his hands to the construction of a grandiose paradigm of anti-modernism, forging an Alternative Science, another theory of universalism which will compete with and oppose Enlightenment universalism itself!'

(Vanaik, 1997: 164). Vanaik identifies a number of mistakes Nandy makes and, in doing so, re-asserts the positioning of the boundaries of debate as a corrective. First, Nandy treats secularism as a synecdoche, therefore connecting the ideology of secularism with the complicities of the nation state system. Second, to accept the ideology of secularism is to accept the ideologies of progress and modernity as the new justifications of domination (Vanaik, 1997: 170). The connection between secularism and statehood filtered through the ideologies of progress and modernity is met with suspicion here. In short we are told that this is not correct. Vanaik, instead, presents his own corrective in contrast to Nandy's formulation and, although not pursued in any great detail here, is largely organised around a defence of the concept.

Vanaik's own defence is based on the premise that:

> secularism itself is not an ideology of statehood; it is an ideology which endorses a particular principle of modern statehood, a principle that emerges historically as part of the modern democratic revolution. That is why, even etymologically, the word secularism comes much after the words secular or state.

This is a new principle of democratic individualism and any consistent assault on secularism, for example by Nandy, will also assault modern notions of democracy and individualism' (Vanaik, 1997: 171). The main point worth emphasising is that Nandy gets it wrong and that this carries with it a set of intellectual, political and moral consequences, which for Vanaik cannot be ignored. Nandy's 'mistakes' add to a growing chain of threatening signifiers and associations. Namely Nandy's strong culturalism (including the chain of signification which follows from this: his anti-modernism, his anti-secularism, his anti-science position, his anti-universalism, his anti-statism and so on and so forth) combined with his scholarly inadequacies.

Vanaik's corrective voice extends to Nandy's psychoanalytic interest in human subjectivity, and the cultural politics of selfhood. Vanaik critiques Nandy's concept of a pre-modern self, which in Nandy's work exists albeit latent within concepts of Indianness and within political culture, as part of an inner and outer dialogue he wishes to reclaim. Vanaik states that, 'all talk by Nandy of the special fluidity of the pre-modern self is utterly mistaken' (Vanaik, 1997: 174). Although Vanaik does not offer an alternative definition, other than to dismiss this fluid concept of selfhood in preference for the ontological security of a self-image grounded in defence of a secular order. Within this argument there is no alternative other than to align Nandy's position with communalism. 'So the religious community must be seen as a, if not the, principal political and social unit in the construction of the desired anti-modernist project' (Vanaik, 1997: 177).

Nandy's position on secularism 'is a credo which in virtually every major respect rests on mistaken assumptions and understandings' (Vanaik, 1997: 177). Nandy takes on the characteristics of an untrustworthy voice, lacking authenticity and moral consistency (Letche 1990: 159). In a number of places this representation of Nandy carrying the weight the phobic object, as lacking authenticity, and bringing forward disruption and threat is repeated. Vanaik declares that, 'his is not just a lost cause, but a non-existent one' (Vanaik, 1997: 177). His intellectual significance reads as negligent and much is made of Nandy's flawed credo. As he emphasises, 'modernity, de-traditionalises tradition, leading defenders like Nandy to do what was never required even of traditional society's elites – rationalizing, justifying and defending tradition!' (Vanaik, 1997: 177). But even this rationalising, justifying and defending of tradition is something that Nandy is unable to fully achieve within his work, even as the voice of anti-secularism. As Vanaik maintains, 'the great irony in this defence is that Nandy displays a weaker understanding of traditionality and the past than he does of modernity and the present, even though his understanding of modernity is also deeply flawed' (Vanaik, 1997: 177).

Nandy's disruption and threat is advanced as he becomes representative of a border or a limit that has encroached upon everything. This includes an assumed immunity from professional criticism, a claim that Vanaik reads as further evidence of 'his commitment to an authoritarian and deeply anti-democratic form of discourse' (Vanaik, 1997: 179). Characterising Nandy as the voice of anti-modernism, anti-secularism and now an authoritarian and anti-democratic discourse reiterates Vanaik's commitment to the secular ideal. In the hands of Nandy's own peculiar modernist interpretation, this 'leads to a dangerous and disastrous seduction' (Vanaik, 1997: 180). And one that is also necessarily constructed within the discourse as outside the boundaries of a humane future. Nandy cast as the abject figure, is threatening, ambiguous and disruptive but also amoral and inhumane. To fall under the seductions of Nandy's anti-secularism or his siren song of anti-modernism, is for Vanaik to side with the inhumane.

Radhika Desai's scathing critique of Nandy in an essay written two years later in 1999 in *Economic and Political Weekly* reignites the question of his commitment to culturalism and the rise of Hindu nationalism. The article 'Culturalism and Contemporary Right, Indian Bourgeoisie and Political Hindutva' is significant for a number of reasons, notwithstanding its critique of political Hindutva, which had translated at the time into electoral victory with the formation of a Hindu nationalist government in May 1998, a coalition government, confirming 'the increasingly authoritarian urges of India's ruling class' (Desai, 1999: 695). While the Hindu Right within India has since received less favourable political results, the presence of a proto-Hindu nationalist cultural identity or Hindu majoritarian nationalism has not disappeared from the complexities of contemporary Indian political life. A presence, which Desai, following Georg Lukacs's formulation, suggests, is governed less by the internal logic of its central theses and, 'more by the exigencies of the times, by the tasks it is called upon to perform at given historical moments' (Desai, 1999: 695). This, in itself, is an interesting proposition worthy of further analysis and to which a number of theorists, Nandy included, have responded. This is overshadowed by Nandy's role in advancing Hindutva's political project.

According to Desai, Nandy's intellectual significance and indeed his complicity with these Hindutva politics is evident in the function he performs. This becomes the vantage point through which to explore the complexities of the intellectual, cultural and political forces that are at play in her essay. Desai questions the conditions for this cultural identity and of an Indianness which is cast and represented as an authentic Indian national identity and, in Hindutva's case, is encapsulated by rigid concepts of Hinduness. The central tenant of her argument is that these culturalist discourses and the intellectual culture, at least within India, sustain them. These conditions have enabled, 'the deployment of the language of particularity, of cultural nationalism which constructs the basis for the authoritarian and majoritarian cultural nationalism' (Desai, 1999: 696). Nandy according to Desai performs a central role in this task. However, the force of Desai's conviction lies not in her argument about the relationship between Hindutva and India's growing bourgeoisie, a point repeatedly made in Nandy's work, but rather that the ideology is being reconstituted by these culturalist discourses in specific ways. The aims and scope of this intellectual discourse must 'be seen as part of this broader effort to change and update Hindutva' and to this extent is complicit with its political aims' (Desai, 1999: 695). Nandy becomes the point of condensation through which these intellectual complicities with political forces are played out. Within Desai's characterisation, Nandy not only epitomises this contemporary culturalism or neo-Gandhian position but also represents the more 'serious and systematic complicities' with 'the political Hindutva,' which he is 'helping to build' (Desai, 1999: 695). Such serious charges laid against Nandy enable Desai to then construct her critique around these phobic features and reaffirm the threat and danger of this position. This characterisation of Nandy as a sympathetic voice of Hindutva and central to its internal workings marginalise and further deauthorises Nandy as critic.

The full force of this discursive mode is evident in Desai's inability to think outside of these symptomatic responses and representations. From the outset there is a dismissal of Nandy's own claims to oppose Hindutva, which she repudiates in the article, in favour of the complicities that he already carries forward. Desai argues that these complicities have not escaped critical attention before, referencing Achin Vanaik's critique of Nandy and Sarkar Sumit's piece written five years earlier as further justification for her own argument (Vanaik, 1997). Desai, then, is not alone in her claims that a figure like Nandy, armed with his anti-secularism and anti-modernism, shares a conceptual space with Hindutva ideology. Yet Nandy, cast as the phobic object, does not have a right of reply within Desai's analysis. As the de-authorised and 'not-yet-entitled-subject' Nandy's own efforts to distinguish his work and intellectual identity from this climate of discontent ultimately only serve to strengthen Desai's existing convictions. As she states, 'Nandy's opposition to Hindutva are signals to reject elements of the received Hindutva in favour of ideas which may be more acceptable and effective components of it in the present context' (Desai, 1999: 695). Nandy's arguments, his ideas and even his voice are overshadowed by his status as 'intimate enemy.' Desai's comments exemplify the intensity of the symptomatic in safeguarding against the threat and disruption that Nandy represents in not affording him a voice, and moreover, a voice that is audible.

This complicity with Hindutva is evident through the mutually dependent relationship between neo-Gandhianism and Hindutva, which Nandy represents. The article is organised around five key arguments that reinforce Nandy's representation as a phobic object and as that, which threatens and disrupts boundaries, abjection. First, Nandy belongs to an intellectual tradition of neo-Gandhianism that nurtures this symbiotic relationship; second, Nandy's dubious academic and intellectual credentials; third, a detailed discussion of Nandy's broad contemporary culturalism; fourth, a critique of Nandy's style and the methodology which finally culminates with a characterisation of Nandy as an irreverent and irrelevant figure; and finally Nandy at his most phobic. What is interesting about these arguments is the way that Desai constructs a chain of association regarding Nandy's phobic features, primarily organised around his intellectual commitment to neo-Gandhian thought.

Similar to Vanaik's criticisms, there is for Desai a collapse between post-modern comments and this culturalism and neo-Gandhian thought. Not much is offered by way of definition of this intellectual tradition, nor does Desai distinguish between neo-Gandhian thought and neo-Gandhianism, arguably an important point of differentiation worthy of further elaboration. Rather, such markers of difference are overlooked in favour of her more general assertions that these discourses are becoming increasingly and disturbingly the breeding grounds for the proliferation of Hindutva ideology. In representing neo-Gandhianism as a mainstream intellectual position and intellectually fashionable she is able to establish the immediate and widespread threat that this presents. The danger is that neo-Gandhianism's nativism lends itself to the contemporary political purposes of the Right and that the impetus for this connection comes from its anti-modernist foundations. Like Vanaik, Desai builds upon a pre-existing chain of signification governed by a persecutory logic. There is a restaging of a series of threatening signifiers, namely that the intellectual neo-Gandhian position is, by definition, profoundly anti-secular and, in turn, anti-modern in orientation.

While Gandhi's critique of western modernity is well-documented, Desai does not engage with the details and particularities of this critique but rather capitalises on a particular representation of Gandhi to make her point. Having invoked this existing phobic threat, clearly anti-modern and anti-secular, she then suggests that Nandy's own neo-Gandhianism establishes an even more disruptive version of this threat with his own contemporary bourgeois formulation, bringing a past threat now into the present. Arguably, the phobic object is firmly fixed in place within the discourse: first with this revival of neo-Gandhianism; and second, via Nandy, who now offers another version or reincarnation of this existing fear. Nandy in similar ways to Gandhi is cast as the bad subject, or even non-subject as his subjectivity and significance is dismissed and not afforded recognition. She questions the validity of this representation of Gandhian thought and the people, in this case Nandy, who uncritically supports it. Desai continues to build upon her aversion towards this intellectual current by maintaining that his institutional setting further deepens Nandy's threatening complicities. She suggests that the Centre for the Study of Developing Societies (CSDS), where Nandy has been based for the last thirty-five or so years, has, since its inception by the late Rajni Kothari in the mid 1960's, 'continued to follow the scholarly fashion of the times—from modernization to suitably de-Marxified versions of dependency in the 1970s to the present Gandhian focus on poverty and social movements (with a preoccupation with the cultural)…' (Desai, 1999: 699).

Ashis Nandy (with the exception of Rajni Kothari who is only mentioned in passing) colonises CSDS, as it were, at the expense of the numerous influential scholars, intellectuals and activists who also emanate from its intellectual and cultural hub. The phobic signifier that determines Nandy's discursive identity carries with it the additional burden of the whole intellectual culture of the institution. The persecutory logic and defensive chain of association within Desai's article grows from (*a*) the connection between culturalist discourses and the contemporary politics of the right to (*b*) neo-Gandhianism and Ashis Nandy as its main exponent to (*c*) being complicit with the reformist agenda of Hindutva ideology to now (*d*) being supported by a prestigious institution, CSDS within Indian intellectual culture which feeds back into (*a*) in an enclosed circuit of logic. Desai, therefore, presents a rather self-contained reading or rather a symptomatic one that faithfully works at keeping these anxieties at bay.

However, Desai's critique remains organised around what she defines as Nandy's own brand of irrationalised elite culturalism. This brand serves to re-work neo-Gandhianism and, in turn, contemporary expressions of Hindutva. A project she interprets in the following way: 'Nandy's version of neo-Gandhianism claims to be more genuinely emancipatory than the West's rationalist and materialist enlightenment discourse, but it is actually an all too fashionable, and by now familiar opposition to the Left, liberalism and reason itself' (Desai 1999: 700). Desai, therefore, constructs her argument around the double threat of Nandy's version of neo-Gandhianism that is undermined and dismissed as a purely oppositional mode. Here she presents Nandy's position of critical traditionalism as a discourse of emancipation used within his work to replace Western Enlightenment rationalism. Set up within this antithesis, namely in opposition to reason itself, Desai can neither see the 'distinctive rationality that critical traditionalism is supposed to embody,' nor see beyond 'these broad generically cultural nationalist arguments' (Desai, 1999: 700). Furthermore, Nandy's conception of tradition, culture or civilisation 'is an elite and conservative [one], and in the case of India, a brahmanical one' (Desai, 1999: 700). These representations enable Desai to project her phobia, at least in intellectual terms, against the irrationalism of Nandy's argument, along with his 'profound potential for authoritarianism' (Desai, 1999: 700).

Such charges of elitism, irrationality and authoritarianism, in addition to Nandy's political alliances with Hindutva, offer very little exegesis or serious engagement with that by which Desai is so threatened, Nandy's anti-secular position. The persecutory logic within which her critique is organised does, nonetheless, give her license to continue her attack on Nandy's mode of address as well as his dissenting position. This mode, which is characterised within generalised terms, reads in the following way: given that all domination is modern and tradition is, in Nandy's view, progressive by definition, tradition, therefore, is where the 'badge of his radicalism' is to be found (Desai, 1999: 701). The formulation, despite its simplicity, misrepresents or rather does not allow recognition of both the significance of critical traditionalism as a conceptual mode of dissent and Nandy's intellectual commitment 'defying given models of defiance' within his work (Desai, 1999: 701). Desai laments the lack of interrogation of Nandy's work especially by the 'unfortunate standard universities of the English-speaking world' where his claims to progressiveness are most successful (Desai, 1991: 701). Commenting on his reputation in the West, Desai attributes this recognition to the 'great deal of heaving from the self-promoting Nandy himself' (Desai, 1991: 701). Although not elaborating on how this is achieved, Desai accounts for Nandy's popularity arbitrarily fashionable in the West driven by a profound ignorance that still exists about India, even by scholars who should know better. 'After all,' she asks, 'how many scholars could take one who claims to be "making myths" as seriously as a peer?' (Desai, 1999: 706). Establishing herself as the entitled subject, the phobic object in contrast, is not granted the status of peer or critic. Nandy's scholarly methods are caricatured as 'casual hearsay' derived from 'after-dinner conversation over drinks,' while his writing we are told, '[is] intellectually undemanding prose with indulgent rhetorical flourishes, in which assertion takes the place of argument, and the convenience of the moment, of accuracy' (Desai, 1991: 707).

Desai is at her most vitriolic in arguing that 'Nandy's views encourage a religious majoritarianism exactly like the BJP's call for Hindu assertion' (Desai, 1999: 707). Nandy's anti-secularism provides not only an ontological threat to the secular subject but also: licenses the 'religious sources of majoritarian Hindutva's content' (Desai, 1999: 707). Desai maintains that he continues to perform a number of functions for Hindutva, notwithstanding his contribution to a construction of a normative pan-Hindu Indian identity and subjectivity. As the phobic object, and as representative of the abject that disrupts boundaries, Nandy constructs a Hindu, brahminical and irrational identity for India's bourgeois ruling class. Desai continues that 'in doing so he reconfigures this bourgeoisie's boundaries (Desai, 1999: 708).

This also reveals Nandy's broader and more destructive aims. For as Desai affirms, 'practically all of Nandy's psychologist writing—whether it purports to be about science or terrorism—is actually about the kind of self his bourgeois audience should have (which is why he sounds so much like another Indian guru, selling his own brand of Karma-Cola)' (Desai, 1999: 708). Nandy's phobic features align him with the branded and commercialised features of yet another Indian guru. Nandy's threat, whether expressed as his anti-intellectualism, his anti-secularism, his culturalism and neo-Gandhianism or his guru-like status, can only continue to perpetuate these anxieties, which Desai's analysis attempts to keep at bay. Nandy, and the form of culturalism which he represents, cannot be afforded the intellectual recognition that would warrant a serious engagement with this position. Desai's warnings continue unabated: 'Thus owning a certain type of dissent and disowning another, India can be made sage for participatory (cadre and lumpen mobilizing) traditional (brahmanical and irrationalist) cultural (religious, anti-secular) democratic (majoritarian) politics suited to India's chaotic political reality' (Desai, 1999: 710). Within this persecutory logic Nandy is constituted as a figure of abjection; the one who incites and perpetuates fear, loathing, chaos and disruption in the wake of his dangerous culturalist complicities.

Public Exchanges and Unvoiced Criticisms

Achin Vanaik and Radhika Desai's critiques of Nandy's 'anti-secular position' cannot be dismissed as academic quibbling, but is indicative of a more complex defence mechanism operating within the debates on secularism. This repetition and re-iteration of a persecutory logic continues to take over and make over Nandy's identity as a critic in over-determined ways. These responses and representations limit the engagement with Nandy's arguments, ideas and methods, and it is his real and perceived threat and disruption that is responded to. In reproducing this logic of argumentation established boundaries defining dissent and debate remain fiercely protected by the symptom, that is 'entrusted with representing important interests,' and which continues to do so with 'a value for self-assertion' (Freud, 1936: 27). The written exchange that took place in 2004 in Indian newspapers and journals between Kuldip Nayar, Ashis Nandy, Sanjay Subramanyam and Amit Chaudhuri moved the debate outside of academic circles and into the public arena. Writing in a widely distributed Indian weekly journal titled *Outlook Magazine* on 31 May 2004, Kuldip Nayar re-opened the debate over Ashis Nandy's contributions to debating Indian Secularism. The article 'Abhor Singularity! The critique of secularism by Nandy et al., confuses tradition with religion', reignites the question of Nandy's contested significance as critic. Nayar begins by recounting a recent meeting with Nandy where he asked him whether his own understanding of Nandy's position on secularism is correct. This being for Nayar that Nandy did not believe secularism was suited 'to the genius of India' (Nayar, 2004: 1). Nandy responded, 'you are more or less correct' (Nayar, 2004: 1). Nayar uses this brief exchange as the basis for revealing the flaw in Nandy's position, his loss of faith in the pluralistic ethos of the country. Nayar laments Nandy's doubt that secularism can preserve national integration and foster pluralism. While this may be worth exploring in Nayar's analysis this possibility is closed off. For Nandy conflates tradition and religion and 'mock[s] at the synthesis the country has managed over the years' (Nayar, 2004: 1). Traditions for Nayar do not equate to religion, and Nandy's opaqueness in clarifying these issues leaves him open to a series of further criticisms.

Nayar invokes a particular chain of association already discussed. Namely that Nandy's reading of tradition is too closely aligned with the political demands of the Hindu Right. Nayar argues that 'our tradition' if one can even speak of a universal Indian-ness, 'is that of accommodating different religions and separate faiths,' of which 'secularism is a product of that process' (Nayar, 2004: 1). Tolerance and 'the spirit of accommodation' are attributable less with the internal workings of traditions and more with the ideological and ontological security found within Indian secularism. What intellectuals like Nandy then fail to realise is that like proponents of Hindutva 'they are making secularism look anti-Hindu and are equating it with minori-tyism' (Nayar, 2004: 1).

Nandy misrecognises the Hindutva position, and even more dangerously does not recognise that which he might have in common with them. Behind such concerns is Nayar's characterisation of the debate of Indian secularism as a fight between secularism and chauvinism; a debate that he tells us is nothing new. For there are distinct continuities in this current debate with what has preceded. Nayar draws on this historical connection by arguing that Nandy is a figure whose work has much in common with the communalism of the mid 1970s. The further assumption is that this wave of communalism during this time also provided the conditions, which led to the assassination of Mohandas Gandhi. In remembering Gandhi's assassination as 'saving the nation from the hot wind of communalism' he stages the victory of official political secularism in the battle against communal forces (Nayar, 2004e: 2). Nandy thus is also attributed with carrying forward these uncanny fears and memories from the mid-1970s. Nandy's phobic status therefore invokes a present threat but also the possible return of an earlier fear and the psychic conditions accompanying these experiences. Nayar warns that, 'what is now accepted as the lure of cultural or traditional impulses was then considered an expression of communalism. But such confusion can't be an excuse for righting a wrong. It only shows that intellectuals like Nandy are faltering in their commitment' (Nayar, 2004: 2).

Ashis Nandy's response to Nayar's article attempts to expose a particular logic operating in the debates on secularism. Nandy's response 'A Billion Gandhi's' published in the same journal on 21 June argues that 'down the ages, a natural tolerance- tinged with faith-has been our subsoil. Why do my friends foist a dry import like secularism upon this rooted ness?' (Nandy, 2004e: 1). Nandy's opening comment makes two key points. First, it re-establishes his position with respect to secularism, as a dry imported concept. The importation of official secularism forecloses tolerance and amity, which exist within Indian culture and life. Second, Nandy challenges the defence of the secular ideal, when he calls for a return to 'a natural tolerance—tinged with faith.' Is secularism the only form of communal amity Nandy asks? Is it in other words, the final arbiter on the question of tolerance in Indian society and politics? Nandy nonetheless continues his lone battle of confrontation and 'working through' by clarifying his position. He states, 'actually, my criticism of secularism is an aggressive reaffirmation of these proto-Gandhian traditions and a search for post-secular forms of politics more in touch with the needs of a democratic polity in South Asia' (Nandy 2004e: 1). Nandy explicitly lays out his intellectual position in noting that his proto-Gandhianism is part of a search for post-secular forms of politics (Nandy, 2004e: 1). The tolerance Nandy has in mind is outside of the established Indian secular ideal. He notes that inter-religious strife; riots and pogroms take place within urbanised and industrialised areas rather than within villages and rural areas. Nandy reads within the Indian village a form of tolerance that continues to endure and prosper outside of these prescribed official modes of tolerance enforced by the Indian polity. As he elaborates, 'to go to an Indian village to teach tolerance through secularism is a form of obscene arrogance to which I do not want to be a party' (Nandy, 2004e: 1).

For Nandy, 'the time has come for us to decipher the language and culture of those humble Indians who live by their inferior beliefs and have made our society liveable' (Nandy, 2004e: 1). At stake is not only whether official secularism should be abandoned but also whether secularism as the dominant ideology occludes and represses other expressions of tolerance. Nandy's invitation is a call to confront that, which has been cast away, that which has been abjected from politics but which lingers like the unconscious within society and within political culture. He asks, 'If secularism only means the traditional tolerance of South Asia, why do we need an imported idea to talk about that local tolerance?' (Nandy, 2004e: 1). Nandy again raises the confronting point regarding the inheritance of the secular ideal from Western political theory and questions its dominant status. Nandy however, recognises that his approach is radically confronting and in doing so reveals limits and limitations within the debates. He concedes that, 'I also know that it is pointless to raise these questions. Some things are just not possible in the dominant, colonial culture of India's knowledge industry and among our official dissenters' (Nandy, 2004e: 2). The question of India's official dissenters brings us back to the constituting boundaries governing the terms of engagement; between the insider and outsider; that is who constitutes official and legitimate forms of dissent. Articulated within these terms the insider or official dissenter receives the benefits not only of the entitled speaking subject, whose voice is heard and engaged with, and whose identity and subjectivity is assured. In contrast, the voice of the outsider, or 'the intimate enemy' remains disruptive and threatening. It follows that the outsider's voice is cast as undermining the integrity of selfhood, the nation, and to this extent must be viewed as anti-Indian.

What is significant about Nandy's contribution to this exchange is that it provides an interruption to the persecutory logic operating within the debates. Nandy interrupts this logic by conceding his own discomfort with his work. He also recognises that his position is unlikely to be heard and is even unable to be heard within these symptomatic responses. Nandy states 'it has taken me many years to turn a traitor to my class—the urban, Western-educated, modern Indians—and to learn to respect the people who have sustained Indian democracy using their tacit theories and principles of communal amity' (Nandy, 2004e: 2). Is Nandy aware of his own abjection when recognising and publicly acknowledging himself as a traitor? As Sarah Beardsworth argues, 'abjection, then captures a condition of the subject that is sent to its boundaries, where there is, as such, neither subject nor object, only the abject' (Beardsworth, 2004: 83). While Nandy maintains that he is a non-believer and a child of modern India, his confrontation with secularism is revealing of a confrontation within his own self. During the last twenty years he claims to have been forced to confront the boundaries of his modern self and into this disruptive mode to address his dissolution with secularism. Nandy's intellectual commitment necessitates confronting a dominant feature of this modern self, described by Gandhi, that those who think that religion has nothing to do with politics understand neither religion nor politics. Or, read through a psychoanalytic frame it acknowledges that that those who think the 'return of the repressed' can simply be further repressed or displaced, neither understand conscious or unconscious life. Nandy's commitment provides his critics with ample ammunition to re-affirm the secular ideal. In this process his views do not acquire the status of 'official' dissent but remain a threatening disruption.

Nandy's interruption in the exchange gives way to a damning rejoinder from Sanjay Subrahmanyam, a Professor of Indian History and Culture at Oxford University in his article Our Only Colonial Thinker' published less than a month later in *Outlook Magazine* on 5 July 2004. It exemplifies the anxiety that Nandy provokes, as 'Ashis Nandy's foundational assumptions on secularism are flawed, uniformed'. The article can be read as a forceful reassertion of the modern secular self; one which is validated by Subrahmanyam's intellectual integrity, in contrast to Nandy's 'maverick thinker' who is 'tiresomely repetitive and profoundly ill-informed' (Subrahmanyam, 2004a: 1). Subrahmanyam though acknowledging Nandy's status as a widely 'celebrated' and 'great thinker,' radically questions these accolades along with Nandy's intellectual credentials and credibility. In re-asserting the already established terms of exchange Subrahmanyam argues that Nandy's reading of secularism, as primarily a European import is fundamentally an untrustworthy formulation. For Subrahmanyam, Nandy's untrustworthy claim is symptomatic of a more general intellectual and moral untrustworthiness. For, 'Nandy's Europe does not exist except in his own imagination. It is a non-place that only exists to be an anti-India and he believes he can attribute anything he wants to it just because it tickles his fancy' (Subrahmanyam, 2004a: 1). Such comments work to reinforce an image of Nandy as a discredited scholar who is intellectually manipulative in order to satisfy a personal whim. From such a vantage point Subrahmanyam is able to differentiate and distance himself from Nandy's anti-intellectualism and scholarly irreverence.

Subrahmanyam represents Nandy as an untrustworthy contributor to the debates because he fails to acknowledge a fundamental historical reality. In not affording Indian secularism the intellectual and political acknowledgement it deserves, Nandy remains a peripheral voice given his illiteracy in the historical reality, Subrahmanyam defends. He is even willing to concede that Nandy's call for traditions and religious concepts of tolerance that have their own long history in India, is indeed a task worth pursuing. Nandy falls short of achieving this task because he is not a credible intellectual source. The phobic object now lacks the scholarly standards needed for reputable research and argumentation. Indeed Subrahmanyam's advice to Nandy is clear as the following excerpt illustrates:

> So perhaps Nandy should begin by reflecting on the rather widespread forms of obscene arrogance and not hand out lessons before doing his homework. If he does so, I am sure he will find plenty of examples of tolerance not just in villages that his rather tired populist rhetoric wants to hold up as an example, but in other parts of Indian society in both the past and present. But it may involve harder work than producing the cotton candy that passes for cleverness in indigenist circles. (Subrahmanyam, 2004a: 2)

Aside from the profound attack on Nandy's scholastic methods, his obscene arrogance amongst other phobic features, Subrahmanyam again invokes the threat of a return to pre-modern concepts of indigeneity and culturalism. Therefore, for Subrahmanyam, Ashis Nandy becomes made over as a true colonial thinker, as evidenced by his arrogant and authoritarian voice. Subrahmanyam regards Nandy as nothing more than a provocateur or peripheral dissenter who is trapped in an image of India that has since long past. He can be located within a 'lachrymose tradition of the romantic under-side of the so-called Bengal Renaissance' (Subrahmanyam, 2004a: 2). This romanticism is accompanied by Nandy's dubious intellectual credentials as a colonial thinker, and representative of a dangerous culturalism. Such a reading keeps Nandy outside of any 'meaning-ful' debate as Subrahmanyam leaves us questioning the intellectual integrity of the phobic object.

Amit Chaudhuri reignites the exchange between Nayar, Nandy and Subrahmanyam by questioning the conditions and boundaries of this exchange. In 'Distant Thunder' published in *Outlook Magazine* on 2 August 2004, Chaudhuri begins by stating, 'back in Calcutta af-ter a month in England, I found that a debate or a public difference of opinion, between two Indian academics had gone all but stale' (Chaudhuri, 2004a: 1). He questions why this exchange has come to a halt, and suggests that this may have more to do with the dissemi-nation of ideas rather than the saliency of the exchange. Chaudhuri argues that, 'there is still no highbrow journal of ideas in our country that could claim to have a decent nationwide circulation' (Chaudhuri, 2004a: 1). Focusing on the question of circulation allows him to explore the ways in which ideas are disseminated through publish-ing channels, though dissemination also denotes the ways in which these ideas are communicated. Hence, his questioning of whether the public exchange thus far might even be conceived as a debate. Chaud-huri's own interpretation leads him to conclude that, 'debate perhaps it is not the right word' (Chaudhuri, 2004a: 1). He characterises the exchange as it has publicly unfolded as a peculiar occurrence, not-ing that, 'I was struck by this business; public airings by academics in India are rare' (Chaudhuri, 2004a: 1). Chaudhuri characterises the discursive field, through which this exchange on secularism has been carried out by noting that, 'all in all, you conclude that in the circles I'm referring to, there has been relatively little scope for the genuine debate, criticism and irreverence in the last two decades; the interest-ing and even important intellectual developments have been swiftly translated into territorial anxieties' (Chaudhuri, 2004a: 1).

Chaudhuri offers an interruption by questioning the constitutive features of the debate, the limits and limitations of this logic. In other words to what extent is genuine debate even possible given the territorial anxieties which Chaudhuri claims are at play. At what point have important intellectual developments been condensed into territorial anxieties? In light of this malaise Chaudhuri welcomes the critique put forward by Subrahmanyam, though he has little sympathy for his argument. For like Nandy's contribution 'it creates a break, a rupture in our monotonous observance of intellectual propriety' (Chaudhuri, 2004a: 2). Yet ultimately he argues that Subrahmanyam falls prey to the discursive logic at play, succumbing to the force of these territorial anxieties. For Subrahmanyam is unable to break away from the symptomatic and invokes a politics of blame through which Nandy's work and his intellectual identity can be understood. Although this is an issue, which extends beyond Subrahmanyam's article, he does repeat and exacerbate these representations in intensified ways. Subrahmanyam's response though cannot be singled out on this basis, but is part and parcel of the symptomatic underpinning this exchange and the debates on Indian secularism. Chaudhuri concludes, 'that in the end, it seemed to reaffirm the difficulties of critical language and thinking, and the unique elusiveness of Nandy in our cultural landscape' (Chaudhuri, 2004a: 2).

The territorial anxiety which Nandy produces even for an intellectual of Subrahmanyam's calibre and indeed working in a very different institutional, political and intellectual setting also gives way here to a deeper anxiety regarding the idiom of Nandy's critique. Chaudhuri rightly connects this to the larger issue of the possibility and audibility of dissent, that is to say the parameters which constitute a recognizable critical language. That there is an elusive quality to Nandy's intellectual identity and significance, or even an ambiguity, has thus far been represented as threatening and disruptive. For a theorist like Subrahmanyam this threat and disruption is contained through the symptomatic. This plays out in terms of Nandy's ill-informed historically inaccurate reading. In response to this, Subrahmanyam's corrective voice reclaims the concept of secularism as authentically Indian and as central to the politics he defends. Such representations leave him to assert that Nandy consequently is ignorant, an innocent, and to question the rationality underpinning his mode of argumentation. Chaudhuri continues to offer a characterisation of Subrahmanyam's own logic that on the surface seems befitting of an established intellectual tradition, 'of polemical debunking: an enfant terrible attacking an older, establishment figure' (Chaudhuri, 2004a: 2). Chaudhuri claims however, that Subrahmanyam achieves the trustworthy and hence authoritative presence by the end of the article. This presence works to overshadow the ignorance, innocence and disruption of the phobic object and leads Chaudhuri to suggest that Subrahmanyam's intellectual integrity wins over in the end. As he states, 'he comes to represent sound historical thinking and knowledge, as well as rationality and logic, in contrast to Nandy's whimsy, romanticism and lack of clear thinking' (Chaudhuri, 2004b: 2). Subrahmanyam's ability to affirm the boundaries of exchange within these terms, serves to cast Nandy as a whimsical, peripheral or at best minor player against Subrahmanyam's intellectual integrity and professionalism. Chaudhuri concedes that Nandy 'is fated to be a minority voice' (Chaudhuri, 2004b: 2). Whether there is a place for such a voice in our community of liberal intellectuals is a more pressing issue.

This possible place is complicated further by the question of the role of the critic and dissenter in Indian public life. For Chaudhuri any discussion of these issues must take into account, 'the paradox of the language of our nationalism; that it contained within it the seeds both of our secular middle class and its fundamentalist other, our pluralism and our intolerance' (Chaudhuri, 2004b: 3). The significance of a critic like Nandy lies in his role as a critic of the post-Independence Indian middle classes that for them is encapsulated in a modern and secular Indian nation state. Chaudhuri though takes Nandy to task for equating modernity with the West. This reading of the Indian middle classes as Westernised leaves Nandy open to a series of criticisms though these issues have less to do with Nandy and more to do with 'the darkness of our inherited language of self-definition' (Chaudhuri, 2004b: 3).

Although Chaudhuri does not necessarily subscribe to Nandy's anti-secular position he is able to acknowledge his critical efforts within the exchange in more complex terms. In such an intellectual and political culture, it is all the more imperative Chaudhuri suggests, that a critic like Nandy in spite of his phobic status, has a presence. The job of a robust, self-critical intelligentsia to recognise the significance of critics like Nandy, rather than revert to the persecutory logic evident within the debate. A critic like Nandy needs to be evaluated in terms of his own contributions to a robust intelligentsia and not in antithetical terms, in terms of supporting an anti-secular view and an anti-modern view. Despite the limitations of Nandy's position whatever these may be for a writer like Chaudhuri he remains a 'provocative and necessary figure' (Chaudhuri, 2004b: 3). Chaudhuri paints a more multifaceted picture of Nandy as an important dissenting voice, one that contrasts Subrahmanyam's defensive caricature of Nandy. Whether or not a figure like Nandy can even carry the discursive weight of the symptomatic explored thus far remains questioned for Chaudhuri. He explains this in the following way by stating that, 'he may be too eccentric, too much a minority voice for us to call him, as Auden called Freud, quoting Alfred Whitehead, a whole climate of opinion' (Chaudhuri, 2004b: 3). Within such a discursive field Nandy is neither a body of knowledge nor a marginal figure but remains the disruptive, ambiguous voice which threatens the established system of organization and of meaning that are the boundaries between secularism and anti-secularism, public and private, self and other.

Chaudhuri's attempts to characterise the logic of debate beckons a less than favourable response from Subrahmanyam. In his rejoinder, 'A Guru and his Followers: A Colonial Thinker' published in *The Telegraph of Calcutta* in 8 August 2004 Subrahmanyam criticises Chaudhuri of his admiration for Nandy. From then on the article reads as a corrective attempt to redress many of these representations that we are told are 'largely unfounded' (Subrahmanyam, 2004a: 1). He begins by challenging Chaudhuri's portrayal of the public debate as limited citing the Journal *Economic and Political Weekly* as one of the key forums for scholarly debate within India. Subrahmanyam raises even stronger objections to Chaudhuri's representation of Nandy as a marginal figure or minority voice. Subrahmanyam's defence against this runs as follows:

> it is a conceit to believe that this best-selling author from Oxford University Press and Princeton University Press, whose books are used in cultural studies and post-colonial studies courses in many parts of the world, is simply a marginal figure, a minority voice, an eccentric. (Subrahmanyam, 2004a: 1)

Subrahmanyam suggests, consistent with his earlier argument that Nandy's significance or status is best understood as a kind of Guru, an influence which extends beyond the Indian intellectual scene. This does not deter him from asking who the followers of this Guru are. He offers a few suggestions beginning with the guilt complexes of the Indian middle class who, 'flock to buy his books' (Subrahmanyam, 2004a: 1). The next category identified is a certain brand of thinker belonging to Subaltern Studies or Post-Colonial Studies. There is another category of followers in the Hindu nationalists, where Nandy's sympathies for culturalism are applauded. The politics of blame is activated here as Subrahmanyam again invokes the political threat Nandy provokes. Nandy as a point of condensation for these ills is taken to its limit with Subrahmanyam's anecdotal relay of 'a frightening occasion' where at a Seminar in London he 'rose to make an impassioned defence of the RSS, *[Rashtriya Swayamsevak Sang]* as true freedom fighters against the Emergency.'[4] The example serves to highlight and warn the reader of the dangers Nandy poses. This is a serious charge to make. Subrahmanyam does not hesitate to implicate Nandy as complicit within these ideological currents and in endorsing this political organization that has a chequered and controversial historical presence within Indian politics. He reaffirms the chain of association invoked in Radhika Desai's work in aligning Nandy's intellectual interests with the political imperatives of the Hindu Right.

Given Nandy's political complicities Subrahmanyam rhetorically asks, 'So who does not find Ashis Nandy today significant, provocative and necessary?' (Subrahmanyam, 2004a: 1). This support base now extends to Marxists, Dalit intellectuals and to even 'sensible historians' who read his attempts at 'myth making' at best as a form of anti-intellectualism and at worst as a form of strong irrationalism. This is contrasted against Subrahmanyam's own intellectualism and rationality that underpins his scholarly commitment, particularly his reading of history. Ultimately, he follows through with the representation of Nandy as a phobic object, focusing on his dangerous political ties and dubious threatening intellectual allegiances. Carrying the heritage of the Bengal Renaissance, Nandy is re-staged as a Colonial Thinker because of 'his utter subservience to Orientalist clichés regarding India's past' (Subrahmanyam, 2004a: 2). No longer is Nandy simply a romantic provocateur for he remains a prisoner of the heritage, of his anti-colonial heritage. Amit Chaudhuri's essay may drip with cultural cringe and the clichéd trappings attached to it as Subrahmanyam suggests but for him such analysis only serves to reaffirm Nandy's own culturalist leanings.

The article which follows this is written by Swapan Dasgupta 'Cultural Cringe: Reducing Colonialism to a single design is poor history' published in *The Telegraph of Calcutta* on August 13, 2004. Dasgupta acknowledges the importance of the exchanges given that 'the impact of official secularism has been horribly divisive' (Dasgupta, 2004: 1). Citing Ashis Nandy's iconoclastic 'Anti-Secularist Manifesto' as triggering the 'first lively debate of the Manmohan Singh era,' he argues that the participants in this exchange have also managed to resurrect a controversy 'that many believe has run out of intellectual steam' (Dasgupta, 2004: 1). For Dasgupta one of the problems with such exchanges is that the debate is too focused around the question of colonialism and its aftermath. This amounts to the, 'comic spectacle of the secularist, the traditionalist and the communalist heaping the same abuse at each other' (Dasgupta, 2004: 1).

Dasgupta takes issue with Nandy for charging the Indian political leadership with a deracination born of colonialism, and then explores how the Hindu nationalists, in turn charge the Marxists and Secularists with pursuing a colonialist agenda. In contrast to this, he suggests the Subaltern Studies group set out to demonstrate their impeccable anti-colonial credentials. He thus references the intellectual differences within the debate as being organised around a (mis)reading of colonialism, Dasgupta falls prey to his own critique. He warns that, 'to reduce it (colonialism) to a monochromatic image and a single experience is good pamphleteering but poor history' (Dasgupta, 2004: 1). Dasgupta reframes the debate in terms of what constitutes good history already established by Subrahmanyam's account of acceptable historical narrative. What is questioned is whether Nandy like the genuine secularists shares the good intentions with respect to wanting India free of sectarian conflict. The other side to such a question is whether the phobic object may speak in a language of good intentions? If Nandy is a traitor to his classes, can he be anything other than the voice of the traitor? While the answer to these questions is already provided by the logic underpinning the debate, Dasgupta too remains locked within these modes of representation.

Audible Dissent and the Question of Narcissism

The article that closes this public exchange by Amit Chaudhuri is 'Natural Proclivities: So little fruitful dissent, so much private discontent.' The piece published on 14 August 2004 in *The Telegraph of Calcutta* was written prior to the printing of Dasgupta's article. Chaudhuri's piece speaks directly to Subrahmanyam's article and clearly re-states his intentions in the following way. 'My article was written not so much to take sides as to consider whether civilized and intelligent debate is part of the discourse of the Indian secular intelligentsia; if not, why not' (Chaudhuri, 2004b: 1). The answers to this question as to why the airing of disagreements and free exchange of ideas is truncated and 'is so difficult in India is evident from Subrahmanyam's article itself' (Chaudhuri, 2004b: 1). For Chaudhuri, the logic he invokes defines him as an uninteresting polemicist. 'Since the debate has descended into personal attacks,' the question remains whether any fruitful dissent can ensue under these conditions, within such logic of persecution? (Chaudhuri, 2004b: 1).

Chaudhuri explores why it is that to paraphrase the title so little fruitful dissent conceals so much private discontent, or why private discontent works to limit the possibilities of dissent. Commenting on Subrahmanyam's characteristic manner it is 'argumentativeness, not argumentation' that is the defining style underpinning his contribution, though this conceals a more disturbing feature in his analysis

(Chaudhuri, 2004b: 1). Chaudhuri questions Subrahmanyam's own methods of critique including the gossip and apocrypha he introduces into the debate with his claim that Nandy once defended the RSS. Such a serious charge, which remains un-referenced and un-validated, is inconsistent with the scholarly benchmarks he is so eager to emphasise in the exchange. This demonstrates the symptomatic at work, as a means of containing the threat and disruption that Nandy, irrespective of his political affiliations, still carries forward. Such statements are recognised by Chaudhuri as dangerous, not least because they operate to affirm Nandy as a point of condensation for a number of anxieties and fears. Although Chaudhuri does not adopt a psychoanalytic framework to explain these representations of phobia and abjection, he argues that these function as an, 'ad hominem attack and the threat of being made into a pariah' (Chaudhuri, 2004b: 1). For Chaudhuri it is this mode of critical engagement, a recrimination and retribution that 'seems to pass for civilized disagreement amongst our secular intelligentsia' (Chaudhuri, 2004b: 1).

Chaudhuri highlights the inability for a scholar of Subrahmanyam's calibre to engage intellectually with his interlocutor, that is to think beyond camps and group affiliations, expressed in the psychic organization of phobia and threat. Rather he focuses on a motley crew, spearheaded by Ashis Nandy, consisting of members or targets that have very little in common with each other. Chaudhuri undermines this logic by aligning Subrahmanyam in service of his personal discontent. He explains this in the following way: 'The creation of this group, then, and the critical method in his piece, are directed principally by Subrahmanyam's narcissism, his unspoken but powerful immersion in what people feel about him and what he feels about people' (Chaudhuri, 2004b: 2). If narcissism defines the driving impetus for critique, all critical exchange is, therefore, set up against this yardstick of confirming what Chaudhuri calls the 'absolute correctness of his own position' (Chaudhuri, 2004b: 2). Here narcissism functions as a defence mechanism against both the territorial and personal anxieties provoked by the phobic object. Where natural proclivities or territorial affiliations characterise the discursive field, and impose the boundaries and limits of critical exchange. Yet again such a symptomatic response is revealing, for the narcissistic structure is crucial in understanding these dynamics of insecurity, threat and disruption that Nandy represents in these debates.

To suggest that narcissism operates within these debates as a defence mechanism is to recognise the boundaries defining the terms of exchange. Narcissism consistent with Kristeva's reading and its connection to her concept of abjection denotes a borderline case, or a case of brittle and precarious borders. In her reading of the abject and abjection in *Powers of Horror: An Essay on Abjection* (1982) she re-works the Freudian account of primary narcissism into these processes. Abjection, then being the 'pre-condition of narcissism' and therefore 'a kind of narcissistic crisis,' but which appears as a regression and for Kristeva is distinctly set back from the *other* (Kristeva, 1982: 13). This is a retreat into a self-referential mode of engaging with the other. As Kristeva elaborates, 'narcissism then appears as a regression to a position set back from the other, a return to a self-contemplative, conservative, self-sufficient haven' (Kristeva: 13–14). The positioning of the boundaries is important given that modern Narcissus, Chanter and Ziarek argue 'is not sure of herself, of her borders, or her iden-tity; she is on the border between security and insecurity, between fusion and separation' (Chanter and Ziarek, 2005: 1). The concept of narcissism adds further to understanding the boundaries operat-ing here. This adds another layer of complexity for thinking through the ways in which the boundaries of intellectual engagement estab-lished through the symptomatic register work to conceal and cover over a state of insecurity. Freud describes the covering over as an il-lusory omnipotence (Freud in Gay, 1995: 545). In *Strangers to Our-selves* (1991) Kristeva develops this need to rupture and re-position the boundaries between self and other in order to heal a narcissis-tic wound. Explored against the backdrop of French national culture where the stranger and foreigner like the phobic object is abjected from view, she emphasises this connection to narcissism. She states that, 'to become capable of loving our neighbour as our self, we have first of all to heal a wounded narcissism' (Kristeva, 1991: 31).

This narcissism prevents us from acknowledging our own radical alterity, the otherness and the stranger who is within. The encounter with that has been cast away and abjected, leads to the breakdown of these narcissistic structures. The other's otherness or radical strange-ness then enables recognition of our own internal and intimate strangeness.

If Nandy is to be recognised within the exchange and the debates at large as the entitled subject then the existing modes of reception and representation, including the relationship between self and other need to be reconsidered. In Kristeva's terms then if the relationship with the other is to be seriously addressed then narcissistic identity must be reconstituted, in order to be able to extend a hand to the other. Thus what is needed she says is a reassurance against the existing defence mechanism. This facilitates the process for reparation, reconstructing narcissism, personality and subjectivity in order for there to be a relation to the other, outside of this pre-existing regressive structure. The reassurance or reparation in our relations between self and other are for Kristeva made possible through a shattering or negativisation of the narcissistic structure. As Ewa Ziarek emphasises, this leads to an acknowledgement, a confronting one at that, of our internal alterity and subjectivity as we come face to face with our radical strangeness.[5] This leads to a profound recognition of 'the strange within the familiar but also to the possible projection of this discovery onto the Other.' (Ziarek, 2001: 127). In these processes the other is afforded a greater complexity. For Kristeva this includes recognition of the other's subjectivity and humanity. The question that remains is whether the participants represented in this exchange demonstrate this capacity in extending a hand to the other. Is this even a question that can be asked given the presence of the symptomatic? Given the complex defence mechanisms Subrahmanyam, Nayar and Dasgupta demonstrate, it is unlikely within this exchange. The exception to this is Chaudhuri who comes close to recognising the possibility that Nandy's radical strangeness provides in disrupting an existing narcissistic logic. As Chaudhuri argues, as long as this narcissistic wound remains unhealed then Subrahmanyam's narcissism, along with this persecutory logic, also operating in these other responses by critics, remains fixed in place.

The healing of the narcissistic wound would entail a break away from the logic structuring the symptomatic. Therefore, where such personal discontent reigns supreme, it is little surprise that such little fruitful dissent ensues; when dissent itself remains confined or subject to these psychic processes. The concept of narcissism that appears, as Sarah Bearsdworth notes when our capacities and relations to others 'are weakened or collapsed,' also sheds further light on the question of dissent (Beardsworth, 2004: 59). It is interesting to note that it is Nandy in this exchange that acknowledges this connection. We may well ask whether it is Nandy's abject status, his own recognition of the instability of meaning that provides him with this capacity? This finds expression as he tells us in demarcating between official dissenters and the others that do not register. The official dissenter is assured then with the ontologically secure position of the insider within the debates. In contrast Nandy whose borderline status elicits responses of fascination and horror is neither an outsider who can be ignored nor an insider to be acknowledged. Nandy's position marked by its lack of recognition therefore raises the question of whether the idiom of his mode of critique is outside of this narcissistic crisis underpinning the politics of blame. In this vein Chaudhuri comes to a poignant realisation in the exchange when he concedes the limitations in evaluating the significance of Nandy within these terms. If Nandy's own mode of engagement is outside and as I argue, breaks away from this persecutory and narcissistic dynamic, then this opens up new possibilities for dissent and critical intervention.

This final example of this logic brings us to the beginning of 2008, where Nandy was cast not only as the disruptive figure, but attempts were made to criminalise the identity of the critic. This took place through the attempts to criminalise his identity by Narendra Modi, Chief Minister of the State of Gujarat for the publication of an article critical of the outcome, and Modi's re-election, in the 2007 elections. This response to Nandy's article 'Gujarat: Blame The Middle Class' in the *Times of India*, 8 January 2008 exemplifies the intensification of Nandy's threat and disruption over time and the perceived need to abject Nandy from view. In the article Nandy consistent with his psychoanalytic approach as advanced in this book, explores the features and subjectivity that defines political culture in Gujarat. Of particular interest are the ways in which a dominant and official culture of fear and hatred against minorities dominates politics and middle-class attitudes. Nandy notes that even if Modi had lost the elections in Gujarat this political culture and its attitudes would have remained unchanged. He states, 'forty years of dedicated propaganda does pay dividends, electorally and socially' (Nandy, 2008: 1). Nandy confronts the processes of subjection operating in Hindu nationalist attitudes and the ways these re-constitute individual and collective subjectivity. He points out for instance that Gujarati Muslims are now adjusting to their new station as second-class citizens. Yet what is interesting about Nandy's analysis are the ways in which his comments and the responses to it work to reconstitute Nandy's subjectivity.

The charges laid against Nandy by the Modi State Government are for inciting animosity between communities. It is understood that Nandy's presence as a public commentator on these issues is underpinned by a more over political and threatening agenda. The logic at play and demonstrated in the criminal charges laid, indicate the full extent of Nandy's real and perceived threat and disruption. Although the charges were laid in response to this particular article, the over-determined response to criminalise Nandy is an accumulation of complex internalised fears and threats. Are these actions simply the reaction and defence of an aggrieved Gujarati Hindu majority? For the 150 academics and activists from India and internationally who protested against these charges, the action taken against Nandy is part of larger processes. They argue that:

> This is the latest case of harassment of intellectuals, journalists, artists and public figures by anti-democratic forces that claim to speak on behalf of Hindu values sometimes and patriotism at other times, especially Gujarat, who have little understanding of either. ('Academics protest against Ashis Nandy's harassment,' *The Times of India*, 19 June, 2008)

These comments set the scene for situating Nandy within larger anti-democratic forces at play within Indian political culture. In confronting the constituting features of these Hindu values and claims over patriotism, Nandy's voice is cast by the state as the anti-patriotic, and by extension anti-Indian, the 'intimate enemy.' It is this voice that is subject to policing and potential criminalisation by the State that draws on the language of civil liberties to achieve its ends. Consistent with Kristeva's concept of the abject, the actions of the Modi Government to criminalise Nandy's subjectivity confirms his abject status. Nandy is cast as that which 'does not respect, border, positions, rules' (Kristeva, 1982: 4). Kristeva continues that, 'any crime, because it draws attention to the fragility of the law, is abject, but premeditated crime, cunning murder, hypocritical revenge are even more so because they heighten the display of such fragility' (Kristeva, 1982: 4). To Kristeva's list of crime we can add the crime of inciting communal tensions not only because it transgresses the official secular political ideal of tolerance but because it also reveals the fragility of the ideal and its defence.

As Nandy publicly states in response to the charges and in response to representations of his subjectivity, 'this is just being done to silence people like me' (http://www.indianexpress.com/news/dont-arrest-nandy-sc-to-modi-govt/330070/). Nevertheless, the charges demonstrate the significance that is afforded Nandy as a dissenting, threatening and abject figure. While the Supreme Court has dismissed the charges, Nandy as the threatening and disruptive figure does not redeem his innocence within representations of his subjectivity but rather retains the slurs of an accused in a criminal matter. The contested hearing was held in the Supreme Court in Delhi, and was dismissed on the grounds that Nandy had no case to answer. The dismissing of the charges reinstate to some extent subjectivity to Nandy that had previously been denied in his representation as an alleged criminal and abject public figure. Despite the criminal matter being resolved, the incident demonstrates the threat and fear that Nandy continues to carry forward in public debates. Cast as the phobic object and as the abject, this questioning of intellectual integrity collapses into a generalised attack on his moral credentials. For as John Letche claims, 'the one who is abject lacks authenticity, that is lacks any detectable moral consistency' (Lechte, 1990: 160). Reclaiming the subjectivity of the abject figure is a task that must be carried forth elsewhere, that is outside of such symptomatic exchanges, responses and representations. How though does Nandy distinguish himself from this existing logic?

Nandy's willingness to confront and furthermore work through the complexities of a fiercely defended secular ideal also demonstrates autonomy of thought. While this autonomy is noted to some extent in this public exchange, the complexity in having arrived at this intellectual destination is overlooked. Therefore the starting point for exploring his willing confrontation must be with those features and characteristics that are deemed threatening and disruptive.

NOTES

1. For a survey of these debates see Needham, A.D. and Rajan, R.S. (2007); Bhargava, R. 1998; McGuire, J., Reeves, P. et al. (1996); Sharma, A. (2001).
2. Dacey (2008); German (2007); Layman G.C and E. G. Carmines (1997); Taylor, C. (2007).
3. On this point see Julia Kristeva. 'The object of fear is, in other words, a substitute formation for the subject's fear caused by the breakdown of any distinction between subject and object, of any distinction between the world of dead material objects and us' J. Kristeva (1982).
4. The Rashtriya Swayamsevak Sangh (RSS) or the National Association of Self-helpers is a voluntary organisation focusing on developing society based on Hindutva—which they claim is the essence of Hinduism. Established in 1925 it was founded by Dr K.B. Hedgewar when he unfurled the Bhagawadhaj-saffron flag-at a camp in Amaravati. Hedgewar talked of a Hindu-Rashra, but it was his successor, M.S. Golwalkar, popularly known as Guruji who expounded its ideology. The RSS has had a colourful yet checked presence on the Indian political scene. It has been banned twice in India, and despite this had remained a strong and popular political force finding support and expression during particular periods of political unrest. It's presence as a political ideology has diminished over the last five to ten years amongst a backlash of criticism, scholarly and public regarding its communal foundations. For further information refer to Kamat's description of this movement

as a sub-culture within Indian culture. http://www.kamat.com/indica/culture/sub-cultures/rss.htm.

5. Ziarek argues that:

> Kristeva analyses many instances of the subject's own unsettling heterogeneity—the abject [which is the main focus here] the uncanny, the death drive, sex and the aporia of primary narcissism—all of which point not only to different modalities of 'the strange within the familiar' but also to the possible projection of this discovery onto the Other.

For a discussion of this refer to E. Ziarek (2001).

4

Critique at the Threshold of Politics

This chapter explores Nandy's willingness to enter into processes of confrontation and 'working through' in greater detail. I argue that this confrontation is fundamental to understanding Nandy's psychoanalytic approach and the way this further distinguishes his work and identity as critic, in the debates on Indian secularism. While Nandy's critics seldom recognise his contributions to the debates of secularism as valid in attempts to deauthorise the voice of the critic, there is a distinct confrontation that takes place. This aptitude for confronting the distortions that the ideology of secularism produces is demonstrated in the autonomy of thought that distinguishes his work, and remains a source of fascination and horror for critics. The other notable feature of confrontation is that it imbues Nandy's work with a reflexivity and self-reflexivity for the inclusions and exclusions operating in politics. In an interview Nandy distinguishes his position by stating '...that instead of looking for other ways of, in which you can achieve the goals of secularism in a more human society, they [secularists] want a higher dose of the same medicine to solve all the problems. And I thought that was a chimera' (Nandy and Deftereos, 2006: 2). This recognition of the secular ideal as a chimera is a distinctive break from an existing and dominant logic of persecution, idealisation and defence that marks these debates. Confrontation here also denotes traversing the fantasy structure that accompanies the defence of secularism. For instance, Nandy confronts and traverses the dominant view that communal amity can only be safeguarded through a more aggressive pursuit and commitment to the ideology of secularism. This recognition of the fantasy structure as chimera enables him to rupture existing meanings and assumptions. This approach also enables him to explore alternatives outside of these structures of idealisation, projection and defence.

The confrontation and ultimately the rejection of the secular ideal enables Nandy to explore features of Indian political culture that are excluded and deemed abject. These border crossings or rather the re-positioning of the boundaries of debate produces a number of dis inct alternatives. Yet while Nandy's voice is 'excluded' and 'deauthorised' in particular ways his critique of secularism takes seriously the question of 'exclusion,' in addition to engaging with the 'excluded' aspects of Indian political culture. For example, Nandy explores the possibilities and internal resources of the non-modern peripheral and their capacity for what he terms is a post-secular awareness. This awareness is an internal capacity within the non-modern peripheral and is also present within Indian culture, though seldom recognised within the official account of Indian political life. In exploring the ways that this awareness can disrupt existing inclusions and exclusions within politics, Nandy furthers his own post-secular commitment. The dissenting forms of toleration largely grounded within the non-modern religiosity of those deemed peripheral, and cast as bad subjects within secular political culture, reconstitutes existing subjectivities and inter-subjective relations. In traversing the fantasy of a western secular ideal, in confronting the viability of statist secularism in safeguarding tolerance, and the ways that alternative accounts of subjectivity are foreclosed by the ideal, Nandy's position threatens and disrupts the modern markers of politics. Though as some critics might suggest, is this a romantic return to a pre-modern India or is this post-secular commitment an alternative political imaginary? Shifting the emphasis to detail the border crossings and exclusions that Nandy raises in his work more closely is needed.

For in confronting that which is deemed abject and 'cast away' in service of a distinct subjectivity in his work, Nandy, according to certain critics, becomes the phobic object, or at least the object of derision and disruption, thus taking on the features of abjection. In critiquing and representing Nandy's confrontation with secularism, but moreover, his willingness to do so, his own identity is cast and made over as disruptive and threatening. Nandy carries the weight of abjection as that which both fascinates and horrifies with its real and potential threat to disrupt subjectivity. In Kristeva's work abjection causes a violation to the subject by, 'blurring the borders of oneself, pushing one towards psychosis where the all-too-real undermines the divisions between self and other and the capacity to differentiate' (McAfee, 2004: 121). This is the discursive burden that Nandy carries forward in the debates on secularism, as that which threatens subjectivity, meaning and thus signification. In *Powers of Horror: An Essay on Abjection* (1982) Kristeva documents at length our profound un-willingness to confront abjection. As she reminds us, 'In short, who I ask you, would agree to call himself abject, subject of or subject to abjection?' (Kristeva, 1982: 209). Nandy in reflexive moments ac-knowledges the unpopularity of his critique and attempts from crit-ics to silence him or render his work and subjectivity irrelevant, but he does not concede to these representations of abjection. Rather what I argue in this chapter is that in maintaining the integrity of his commitment to psychoanalytic confrontation as a method of critique that enables Nandy through these processes to confront the bound-aries of inclusion and exclusion, operating in politics. As he explains, 'not only must politics work with – and work out – the contradictions in human subjectivity, *[but]* that subjectivity in turn concretises, per-haps better than any action, the state of politics in a society' (Nandy, 1980a: vii).

The argument continues around Nandy's willingness to confront those areas of Indian life—ambiguities, contradictions in human subjectivity and within Indian traditions and culture that remain threatening and destabilising to an Indian secular political culture. This task of willing confrontation for Nandy extends to confronting parts of his own self, in order to generate his approach and main-tain his commitment to confrontation and a psychoanalytic working through. In doing so, I argue that Nandy's critique rejects the ontolog-ical security of certitudes in favour of a more ambivalent positioning of the boundaries of selfhood and politics. The features of his will-ing confrontation are considered in two replies that Nandy makes to critics, Achin Vanaik and Kuldip Nayar.[1] These replies provide insight into the features of confrontation, the reflexivity and receptiveness that result from these processes. These replies to critics also strength-en the argument regarding the psychoanalytic focus of Nandy's work; namely, his commitment to confrontation and a working through. It is also important to note that these responses are uncharacteristic, given Nandy's notable reticence to enter into existing academic de-bates and in responding purely to academic voices. As he states, 'you know I never respond to purely academic critics. I respond only to those who are involved in movements or who are doing something in India or in South Asia in general' (Nandy and Deftereos, 2006: 2). He continues:

you see even if Kuldip Nayar and Achin Vanaik have not said something sub-stantial the fact remains that their words count because they are fighting the battles in India, because they are writing in India, so you know I would like to respond to them. (Nandy and Deftereos, 2006: 5)

In what are Nandy's only official responses to critics within the debates on secularism, confrontation is clarified further as is his ability to work through and reflect on parts of his own identity as critic, as features of his approach to critique. Confronting and working through the complexities of the secular ideal and position in defining Indian politics and political culture, Nandy comes face to face with a number of resistances and deeply imbedded defences. While these defences may function as a protective structure against the threat of the loss of ontological security, this only works to consolidate existing and dominant processes of inclusion and exclusion. In Nandy's responses to critics these resistances and defences are radically confronted, worked through and reflected upon in order to generate a broader conceptualisation of politics. In disrupting the boundaries of inclusion and exclusion operating in politics he builds a case for the necessity of democratic pluralism. This as he notes is 'always helpful even if it is crude, impractical or wrong' (Nandy and Jahanbegloo, 2006: 68). For in Nandy's analysis acknowledging and facilitating pluralism and diversity within politics leads us towards an equally important possibility. This possibility is described as the inclusion of a post-secular awareness within a regenerated conceptualisation of politics. This new and alternative political imaginary though remains radically threatening and disrupting, because of its invitation 'for seeing difference as an ontological possibility for subjectivity' (McAfee in Oliver, 1993: 131).

A Personal Statement on the Threat of Indian Democracy

Nandy's response to Achin Vanaik in 'Closing the Debate on Secularism: A Personal Statement' (Nandy, 2002h) is part of a broader debate about the threat of democratic processes. For critics such as Vanaik, democracy remains an important feature of Indian political life. As Vanaik's critique of Nandy's 'anti-secular' position emphasises, secularism has been important for expanding the world's largest democracy. For Nandy, the more relevant question is how democratic pluralism, including the expansion of political representation has presented challenges to the operation of the secular ideal in Indian political culture. Writing in the aftermath of the horrific political violence witnessed in the Gujarat riots of 2002, Nandy re-affirms the need to confront the sustainability of the ideology of secularism in India. He argues that the atrocities witnessed in Gujarat 'should make us openly admit what we all secretly know but cannot publicly acknowledge' (Nandy, 2002h: 1). At this moment of forced engagement, there is for Nandy an invitation available to confront a secret. The national secret that cannot be publicly revealed and is voraciously defended against is the inability of secularism to safeguard tolerance and address social and political amity. Nandy questions whether the ideology of secularism contains the internal resources to address the threat of militancy, xenophobia and fanaticism witnessed in India. What is interesting about Nandy's confrontation and acknowledgement of this secret is that this knowledge about secularism is known but unable to be communicated in public life. Gabriel Schwab, in a different context has argued that when this knowledge operates as a national secret then 'it becomes a tacit knowledge, shared by everyone yet treated like a taboo subject' (Schwab, 2004: 186). Consistent with this public disavowal or repression Schwab confirms Nandy's experiences as an 'intimate enemy,' in noting that it is not surprising that 'people who bring it to the surface are often treated with passionate hostility as if they threatened a fragile sense of balance' (Schwab, 2004: 186). This too is the case with Nandy whose efforts to confront and expose this national secret threatens precarious process of self and national identification.

Nandy sets himself the task in the essay of analysing this defence further and the inability to publicly acknowledge the problems of secularism, outside of its obvious state of 'crisis.' This takes us back 'to square one,' to the birth of the independent Indian modern secular state. In addition to the socio-historical context, Nandy argues that violence, and in particular the violence witnessed in Gujarat cannot be viewed as an aberration. To do so not only perpetuates the silences that the 'national secret' preserves but also denies continuities within episodes of violence in Indian politics. For Nandy, there is continuity between the current outbreaks of violence in contemporary India, especially the events at Gujarat with the partition riots of 1946–48. According to Nandy this is evident in the way in which the violence took place, first originating in cities and then spreading to villages across Northern India. What also bears a 'family resemblance' is the way the Gujarat riots, like the riots of the Partition were supported and legitimated by an official public discourse of hatred. Acknowledging the complicity between the independent Indian postcolonial state's own process of *becoming* with these discourses of hatred, and the continuities of these discourses in defining Muslim and Hindu identities and communities in contemporary India, is nonetheless a confronting proposition. Nandy continues this willing confrontation by exposing these issues further whilst reflecting on the difficulties of confrontation. As has been discussed the 'autonomy of thought' that Nandy demonstrates, and the representations of him as an abject figure, including the attempts to criminalise his identity, come at a significant cost. The title of the essay 'A Personal Statement' provides a reflexive space for the critic to explore why confrontation is vital in the production of critique. This provides a space, outside of these existing discursive representations to continue to challenge and confront the resistances, the fantasies and defences, which prevent this national secret from being publicly acknowledged. If for instance, the 'secret' cannot be publicly acknowledged and attempts are being made to deauthorise and even criminalise the voice of the critic who attempts to bring this into public debate, then to what extent does the 'personal' realm emerge as a response? To what extent does Nandy use the 'personal' to counter the way his voice and identity as critic has been cast as threatening and disruptive, as a means of reclaiming subjectivity? That what he presents us within is a 'personal statement' also plays on the political private and public divide, and the inner and outer division, which his work problematises.

While Nandy's own doubts about the efficacy and sustainability of secularism have been met with suspicion, he argues that secularism's 'decline' is substantiated by empirical evidence. In consulting empirical evidence he confirms that for the first three decades of Independent India the record of secularism could not be disputed. The ideology of secularism did have an important role to play in establishing the independent post-colonial Indian nation state. However, in contemporary India an analysis of the role of secularism, including debating just what this role should be, has been foreclosed. What is 'strange' he tells us is that when he first raised doubts about secularism twenty-five years ago in an 'An Anti-Secularist Manifesto,' his position was 'already a cliché among activists and scholar-activists.' (Nandy, 2002h: 2). Nandy makes the argument that those who were involved directly in political and social movements already understood the issues raised in his essay. There was an existing consensus or rather diagnosis of the 'bad health' of secularism that cut across political and intellectual ideological boundaries. According to Nandy it is important to acknowledge that there was a prior recognition of these issues, but which at a certain point have become foreclosed by the continuing defence of the secular ideal.

The other concern that Nandy addresses in the essay is why this confrontation with the secular ideal, and the fantasy structure that accompanies its continuing defence, cannot be aired in public. Particularly, given that those working on the ground have already aired this in public. That this consensus cannot be publicly acknowledged after all this time, and during the period of post-Gujarat national reflection, becomes all the more arresting. There is a deeply imbedded defence mechanism at play, which for Nandy operates on individual and collective levels and across the private and public realms. The defence that operates blocks the possibility for confrontation, let alone a willing confrontation that he enters into. According to Nandy the differences of opinion that do exist amongst activists, public intellectuals, between the main political parties and even within the academic debates which have ensued, are more lateral in their focus. A greater emphasis is given to explaining the reasons and responses to this decline in the faith of secularism rather than confronting the psychological viability of the ideal itself. As he notes 'few have cared to argue or examine the issue of political cultural sustainability, which I thought would be of interest to even dedicated secularists.' This creates a characteristic limitation within the range of ideas and positions expressed in debate, creating in effect homogeneity in the dissenting viewpoints expressed.

The confrontation that Nandy *willingly* enters into is largely absent from these debates, as he distinguishes himself from other approaches and contributions. What characterises Nandy's contributions to these debates is this capacity to willingly confront the ideology of secularism and furthermore, in publicly acknowledging the necessity for confrontation. Articulated as a personal statement, he recognises that it is 'obviously an unpopular stance; it smacks of class-betrayal' (Nandy, 2002h: 10). Nandy defines confrontation as a form of betrayal in turning against one's class, and to this extent as a turning against parts of self. Why though is Nandy able to enter into this betrayal that distinguishes him, and turn against his class in this way? Although a direct answer to this question is not provided, an indirect response can be found in his analysis of why others are unable to follow through with the task of confrontation. In the case of critics the reluctance to enter into these processes of confrontation and subsequent denial of Nandy's own method of confrontation, can be explained in the following way. Nandy cautions that such a task is not an easy one but more importantly necessitates an internal dialogue. Critics' condemnation of Nandy's ability to do so, results in a counter-defensive argument.

As Nandy concedes condemnation is a defence mechanism 'because they have to fight it within themselves these conclusions they have drawn, *[and]* they feel disturbed, guilty and complicit when someone else brings them to the fore' (Nandy, 2002h: 2). The connection established here between an inner and outer confrontation is important for understanding the way the 'secret' about secularism is reinforced through a private (inside) and public (outside) border.

The personal and public threat is projected onto Nandy, whose own willing confrontation and betrayal must be defended against. These defences and projections are for Nandy part of more complex and deeper resistances to confronting aspects of postcolonial Indian identity, and the psychoanalytic 'turning inwards' that such questions necessitate. The resistances prevent these issues from being publicly acknowledged and also demonstrate an inability to 'work through' the cultural and psychic resistances that otherwise block an appreciation of the damage and distortions that the ideology of secularism has entailed. The intensity of this defence is for Nandy demonstrated by theorists like Mukul Kesavan, who in order to protect his familiar world 'stretches the meaning of secularism to include in it all forms of non-communal attitudes'[2] (Nandy, 2002h: 10). For Nandy figures like Kesavan and to this he adds Achin Vanaik, these defences, including their defence against him, 'act as forms of exorcism' (Nandy, 2002h: 2). For Nandy though, this 'exorcism,' functions as foreclosure and to that extent remains as a defence of secularism and moreover, a psychic defence. In continuing to recognise that secularism is a withered concept, even if this is in private, whilst maintaining a public commitment to the ideology, generates enough internal conflict and anxiety of its own accord. The process of internalisation, that maintains the disjuncture between tacit knowledge and public knowledge, generates its own discontents, irrespective of whether this is projected onto the phobic object. As Nandy maintains, this internal conflict is a dynamic that continues on its own accord irrespective of the role of the phobic object in these debates. As the critical analytic voice that stands outside of these psychic structures Nandy reiterates that, 'that they know what they do not want to know and fight against this,' perpetuates these defensive 'counter-phobic' attitudes (Nandy, 2002h: 2).

The anxiety that defines these internal dynamics is connected to a larger external issue. One that Nandy concedes has little to do with his own intellectual position or even his status as the threatening and disruptive figure in these debates. The complexity of these internal defences (internal to both self and nation) needs to be conceptualised within the larger threat that Indian democracy presents. For, concepts of democratic pluralism along with democratic processes also threaten these precarious cultural and psychic structures of defence. Moreover, this fear of democracy or a fear of the people disrupts accepted boundaries because it threatens the inclusions and exclusions operating in Indian political culture. For Nandy the homogenising and standardising features of the secular ideal are confronted by democratic pluralism. The threat of pluralism is not unique to India but symptomatic of a 'fear of democracy' underlining democratic culture itself in modern liberal democracies. For Nandy this fear is a feature of all modern liberal democracies. In the work of the political theorist Chantal Mouffe this fear is described through what she terms is the 'democratic paradox (Mouffe, 2000). In *The Democratic Paradox* (2000) Mouffe argues that this paradox ensures the continuation of these tensions as an antagonistic feature of politics. This fear then can also be understood alongside the paradox that exists within all liberal democratic societies. For Mouffe this paradox, a necessary feature of all democratic societies is useful because it denotes a continuing dynamic that cannot necessarily be resolved. In Mouffe's work this antagonism is critiqued in favour of an agonistic account of politics, as a field of struggle where contesting groups with opposing interests vie for hegemony. Mouffe argues that by denying the existence of partisan adversarial interests based on collective identities, modern liberalism has foreclosed the symbolic space for such conflicts to occur.[3]

In Nandy's account the importance of this antagonism and the alternatives that can be preserved within public life is paramount. Nandy's 'anti-secular' critique reiterates the ways in which the symbolic space of debating secularism has been truncated, and its distortions threaten to compromise democratic pluralism and democratic processes. In 'An Anti-Secularist Manifesto' Nandy affirms that democratic processes have expanded representation in Indian politics, as excluded peripheral and abjected voices are finding a place in politics.[4] Over the last twenty years political representation has expanded significantly and the secular state has been increasingly unable to screen those entering politics for their commitment to the secular ideal. For Nandy, this has the effect of regenerating democratic pluralism given that these processes have placed distinct limits on secularisation within India. Nandy adds to this with 'now that secularisation of the Indian polity has gone far, the scope of secularism as a creed has declined.' There is in his analysis another paradox that is identifiable. He explores this as part of what he terms the secular paradox, that secularism as an ideology can only thrive in a society which is predominantly non-secular and that when the dynamics of that society begin to change through secularisation, then the political status of secularism changes. Nandy's questioning continues as he asks: 'And in a democracy what kinds of rights do you grant to ordinary citizens? How do you de-expertise a democracy?' (Nandy and Deftereos, 2005b: 7). Such questions must be seriously addressed if the democratic paradox is to be worked through. This paradox and its accompanying features of antagonism, for Nandy create the possibility for a working through to take place, and in the process challenge established inclusions and exclusions operating in politics. The following statement supports this concept of antagonism in politics:

> In some fundamental sense this combination of the ability to tolerate and live with enormous diversities, and simultaneously use an open political system to change or alter existing intra-communal social relations, existing social relations and hierarchies has been the real clue to the success of democracy and the democratic experiment in India. (Nandy and Deftereos, 2005d: 10)

The success of the democratic experiment in the world's largest democracy is contingent though, like in all liberal democracies, on its own internal capacities and resources to negotiate this paradox. In Mouffe's account of the democratic paradox and in Nandy's analysis of the Indian context this process of negotiation is always a complex task. As Mouffe explains, it is not just a question of abandoning a political ideal, for 'pluralism also means the end of a substantive idea of the good life, what Claude Lefort calls 'the dissolution of the markers of certainty' (Mouffe, 2000: 18). Nandy too recognises the complexity of these processes in confronting, working through and abandoning the secular ideal. However, in his account the distortions of the ideology, and its accepted state of 'crisis' already represent the evidence needed that secularism is at 'the twilight of certitudes.' While the cultural and psychological viability of secularism is dubious, both Mouffe and Nandy acknowledge that pluralism itself implies a profound transformation in the symbolic ordering of social relations. Nandy, like Mouffe recognises the possibility carried forward within concepts of democratic pluralism to disrupt the borders of inclusion and exclusion in Indian political culture and to transform these relations.

Despite the emphasis Nandy places on the ways democratic processes confront and destabilise the markers of certainty, the threat of
democracy, as a fear of the people remains. People though do bring
into politics a range of peculiarities, ambiguities, contradictions,
competing ethical systems, including views and knowledge systems
considered non-modern. For Nandy, pluralism of this kind is also expressed through different accounts of subjectivity and of Indianness
and carries forward the possibility of radically destabilising inclusions and exclusions in political culture. These threats play out within
Indian political culture and amongst intellectuals debating these
issues, as an inability to accept ambivalence and pluralism. The defensive response to these threats, as demonstrated in the Hindu nationalist movement, is to contain and abject ambivalence and pluralism.
As Nandy explains, 'a lot of people have wanted democracy but also
wanted the people to democratically choose what they want them to
choose!' (Nandy and Deftereos, 2005d: 2). Though importantly this
is not exclusively an Indian experience but part of the global experience with democracy, this attempt to foreclose the dynamism of
democratic processes and contain the uncertainty of the paradox
finds expression in two dominant political assumptions. These assumptions also work to affirm established boundaries of inclusion
and exclusion operating in politics. The first assumption operating
in defence of this view is that those who do not speak the language
of secularism are unfit for citizenship. Thus from this perspective
there is a need to re-affirm that which must be abjected, excluded
and prohibited from politics. The second assumption that follows is
that those who do speak the language of state secularism have 'the
sole right to determine what true democratic principles, governance
and religious tolerance are' (Nandy, 2004a: 118). However, for Nandy
to accept democratic pluralism, including the paradox of democracy,
is to recognise that the disruptive interests, preferences and choices
of the non-modern peripherals are part of politics. This for Nandy
is connected to recognising the subjectivity of the non-modern peripheral as political, and not in exclusionary terms to cast them as
Seyla Benhabib acknowledges as pre-political subjects. There is then
a connection between recognising difference within subjectivity that
is imperative to pluralism and democratic politics.[5]

Nandy concedes that recognising the non-modern peripheral as a
political subject, and as central to working through the democratic
paradox, is a confronting issue. In his reading this is complicated further by the fact that 'they [the secularists] want India to be diverse

but only as long as that diversity is subservient to Modernity' (Nandy, 2004c: 2). The defensive logic that prevails is intimately tied to the modern features of Indian political culture and to a modern self, a modern Indianness that is fiercely protected. To challenge and confront these constitutive features is radically destabilising on both national and on personal levels as a dominant and preferred self-understanding and self-representation is threatened. Nandy explains the threat of confrontation in the following way. He states:

> ...that such knowledge might lead to large-scale displacement or uprooting in the domain of intellectual work, that the familiar world of knowing might shrink, if not collapse and, in the new world that may come into being, there would be less space for the likes of us. (Nandy, 2003: 1)

What will be my place in a non-secular or non-modern world? Nandy rhetorically asks mimicking the voices of 'India's newly empowered urban middle class *[who]* just cannot conceive of a good society without its ideas and itself at the helm' (Nandy, 2003: 1). Consistent with the ego-defence at play, there is a narcissistic feature to this defence. For protecting and defending against the ontological threat of disrupting and boundaries of subjectivity is the role of the ego. Nandy argues that this powerful psychic investment in the defensive structure, protecting a dominant account of self, is analogous to Freud's account of the inescapable human fantasy of immortality. This fantasy is governed by a narcissistic ego questioning whether 'will and more importantly *can* life continue after my death?' In Nandy's analysis there is a similar narcissistic fantasy structure operating in the defence of the secular ideal operating within Indian political culture and in the intellectual culture that theorists like Achin Vanaik, seek to preserve.

Thus far what is discernable from Nandy's reply to Achin Vanaik is that confrontation takes place on a number of different levels in his work. This includes a willingness to confront the secular ideal and the complicity of this ideal in the violence of Gujarat. Confrontation is explained as a personal statement as Nandy enters into a confrontation with aspects of his self, including the expectations of his class. Confrontation also takes place in working through the fear of democratic pluralism and the democratic paradox that underpins all modern liberal democracies. Nandy's own reflections of these confrontations indicate that this takes place as something more than autonomy of thought. These processes of confrontation and working through complex individual and collective defences, are central to

Nandy's psychoanalytic approach to generating social and political criticism. Confrontation and working through reference processes that enable the defence to be identified and explored in order to reveal what is being covered over by the defence. There are strong affinities between working through in a psychoanalytic therapy and the way Nandy works through the cultural and psychic resistances within self and society, that otherwise block an appreciation of the damage and distortions that the ideology of the Indian secular state has entailed. The discussion continues as to how this takes place in Nandy's 'personal statement' to Achin Vanaik.

The voice of the political psychologist offers four different possible diagnostic features given for secularism's ill health and decline. For Nandy, rather than confronting and working through this decline, a series of diagnoses and rationalisations emerge. This is a further point that distinguishes Nandy's aptitude for confrontation, especially in confronting the positioning of the boundaries of debate. The first diagnosis is from the Hindu nationalists who claim that secularism's decline is due to the political appeasement of minority interests, particularly from the Gandhians on the Left. This reactionary attitude against ambivalence, difference and pluralism emanates from a perceived internalised wound or discrimination, which such nationalists claim Hindus have experienced. They carry forward a belief that secularism of the kind demonstrated within Indian politics has been biased against Hindus, notably with the introduction of the Hindu Code Bill after Independence. The reaction in simplified terms then finds expression in militant calls for genuine secularism as opposed to the pseudo-secularism they claim has been witnessed in India. For Nandy, 'the policies and actions of the Hindu nationalists may often have not been secular, but a part of their soul has always been' (Nandy, 2003: 1). Cast again as an internal question the complexities of this political subjectivity have been discussed in relation to the zealot, who epitomises the self-loathing projected towards one's disavowed cultural self, along with a more generalised hatred and fear of difference.

The second diagnosis offered is that secularism given half the chance, that is, if governed and nurtured by the right kind of people would still prosper. This solution is for Nandy 'offered by the loveable innocents,' whose innocence is preserved by the repetition of the pursuit of secular ideal. For these innocents, which Nandy identifies as the historian Mushirul Hasan, the sociologist Dipankar Gupta and journalist Praful Bidwani 'heavier doses of the same medicine, is the only possible remedy for the ailment called religious violence' (Nandy, 2002h: 5). In addition to the fantasy that secularism remains the solution to inter-religious tolerance and amity is that the violence witnessed is definable by its religious and not political characteristics. Nandy contradicts this in arguing that this violence is not a symptom of a non-modern, regressive, traditional and religious India.

The third response is an extension of this diagnosis by those who maintain that the Indian state has never been entirely secular and policies of appeasement demonstrated towards minorities have pre-vented this ideal from being realised. This is linked to the fear of the divisiveness of minorities and the diversity which religious and eth-nic plurality introduces into a nation state. Therefore all religions and ethnic divisions become hurdles to nation building and state forma-tion, and as dangers to the State and political processes. According to this view the State has made a series of consistent concessions start-ing with political slogans of 'equal respect for all religions' or 'sarva-dharma-samabhava.' The remedy is in a tough dose of Western style secular tolerance. Nandy alludes to wanting to be sympathetic to such a response, for he recognises this as an easier option, but in hav-ing confronted the abject and traversed the fantasy, he is unable to return to this position. For, behind the compliance to this fantasy of security provided by the secular state are deeper attachments to the ideological formation of the nation state. Nandy states:

> the kind of agency and coherence often imputed to these impersonal enti-ties *[the State]* is usually a projection of our inner needs and anthropomor-phic fantasies of a parental state; such feel good attributions are a tribute to our trusting nature rather than to political acumen. (Nandy, 2003: 2)

This psychic investment in the state and state apparatuses creates a dependency and attachment that Nandy questions and ultimately, is unwilling to accept. Moreover, this trusting nature or 'blind faith' that secularism demands and that secures attachments to the State is theorised by Nandy as constituting a dangerous psychic state. Nandy describes this attachment by using what the psychologist Rollo May defines as a psychic state of 'pseudo-innocence' (May, 1972). The illusion established by this trusting nature and its conditions can be explained through May's concept of 'pseudo-innocence.' In May's work this references a narcissistic defence that takes one back, psy-chologically speaking to an infantile psychic state. For May, it is a childlike naiveté, riddled with insecurity that covers over the possi-bility of confronting questions too provocative or horrendous for the

self to contemplate. The defence takes over to protect the self to preserve an existing psychic state. May explains, 'we tend to shrink into
this kind of innocence and make a virtue of powerlessness, weakness
and helplessness' (May, 1972: 49). In Nandy's critique applying this
concept of 'pseudo innocence' to understand the defence of secularism, alerts us to the dangers of this position. For, it validates a fantasy structure, and a concept of a helpless self, that forecloses the
impetus to confront perceived and real dangers to selfhood. For 'it is
this innocence that cannot come to terms with the destructiveness in
one's self or others…that becomes self-destructive' (May, 1972: 49). In
Nandy's analysis, it is a 'pseudo-innocence' that underpins the defence
of state secularism and that state secularism can safeguard tolerance
and amity in India. To support this position and to continue to defend
it is therefore, to fall back into a psychic state of pseudo-innocence.
It represents a deferral of power to an external ideal, which continues
to prove ineffectual in politics but also does so at the expense of our
individual and collective capacities to negotiate subjectivity, including
our own. This psychic position is a stark contrast to the more creative
possibility of an 'authentic innocence' that May distinguishes. In contrast to the concept of 'pseudo-innocence' this 'authentic innocence' is
a different psychic state that relies not on a fantasy structure but a dynamic interplay between parts of self. It is this latter expression of innocence that Nandy advocates as creative and a more complex form
of psychic organisation, central to a dynamic account of subjectivity.

The final diagnosis offered for the decline in secularism comes
from the part of society that does acknowledge that Indian experiences of secularism cannot be those of Europe's. Nandy suggests
that this is a 'post-secular awareness' that enters into the debates
(Nandy, 2003: 2). More significantly, this awareness emerges though
from having worked through the realities of the democratic paradox,
rather than maintaining fantasies of Indian democracy and Indian
political culture, along with the experiences of democratic pluralism.
This awareness acknowledges the presence of alternative subjectivities, including aspects of Indian selfhood or a cultural self, abjected
by a secular ideology. Therefore, according to this view the ideology
of secularism can only have a superficial presence in Indian politics
and political culture. Affording secularism a superficial status in Indian
democracy though would entail an acceptance that pluralism and
diversity within a democracy includes all kinds of citizens. This final
diagnosis remains threatening and disruptive because it challenges
existing structures of inclusion and exclusion in politics. As Nandy

explains, 'if you allow me the right to my own cliché, these are societies that enjoy the luxury of electing their political leaders periodically but alas, to the chagrin of their progressive academics, not the right to elect their people' (Nandy, 2002h: 5). This position reinforces what Mouffe describes is 'the typical illusion of pluralism without antagonism' (Mouffe, 2000: 20).

In the final parts of the article Nandy reflects on the intellectual culture and his positioning within it. He notes that within such a defensive culture his own contributions to debate cannot be accepted as a constructive contribution, given that it is predicated upon a confrontation of these very defences. Is this the symptomatic register foreclosing the possibilities of confrontation and working through? Nandy's position is nonetheless unequivocally made despite its contested value to the debates on secularism. As he concludes, 'I have given a pathologist's report and declared the patient incurable' (Nandy, 2002g: 2). This is a diagnosis and intellectual position that has been arrived out through a serious and complex confrontation with the secular ideal, despite critics' assertions otherwise. More importantly, it is not he who qualifies for a plea for 'euthanasia' (Nandy, 2002g: 2). For Nandy the time has come to 'give up on the patient and look towards a new generation of concepts' (Nandy, 2002g: 2). What distinguishes his confrontation from other theorists is that this confrontation, rejection and traversal of the secular ideal are as he describes also executed 'with a touch of glee, without obediently shedding tears for secularism' (Nandy, 2002g: 2). Vanaik 'the Sikh Samurai never lost for words' has wasted his breath in his efforts to redress Nandy's confrontation. Nandy acknowledges critics' dissatisfaction with him when he states that, 'critics have reasons to be bitter that I do not want to save my skin under their expert guidance, by declaring my allegiance to the textbooks and ritual the benevolent guides have borrowed for my benefit from Europe's past' (Nandy, 2002g: 2). Nandy thus maintains the integrity of his commitment to confrontation through his formal reply to Vanaik. This though does not prevent him from acknowledging the difficulties of this position. For as he states, 'I am perfectly willing to accept that this alternative might be second-rate' (Nandy, 2002g: 2). He cautions that is not because he believes that people deserve a second rate solution. Rather it is because living in a democracy and in *working through* and *living with* the democratic paradox, 'we have no option but to build upon the second-rate that the majority prefers' (Nandy, 2002g: 2). The inability of critics to accept his position is all the more revealing of the defence mechanisms operating given that 'studies of resistance at the ground level' repeatedly confirm his view. 'It is not my fault,' he confronts 'that these secularists fear their own data and experiences' (Nandy, 2002g: 2). The defence is also reinforced through what Gyandera Pandey has argued are the complicated relations with western knowledge in the development of the social sciences in India.

Nandy identifies three irreconcilable contradictions that he argues need to at least be recognised, even if critics are not prepared to confront and traverse the sanctity of the secular ideal within these debates. First, if the boundaries between religion and politics are so easily distinguishable then why do secular Indians invoke the non-secular into concepts of selfhood? Why for instance, is a political figure like Nehru only remembered and celebrated as the ideal secular statesman, when his own identity and political personality is far more complex? 'Many [Nandy included] have been forced to search for new heroes who would make some sense to ordinary citizens' (Nandy, 2003: 2). The second contradiction that remains unresolved is in response to the boundaries defining the debates of secularism. To defend the secular position is as he suggests a destructive form of innocence not least because critique and debate, and the normative boundaries of debate are not confronted. He asserts that, 'secularism has become the last refuge of the intellectually lazy, of those who refuse to confront the logic of their own political and cultural choices' (Nandy, 2003: 2). The deferral to a defensive and persecutory logic reinforces the internal resistances to an analysis of these issues within this intellectual culture. The third and final contradiction is that in confronting secularism as a sterile source of social creativity, he enters into a critical and psychoanalytic engagement with theses secular icons and ideal types. In not being invested in the defence of secularism, 'by doing so, I believe that I have taken the secularists more seriously than they have done themselves' (Nandy, 2003: 2). This provides Nandy with the conditions to explore the peripheral and creative forms of resistance, which continue to exist within India, against the pathologies of state secularism (Nandy, 2003: 2). In defence of his own position and by way of expanding on the features of his confrontation, he says the following about his approach. 'I have built on what creative, successful resistance against such pathologies has done and said it has done over the centuries, rather than on the ideological baggage secular fundamentalists have thrust on it' (Nandy, 2003: 2).

Nandy's intellectual commitment continues around developing the resistances and human potentiality to be found in Indian democracy and within post-secular forms of awareness. This commitment continues alongside the recognition that in the culture of democracy his efforts remain threatening and disruptive. Irrespective of this threat, Nandy's own resistance, defiance and confrontation are unrelenting and consistently affirmed in the essay. He maintains his '...vague, anxious suspicion that much of the citizenry might not need vanguards, experts in multiculturalism, or ideologically-drive, politically correct, Orwellian thought police' (Nandy, 2005f: 1). Where this personal statement to Achin Vanaik addresses the threat of democratic pluralism, operating at the threshold of Indian politics, Nandy's reply to Kuldip Nayar directly responds to the fear of a post-secular awareness that operates in Indian political culture.

BOUNDARY CROSSINGS: TRAVERSING THE FEAR OF THE POST-SECULAR

Having confronted the threat posed by democratic pluralism in his response to Achin Vanaik, Nandy turns to explore the fear of post-secular forms of awareness. Written in 2005, three years after his reply to Vanaik, the article 'The Return of the Sacred: Post-Secular Reflections on the Language of Religion and the Fear of Democracy' responds to Kuldip Nayar's criticisms levelled at him in the 2004 exchange, and functions as a platform for re-affirming his commitment to confrontation. Nandy revisits the question of the psychological viability of secularism in an age where religion returns in Indian politics now in a pathological form. Religion he tells us, '...has re-emerged at the end of what could only be called an age of ideologies, not in its pristine form but bearing the imprint of the age of secular ideologies' (Nandy, 2005f: 1). In Nandy's analysis religion returns in politics carrying the wounds of the processes of subjection. Nandy argues that since the beginning of the twenty-first century and across many democracies 'religion has become a phoenix that has risen from its own ashes and now wears the ashes as a sign of its new triumph' (Nandy, 2005f: 2).

The reasons for the return of religion and the conditions of return are widely debated. Nandy adds to the reasons in noting that issues like the ills of globalisation, the excesses of consumer society, uncritical individualism, the growth of violence including gratuitous violence, and the decline in the sanctity of life are all relevant factors. In the Indian context though what also bears significance is that a number of modern values held sacrosanct are 'losing their shine' as new forms of dominance and despotism are taking shape (Nandy, 2005f: 1). This return to religion must similarly be recognised as a response 'for the excesses of secularisation during the last one hundred and fifty years in human affairs' (Nandy, 2005f: 2). It is not the disputes, as popular opinion maintains, simply a case of the ethnic backwaters of India advocating this return and who in having remained untouched by the processes of modernisation and secularisation are yet to catch up with a dominant political culture. Even if populist opinion is accepted this does not adequately account for the conditions of this return. Is this return of religion in contemporary Indian political life the reassertion of faith or is it the return of a pathological expression of religion as ideology? In asking these sorts of questions Nandy disrupts what he sees as a facile separation between religion and politics maintained by secularists. In noting that religion returns as re-made political identities, he confronts the political conditions of this return.

The remedy is not with single-key solutions or with perfect institutions and systems. Rather in Nandy's account the vernacular of political certitudes and the search for ideal solutions is part of the problem. For all world-views, whether one acknowledges the Enlightenment vision or the alternative cosmology of the non-modern peripherals via the sacred and religious, have this capacity for inclusion and exclusion. What does distinguish these non-modern visions of the good life is that this subjectivity has the potential to challenge these divisions. According to Nandy 'seemingly these visions convert a part of the drive for power to a drive for power over self, particularly over the unacceptable parts of one's self' (Nandy, 1987a: xviii). These non-modern visions of the good life have the effect of creating a confrontation within the self. It is this psychoanalytic focus that is celebrated as the inclusions disrupt these power relations. This is not to say however, that inclusions and exclusions are eradicated but that there is a greater complexity afforded to the self in this perspective, and by extension self/other relations. There is a vital recognition and awareness within this internal focus, internal to subjectivity and culture, with what Nandy terms is an isomorphism at play. Elsewhere, Nandy has described his use of the concept of isomorphism, crudely speaking as an awareness that 'what we do to others we do not only to ourselves but also to our cognitive ventures' (Nandy, 1987a: xviii). This emphasises the psychoanalytic focus of Nandy's perspective and the ways that these internal dynamics can restructure subjectivity and inter-subjective relations. The recognition of this dialectic at play in the non-modern peripheral between these outer and inner powers is fundamental to understanding the confrontation Nandy is interested in. This requires a different configuration of selfhood.

For Nandy the non-modern peripheral carries forward a post-secular awareness present in these alternative non-modern ethical and knowledge systems. This awareness is not present in the return of religion as ideology. For as explored in his critique of secularism, the internal resources and psychic state of the Hindu nationalists or the zealot, is similar to the modern political secularism. The use of violence for political advantage is central to both these groups. Violence in any form, including violence to self, is in Nandy's account incompatible with the appeal to internal resources that he makes. It is important to note that even when violence is adopted as a political tool, it is still radically disruptive to subjectivity and the boundaries of political culture.[6] For violence in its extreme form represents in the most confronting way the collapse of limits; the limits between self and other and the collapse or loss of the sanctity of life. In Kristeva's *Powers of Horror* (1982) she explains that 'of things abject, the corpse is the most abject' (Kristeva in Humphrey, 2002: 17). Political violence of the kind witnessed in contemporary Indian life, particularly over the last decade, is for Nandy a violation, or the most positively negative sign of the abject functioning. This is a violation to social relations and to self, where total disintegration of subjectivity or abjection is made possible. While violence alerts us to the threat of abjection in an immediate and horrifying way, he radically questions whether this violence is attributable to the return of religion. Nandy qualifies though that while religious violence does take place, comparatively it has not caused the loss of life in nearly the same numbers that secular states have been responsible for.[7] The solution that he is interested in developing takes place through yet another confrontation. As he claims, 'however uncomfortable the thought might be the intellectual challenge of our times may well be to identify the means—the institutional structures and personality resources—that can reconcile diversity with exclusions that are not radically destructive or driven by hatred' (Nandy, 2005f: 2). This 'tolerable ethnocentrism' is in Nandy's reading, an inevitable part of a living culture. This is controversial in his work… This intellectual commitment to identifying the means (within the self and within Indian culture) to address questions of diversity and pluralism in less destructive terms forms the main argument of the article. Nandy, therefore confronts the underside of Indian democracy—the language and cosmology of religion—in order to work through these possibilities.

If one is to have access to 'a huge majority of those staying in the God-forsaken parts of the world' then religion cannot be abjected from view. Nandy argues that in places like Latin America, Africa and Asia, people have partial or no access to the language of secularism and citizenship (Nandy, 2005f: 2). Without some minimal contact with this language and cosmology then one is reduced to a spectator of politics in most parts of the southern world. The spectator for Nandy occupies the privileged voice of inclusion and dominance, then bemoans the regressive and irrational choices that the abject and 'irresponsible electorates' make (Nandy, 2005f: 2). It is doubtful whether this spectator of politics has the capacity including the internal psychic resources, to recognise and publicly acknowledge this democratic right of every citizen to bring into public life the language or cosmology of their own choosing. Can another ethical framework and knowledge system be tolerated, given that as already discussed 'the framework may not satisfy the criteria set up by his or her earnest well wishers?' (Nandy, 2005f: 2). The confrontation with the abject irresponsible electorates becomes intertwined with a confrontation with an alternative world-view. The message is that once you accept that citizens will bring their own visions of a good life into politics then you cannot, as Nandy says, attempt to police this. You cannot ensure that the good parts are brought into public life and the bad parts are abjected from public view and democratic political processes. The spirit of accommodation that Kuldip Nayar accuses Nandy of misrecognising within the secular ideal is for Nandy a feature of democratic processes and not as Nayar would believe attributed to the ideology of secularism.

Nandy argues that there are homegrown, hybrid and multiple versions of this spirit of accommodation already present within religious communities. Confronting the fear of the post-secular is to recognise the pluralism and diversity that exists within India. The intrusion and disruption that religion brings is that it draws political attention to these competing ethical and knowledge systems. Another aspect to the fear of this post-secular is with the ecumenical and the scope of disruption it can cause given that for Nandy 'such dialogues of faith can transcend history'[8] (Nandy, 2005f: 6). These anxieties and fears become all the more annihilating, 'particularly when combined with the fear and contempt for the people and their worldviews and categories that have constituted the underside of both democratic politics and political radicalism for at least two hundred years in much of the world' (Nandy, 2005f: 7).

The cost of not confronting this underside is that India's cultural past along with the pluralism of Indian democracy remains unacknowledged and can manifest in pathological form. This cultural past includes distinctive traditions of cosmopolitanism and plural accounts of subjective and inter-subjective relations that exist in India and which constitute an all-together different spirit of accommodation.[9] At stake are these alternative political imaginaries that exist within India's cultural pasts. An interesting example of this effort to preserve these alternative political imaginaries is developed in Nandy's essays collected in *An Ambiguous Journey to the City* (2001). Here, he links the return to the village from the city as often a search for alternative cosmopolitanism and, 'that cosmopolitanism has a place for the humble vernacular, often incompatible with any iconography of the nation state, with the compulsions of the global market, and with the demands of a global knowledge industry' (Nandy, 2001: ix.) Nandy notes, 'human beings have invested some of their best cognitive and affective resources in the spiritual and the religious' (Nandy, 2005f: 8). He is again willing to acknowledge, but not to accept the fear and threat that accompanies this creative post-secular awareness as an alternative political imaginary, and the need to defend against this possibility of disruption to an existing political imaginary with what he terms is a principled forgetting. Given his confrontation, this remains a source of tension in people's willingness to forget the secular world's capacity to endorse evil, yet retain their fear of religion in any form and its capacity to endorse evil. As he states, 'civilization, as we know it, is largely the achievement of the religious way of life, though we try hard to forget that part of the story' (Nandy, 2005f: 8). In continuing to submit to the repression and processes of disavowal at play then 'how' he asks, 'can we acknowledge the achievements of a part of our self that the Enlightenment vision has declared a terra incognita?' (Nandy, 2005f: 8).

The other confrontation Nandy brings to Nayar's criticisms is in recognising the internal built-in contradiction to his own argument. While he continues to build a case for understanding the religious worldview as 'a means of entering popular consciousness and the normative frames that shape the democratic process,' his account equally recognises the ambivalence this leaves in its wake (Nandy, 2005f: 9). Though arguably not threatened by the possibility, which this ambivalence brings in regenerating the boundaries of the political, Nandy does concede that, '... it remains an open question how far this worldview and normative frames directly shape democratic choices and how far they are mediated or altered by the packaged interpretations of religion floating around in the public sphere' (Nandy, 2005f: 9). This open question for Nandy does not justify the reproduction of these defensive and narcissistic structures.

For learning to live with difference, ambiguity and contradiction is essential to the complexities of human subjectivity and in our capacity to extend a hand to the other. Similarly, a more fluid and ambivalent interpretation of religion is offered, which he suggests carries forward an awareness of these complexities, thus displacing a dominant concept of religion as ideology from the political. In reinvoking a key Gandhian tenet, this entails a confrontation with high versus low accounts of religiosity, particularly in the fight against the re-brahminisation of belief. It is what he terms the low brow, folksy and non-canonical accounts imbedded in everyday vernacular and practices that challenge the lack of the spirit of accommodation present in politics. Yet while this intellectual culture perceives this as an embarrassing challenge, for Nandy it is in bypassing this very division between high/low, which can lead to a regeneration of meaning. This process can lead to a reconfiguration of selfhood and to a cognitive and political space of human sensitivity. As he explains,

> ...The real challenge is to bypass this division and discover the frames of sensitivity within which the respect for – and celebration of – the unthinking casual, everyday forms of religiosity converge with serious scholarly visions of a sacralised cosmos and sanctity of life. Let me call it the first step towards a post-secular social and political awareness. (Nandy, 2005f: 10)

This is an analogous plea to what Mouffe identifies is the need for democracy to become dialogic, in order to actuate this possibility for human sensitivity in the politics. This coincides with her call for a life of politics capable of confronting and incorporating a 'democracy of emotions' into its repertoire (Mouffe, 2000: 15). In Nandy's rendition the dialogic feature of democracy would facilitate the incorporation of diversity, including post-secular frames of sensitivity and aware-ness into political culture. This post-secular awareness as highlight-ed carries forward a disruptive element, none the least because of its emphasis on the internal aspects of self and culture. It implies an al-together different internal reflexivity for the self and within a culture, in which the possibility of transforming the boundaries between self and other, public and private, secular and non-secular are reaffirmed. Reclaiming this possibility is central to Nandy's argument and arrived at through his psychoanalytic approach. For Nandy a similar way to working through carried out in a psychoanalytic therapy, also works through the cultural and psychic resistances that otherwise block an appreciation of the damage and distortions that the ideology of the Indian secular state has entailed. For Nandy, it is like the psychoanalyst's interpretation of the patient. Even when the interpretation is wrong it is therapeutic because it ensures self-reflection. Diversity expands the range of human cognition and re-establishes an open dialogue between knowledge and feelings, even when it includes the bizarre and eccentric. (Nandy and Jahanbegloo, 2006: 68)

Nandy's position can be understood as an invitation to explore the dialogic features of democracy, to live with difference, ambivalence and pluralism and in doing so to work with these dynamics. In reflecting on the criticisms already made of him by Nayar, Nandy suggests, 'readers may like to look up more serious scholars on the subject' (Nandy, 2005f: 11). These issues however, extend beyond the territorial anxieties of the Indian intelligentsia and Nandy's contested place within it. This fear of the post-secular in Nandy's account is intimately tied to the complexities of the democratic paradox. In this account it is both the pluralism of the people along with their own internal resources that can transform the positioning of the boundaries constituting politics. In advocating this view in his two replies to Achin Vanaik and Kuldip Nayar, Nandy locates his analysis at the threshold of politics, and within the possibility of a new political imaginary.

THE POSSIBILITY OF AN ALTERNATIVE POLITICAL IMAGINARY

It is important to emphasise that Nandy's willingness to confront aspects of Indian identity and political culture deemed abject, is not an effort to eradicate abjection. Rather Nandy's efforts are located in recognising the positioning of boundaries constituting individual and collective subjectivities, and in preserving the possibility of challenging and regenerating subjectivity. This extends to the possibility of transforming our relationship to our selves and to others. Noelle McAfee raises a pertinent question in relation to Kirsteva's work, and the point is equally relevant for understanding Nandy's critical intervention in questioning secularism. McAfee questions whether it is even possible or even desirable to rid us of abjection? For 'without abjection, would personal and political identity (self-same and different from others) [even] be possible?' (McAfee, 2004: 124). I have argued that Nandy's willingness to confront that which is abjected from a dominant Indian secular political imaginary, and to traverse the threats posed by the democratic paradox and the post secular, is underpinned by his sensitivity to the ways that processes of internalisation and externalisation. Nandy's capacity to raise these issues and his analysis of the ways in political identities are formed.

Although Nandy does not articulate his efforts in these terms I have argued that these psychoanalytic concepts enable us to conceptualise Nandy's own psychoanalytic focus further. In confronting the abject there is a possibility for an alternative in this moment though, and it is this moment of reconstituting meaning and subjectivity that Nandy willingly confronts in his critique. In doing so Nandy's approach can be further understood with what Julia Kristeva notes is 'the double time of abjection' (McAfee, 2004: 121.) As Kristeva clarifies while abjection is 'a time of oblivion and thunder, of veiled infinity' it is simultaneously also 'the moment when revelation bursts forth' (Kristeva in McAfee, 2004: 121). In other words while it is overwhelmingly threatening and destabilising to confront that which is abject and traverse the security of the secular fantasy, this moment is as Nandy's critique of secularism demonstrates, also a moment of possible transformation. It is a possibility to re-position and transform the positioning of established boundaries of meaning: secularism and religion, the public and private and self and the other. In Nandy's work this leads to a regenerated understanding of politics in which the ambivalence, contradiction and pluralism within human subjectivity and Indian traditions is afforded political recognition.

Politics for Nandy is intimately and necessarily so, tied to 'the challenge of the breaking down and the reconstitutions of the imaginary field that defines a society' (Sjoholm, 2005: 81). This leads in his work to a radically different understanding of politics. In Mouffe's work what is identified as the fear of the antagonistic feature of democracy, should be allowed expression she argues in an agonistic form, in order to preserve the vital tensions between consensus and dissent. Here the drawing of boundaries between 'we/they' must be done so in ways that are compatible with the pluralism constitutive of democracy. Nandy, too, is not interested in eradicating the tensions within Indian democracy and Indian politics. For it is within these dynamic tensions that the very conditions of the political culture he is interested in fostering are to be found. This is not an idealised vision of a pre-modern India returning to view, as perhaps some of his critics might claim, but a confrontation with the ways this pre-modern India continues to exist in tension with the modern. This willingness to question what has been abjected in service of self whether this is an individual or national self is a distinctive feature of Nandy as critic. For Nandy this is where the threatening democratic paradox and the pluralism within Indian democracy is not contained or reconciled but *lived* with. It is also where traversing the fear of the post-secular leads to a 'multiverse dialogue' between disavowed parts of one's self, including one's cultural self. This also brings us back to the question of the fear of democracy and the need for democratic pluralism and the 'multiverse dialogue' within democracy to be lived with.[10] These processes are nonetheless confronting and not without considerable internal struggle and resistance. For Nandy, the ability to extend a hand to the other is only ever possible when the disavowed, repressed and abjected parts of one's own subjectivity, one's own radical alterity is confronted. What is possible externally within a political imaginary is intimately tied to our internal capacities, within the boundaries of psychic life. In Nandy's critique this necessarily includes recognition of the internal resources within human subjectivity but also the internal resources available within Indian traditions and culture.

Nandy, armed with his psychoanalytic approach to these issues is not just the voice of the provocative diagnostician in these debates on secularism. Nandy is not only the voice declaring the pathologies of the patient incurable, for he cannot entirely be the detached outsider. Rather what passes as a detached outsider's gaze with respect to his identity, is attributable to an internal dynamic operating within his work and identity as critic. The confrontation and working through already noted as features of Nandy's work and fundamental to his approach needs to be explored alongside his *willing* capacity to enter into these psychoanalytic processes. In a similar point made by Jacqueline Rose regarding Freud, Nandy can be seen 'more squarely inside the dilemma of identity which he describes' (Rose in Said, 2003: 70).[11] In articulating the complexities of identity and *becoming* Nandy's mode of critique reclaims a dialectical between inner and outer incentives; one which also must be confronted in the voice of the critic. This willingness to confront the abject in Indian political culture and to traverse a dominant Indian secular political ideal demonstrates a distinctive sensitivity for entering into psychoanalytic processes. Psychoanalysis not only underpins the focus of Nandy's interventions but also informs his identity as critic. This internal questioning, or 'turning inwards' therefore precipitates a sensitivity, reflexivity and capacity to address these issues of subjectivity in his work. This does not detract from the fact that these processes of confrontation remain deeply threatening and disruptive, particularly for one's preferred understanding of themselves, including the postcolonial critic. For the fixtures of identity, including in this case one's intellectual identity is to follow Rose's comments still 'something, which is hard to escape' (Rose in Said, 2003: 74). Once committed to this internal confrontation and analysis, including working through these complexities and struggles that accompany such a task, Nandy's work and his identity as critic, moves us into the vernacular of the psychotherapeutic.

Notes

1. The first piece is a response by Nandy to Achin Vanaik's detailed critical reading of his work in Vanaik, A. (1997). See Nandy (2002h).
   The second response is to Kuldip Nayar. See Nandy (2005f) and Kesavan (2001).
2. See also Kesavan's text where he imbues in the concept of secularism a historicity that he claims is peculiar to India. Kesavan defines secularism as 'anti-hegemonic, pluralist and all-inclusive.' These qualities are for Nandy peculiar not to secularism, but to the diversity within the Indic civilisation with its many traditions of toleration and cultures of religiosity. Kesavan (2001).
3. On this point see Tally, R.T. Jr. (2007).
4. On this point see Nandy (2002a).
5. In Seyla Benhabib's work this recognition of difference within subjectivity is imperative to the democratic deliberative politics she advances. For a discussion of this refer to Noelle McAfee's discussion of Benhabib's work in the chapter 'Complimentary Agency in McAfee, N. (2000). *Habermas, Kristeva, and Citizenship,* Ithaca: Cornell University; See also Benhabib, S. (1992); Benhabib, S. (1996).
6. This relationship between violence and the abjection has been explored at length. Some examples include: Das, V. (1990). Das, V. (2001). V. Das (2000). M. Humphrey (2002). J. Kristeva, (1982). J. Kristeva (1991). M.J. Reineke (1997). J. Butler (2004). Zizek, S. (2008).
7. Refer to data cited from Rummel, R.J. (1994). Elsewhere Nandy states referencing this data that:

   > they seem to suggest that in the last one hundred years, less than five percent of those killed in mass violence have died in religious wars and riots. A little less than eighty per cent have died at the hands of the state, a huge majority of them in the hands of their own states, espousing secular, rational, scientific values.

   For a discussion of this question of modernity and violence see Nandy and Jahanbegloo (2006: 71).
8. This disruption to history is explored at length by in Nandy in his essay in Nandy (1995d).
9. This theme has also been developed by Nandy in the essay 'Coping with the Politics of Faiths and Cultures: Between Secular State and Ecumenical Traditions in India,' published in J.D. Pfaff-Czarnecka, and D. Rajasingham-Senanayake (1999). For a discussion on cosmopolitanism see 'Time Travel to a Possible Self: Searching for the Alternative Cosmopolitanism of Cochin' in Nandy (2002b).

10. Refer to Nandy and D.L. Sheth (1996).

11. Said, 2003.This point is made in a reply provided by Jacqueline Rose to Edward Said's essay 'Freud and the Non European.' Here she is responding to Said's point regarding the ambivalence of Freud's identity, which Said argues, underpins his work, particularly his text *Moses and Monotheism*. Rose states that in Said's reading, it is:

> through his complex, ambivalent relationship to his own Jewish identity, Freud precisely as outsider, was able to tear away the façade of European perfectibility long before the horrors of the Second World War and the violence of anti-colonial struggle would bring crashing to the ground. (Said, E.W. 2003)

5

Revolt and the Role of the Critic

Nandy's critique of secularism and his call for a 'post secular aware-ness' demonstrates a radical confrontation with the ideology and autonomy of thought from existing arguments within the debates on secularism. Nandy's anti-secular thinking displaces and traverses the secular political ideal, foundational within a post-colonial Indian political culture. In rejecting the reiteration of the norm in defence of secularism, his analysis flouts popular slogans that 'secularism is India's destiny' as advanced by the Congress Party (Gandhi, 2002: 1). The autonomy of thought that Nandy demonstrates in rejecting con-formity to the secular ideal reinforces an aptitude for confrontation and 'working through.' This is evident in his distinctive willingness to confront and question aspects of Indianness deemed threaten-ing and disruptive to Indian secular political culture and to political identities. However, that which is deemed threatening within Indian secular political culture, including those 'other selves' that threaten to disrupt dominant processes of identification, need to be conceptua-lised alongside a fear of pluralism. This is a fear of pluralism not only within Indian democracy but also within human subjectivity and ex-perience. Nandy's anti-secular thinking in part provokes and divides because it beckons a confrontation with the constitutive features of modern Indian selfhood and the threat of people's choices within the world's largest democracy. In identifying these fears, in confronting and working through these defences, Nandy is able to distinguish himself as a critical voice that traverses a narcissistic fantasy of the secular ideal. Nandy's intellectual autonomy, and his capacity to con-front, work through, and traverse the effects of the distortions of this dominant secular ideal have been explored through the psychoana-lytic concepts of the abject and abjection. Nandy's confrontation with secularism and the autonomy of thought demonstrated is a confrontation with the abject, as that which is at once most marginal and cast away from view. Such a reading provides a deeper engagement with the threat that Nandy represents in confronting aspects of selfhood and culture that have been abjected or cast from view in processes of subjection to the secular ideal, in pursuit of the formation of the modern secular self and political culture.

Nandy's disruptive presence and his anti-secular position in which meaning, identity and boundaries collapse demonstrates that 'the time of abjection is double.' As Kristeva explains the time of abjection is 'a time of oblivion and thunder, of veiled infinity and the moment when revelation burst forth' (Kristeva in McAfee, 2004: 121) Nandy confronts that which is deemed abject as a feature of his approach and identity as critic, and demonstrates this double time of abjection. For while on the one hand abjection 'represents the strangeness of the speaking being, the original repulsion, disgust,' on the other it marks 'the process of his autonomy and access to signs.' (Kristeva, 2002a: 158). This 'double time' is evident in the way that Nandy's own confrontational strangeness, that is, his anti-secularism, is responded to and represented in the debates on secularism. However, in this moment of confrontation that Nandy enters into, in confronting as I have suggested that which is deemed abject or has been 'cast away' in the formation of political culture, there is also paradoxically the potential for new meaning. For instance, this is demonstrated in Nandy's capacity to retrieve back into view aspects of Indianness deemed threatening and disruptive to an Indian secular culture, but which remain as the underside of politics. These ambiguities are welcomed in Nandy's analysis as fundamental to understanding the complexities of subjectivity, Indian accounts of selfhood, democratic processes and the post-secular. These ambiguities are contained by dominant meanings and established boundaries underpinning politics, but in Nandy's account, represent moments of possible regeneration. This includes regenerating established, norms, meanings and identities, as he confronts the positioning of the boundaries of secular and non-secular, public and private and self and other. Therefore, it is through what I have detailed as Nandy's willing confrontation with the abject, that the imaginary and symbolic regeneration and re-articulation of politics is made possible.

Ewa Ziarek explores this connection between the concept of abjection and autonomy of thought in emphasising the possibility for transformation. Ziarek states that, 'such an encounter with the abject—with what is intolerable and irreconcilable with not only imaginary but also symbolic identifications of the subject enables the negativisation of the narcissistic ego and the interruption of narcissistic economies in love and social relations' (Ziarek, 2001: 132). In applying Ziarek's descriptions—the negativisation of the narcissistic ego and the interruption of narcissistic economies—the following can be noted to further understand the confrontation with the abject that Nandy enters into. First, Nandy begins by radically questioning the centrality of a narcissistic secular ego-ideal dominant within Indian political culture and in political identities. His discussion of the ways this narcissistic ego makes over ethnic identities into political identities through processes of subjection demonstrates this. Nandy confronts the ways in which these processes ultimately lead to a series of distortions within the ideology, namely an inability to safeguard tolerance and political amity. However, the dominant narcissistic ego underpinning processes of identification is also evident in the way that secularism is fiercely defended. Nandy consistent with his efforts to disrupt the dominance of this narcissistic ego, exposes this continuing defence of secularism as, at best naïve, and at worst, dangerous. Nandy's analysis of the ways in which the political subject is formed in accordance with this ego ideal enables him to account for and explore latent features of self and of political culture, which, as he claims, are essential to understanding Indian political culture. In exploring both the deviations and distortions from the ideal, Nandy radically confronts the dominant position of the secular political identity. Simply stated, there are other accounts of selfhood, like that of the non-modern peripheral armed with their alternative accounts of secularism that resist the dominance of this secular ideal. This possibility or alternative that Nandy brings back into view as a feature of Indian political culture, and which attracts such contestation constitutes to paraphrase Ziarek's terminology 'an ethics of dissensus.'

The second feature of Nandy's intellectual autonomy is his capacity to traverse the deeply imbedded structure of fantasy underpinning the defence of secularism. This ability extends to Nandy's capacity to traverse the fantasy, which operates in parallel ways to fiercely protect the status of secularism in the debates on Indian secularism. I have already detailed the ways in which this traversal of the fantasy also enables Nandy to recognise alternative possibilities, already present within concepts of Indianness, Indian democracy and within Indian culture and traditions. However, Ziarek states that, 'the traversal of fantasy confronts the subject with ab-jection as its most intimate exteriority' (Ziarek, 2001: 132). If this is the case then the way Nandy confronts this 'intimate exteriority,' and how this informs his identity as critic, needs to be explored as a feature of his intellectual autonomy. Nandy's own awareness of this intimate exteriority, is noted by what Makarand Paranjape has identified is the 'self-representation and self-engineering' that goes on in his work (Paranjape in Lal, 2000: 234). This reflexivity and self-reflexivity has also been noted in the two replies Nandy provides to critics Achin Vanaik and Kuldip Nayar. In his two written replies to these critics Nandy explains this intimate exteriority in terms of the class betrayal that he enters into. Nandy is fully aware that his con-frontation with secularism necessitates a betrayal or a disloyalty, in rejecting the secular ideal that is supported by his contemporaries and his middle class counterparts within the Indian intelligentsia. However, Nandy also acknowledges that this betrayal involves a nec-essary counter-intuitive self-betrayal. As he explains, 'I belong to the middle class. I am a product of the middle class and I feel most com-fortable with the secular world view; I am not a believer' (Nandy and Deftereos, 2005d: 26). Such comments point to the importance of the internal betrayal that Nandy enters into, as a betrayal against domi-nant parts of self, in order to generate social and political criticism.

In having transgressed the narcissistic secular ego ideal and the fantasy structure of defence, Nandy unapologetically wears his self-professed anti-secular badge, and class betrayal, firmly on his sleeve. What role does this betrayal play though in understanding the dis-sent that he enters into as critic of the state and the critiques that he produces? In this chapter this betrayal is conceptualised as part of Nandy's psychoanalytic approach to producing social and political criticism. Nandy reveals something of this approach when he explains that, 'I don't think any social criticism is worth it unless it challenges one's own interests in some fundamental sense' (Nandy and Deftereos, 2005d: 26). Elsewhere Nandy expands further on this feature of cri-tique by stating the following: 'you know there is an inbuilt criticism in many of my remarks. A psychiatrist once said to me, 'What I miss in your writing is self-criticism. Well that is where it comes out. What's the point of saying Indian's suffer from a range of pathologies if one exempts oneself from criticism by cleverly defining oneself as an en-lightened liberal declassed exception?' (Darby, 2006). What Ziarek cautions then, is that a confrontation with one's most intimate exte-riority, is crucial to understanding Nandy's capacity to confront the abject, and the intellectual autonomy that follows from this. There are then internal processes within the identity of the critic that need to be accounted for including the way Nandy confronts the boundaries of his own identity, turns against dominant parts of self, and radically confronts his own certitudes, introjections and projections. In short, Nandy displays a commitment to psychoanalytic processes that need to be characterised. This is central to further understanding Nandy's intellectual autonomy, as his own explanation of this as betrayal does not fully account for how he is able to enter into these processes. The question remains as to what actuates and precipitate's Nandy's own willingness to enter into these states of intimate confrontation and analysis? What enables Nandy as critic to repeatedly enter into a mode of engagement predicated on 'defying the given models of defiance?' (Nandy, 1987a).

INTELLECTUAL AUTONOMY AND DISSENTING ANALYTIC ATTITUDES

I have suggested that there is a greater complexity to understanding Nandy's willingness for confrontation demonstrated in his work. This is explored and developed in this chapter by characterising Nandy's mode of critical intervention. Some of the features of this mode are already discernable through the discussion of his critique of secularism, which I have argued is characterised by its psychoanalytic focus. Nandy's own training as a political psychologist, including his clinical training with a psychoanalytic orientation, predisposes him to these issues, questions and concerns. His idiosyncratic use of psychoanalytic concepts and language is evident in his emphasis on internal and external tensions within the self and society, the psychic life of power, and concern for the positioning of the boundaries of inclusion and exclusion. In critiquing secularism in terms of its cultural and psychological viability, and in questioning the secularisation of the Indian self, Nandy demonstrates this psychoanalytic dimension operating in his work. This sensitivity for analysis is similarly evident in his capacity to reflect on his betrayal.

Consistent with the discussion of Nandy's identity thus far, this presence of the psychoanalytic in his work is not marked or rather dominated by a specific interpretation; in being for instance, classically Freudian. What is cultivated rather is a distinctive 'analytic attitude,' one which importantly does not follow a given disciplinary pathway or disciplinary directive.[1] As Nandy explains it is 'no longer the psychoanalysis I was taught and exposed to' (Nandy and Deftereos, 2005a: 7). The 'analytic attitude' that is discernable 'has become somewhat very personalized and generalized' (Nandy and Deftereos, 2005a: 7). The analytic attitude that is present is referenced in more subtle terms and consequently, is not always recognised as an application of psychoanalytic theory. Nandy reflects on his commitment to an analytic attitude in the following passage. He notes:

> So in the later work you will find that I have learned how to use this language in such a way that when I use psychoanalytic terms, the psychoanalytic person conversing with this is comfortable, but the ordinary reader also gets the hang of what I am trying to say. So turning against the self or rationalizations, identifications, projections these are very important. These are used technically. But also I have learned over the years how to use them in such a context that those who don't, who have not read a word of psychoanalysis, will still get an idea of what it is about. (Nandy and Deftereos, 2005a: 8)

There is the issue then of how Nandy uses and applies psychoanalysis in his work to generate critique, with what has been noted as his characteristic de-professionalised gaze. We might add that this approach, his de-professionalisation of self, is celebrated in Nandy's account for its lack of formality, and because of its idiosyncratic and personalised application. This autonomy of thought demonstrated in his application of these concepts and methods in this way remains though a source of fascination and horror for critics. Vinay Lal argues that this autonomy in Nandy's approach is consistent with the democratisation of knowledge operating in his work and advanced through his role as scholar and public intellectual. This along with Nandy's defence of democracy and democratic processes renders him in Lal's appraisal as 'the ultimate dissenter' and as a 'radical democrat' (Deftereos, 2005d: 5). Lal's appraisal is consistent with Nandy's search for a mode of dissent that radically challenges the Enlightenment vision of standardised developmentalism and the modes of dissent it has produced. Nandy notes that:

> The fact remains that this dissenter [the dissenting children of modernity] uses the language of the Enlightenment. So in some sense this is not at all adequate for those who speak entirely differently, outside of this. And who has found the Enlightenment to a great extent self-complicit. The Enlightenment consciousness is complicit with the violence, uprooting, and the de-culturation they have confronted in their lives or in their pasts of their communities. They need a different kind of life. (Nandy and Deftereos, 2005b: 6)

These efforts underpin the mode of dissent or mode of critical intervention he is interested in developing. For as Nandy cautions even the dissenting voice of Freud along with his dissenting analytic atti-tude can become contained 'within the citadels of modernity' (Nandy, 2004d: 2).

Written in 2004 'Freud, Modernity and Postcolonial Violence' warns against the processes of conformity, domestication and homogeni-sation that can form within dissent and within psychoanalysis more broadly. In this essay Nandy builds a case for a dissenting analytic atti-tude that challenges and confronts existing traditions of dissent with-in modernity. To this extent the essay repeats a continuing thematic concern with the positioning of boundaries of 'acceptable' dissent. This sensitivity for the inclusions and exclusions operating within the protocols of dissent is a consistent theme. In 'Shaman, Savages and the Wilderness' this issue has been explored in terms of what consti-tutes audible and inaudible dissent. Nandy affirms his commitment to psychoanalysis, albeit an idiosyncratic and personalised commit-ment, and to a psychoanalytic perspective by stating that, 'the body of work that challenges the Enlightenment vision, when not directly dependent on psychoanalytic insights, has borrowed heavily from clinical work and therapeutic visions' (Nandy, 2004d: 1). While he of-fers a number of reasons for this, it is namely that Freud, a product of multiple cultural traditions, including what Edward Said describes as his 'outsider status,' remains one of the rebellious children of moder-nity (Said, 2003). Freud did not necessarily reject the Enlightenment vision, but his rebelliousness is evident in his primary discovery of the unconscious that radically rallied against the accepted norms and ideals of the time. It is often overlooked just how controversial Freud was during his time. George Makari's text *Revolution in Mind: The Creation of Psychoanalysis* (2008) is a timely reminder of the exclu-sion Freud faced in the scientific community. This includes Freud's radical critique of the idealisation of the rational Cartesian subject in Western discourse. It is precisely this dissenting Freud that Nandy describes as being today a 'stranger to many.' As Nandy continues, 'the problem is compounded by the various schools of post-Freudian psychology, which are mostly progenies of the theoretical frames that crystallized as forms of dissent within the Enlightenment' (Nandy, 2004d: 2). These dissenting features have been foreclosed by a num-ber of contemporary post-Freudian interpretations of psychoanaly-sis and of Freud's legacy. These contemporary readings of a Freudian analytic attitude have contributed to co-opting this tradition of dis-sent into conformity. This conformity takes effect through the ways these 'stalwarts who contributed to the Enlightenment vision, tended to nurture one particular kind of critical attitude' (Nandy, 2004d: 3). This attitude is further validated by 'the global triumph of rationality, sanity and progress (encased in an expanding global culture of common sense and conventionality)' that resides within contemporary Indian middle-class culture. (Nandy, 2004d: 3). This common sense and conformity now applies to an analytic attitude that is accepted as a mode of demystification or unmasking. It is assumed that manifest reality after a point needs to be demystified. The processes of unmaskings assume that a truth claim (or a claim closer to the truth) can then be made. This process of demystification as a mastery of one's reality, is however deeply problematic. For Nandy this critical tradition leads to the establishment of a second order reality. This provides the conditions for a new set of certitudes, through which 'a new society, a new social vision, and even a new human personality could be built based on this new hermeneutics'[2] (Nandy, 2004d: 3).

What Nandy celebrates as the critical impetus within the Freudian analytic attitude now becomes subject to processes of standardisation, homogenisation and containment. The consequences of striving to domesticate an otherness, that psychoanalysis already recognises as unable to be domesticated, carries an ethical and political dimension in Nandy's reading. Nandy warns that, 'one-way style of demystification has not merely become a new source of certitude, but also a new means of legitimising the forced obsolescence for those marginalized by the world system' (Nandy, 2002b: 208). The only mastery that is ethically acceptable in Nandy's account of the analytic attitude is within these psychoanalytic processes of self-knowledge and awareness. As has been argued of the Freudian psychoanalytic process the only mastering that is possible is in the ways in which psychoanalysis as a psychotherapeutic practice leads one into an unmastered past as a sequence of steps in self knowledge. What in Nandyan terms constitutes a 'politics of awareness'. It is the Freudian psychoanalytic experience of remembering, repeating, working through, which creates the conditions for a psychoanalytic rebirth of self as a dynamic and continuous process. Alternatively expressed in the work of the French psychoanalyst Julia Kristeva it is the return to the timelessness of psychic life that enables this analytic rebirth.

In critiquing and challenging processes of closure within 'one way style demystification' and dissent Nandy's own intellectual commitment to a mode of social and political criticism cannot be defined in these terms. What distinguishes his analytic mode as critical intervention is this confrontation and willingness to work through stagnation, standardisation and homogenisation within meaning, knowledge construction and human subjectivity. The task of critique then becomes one of creating a dynamic interplay with alternatives. This analytic mode of engagement arguably already operates in the following statement when he tells us that,

> ...In that sense I think we have to extend Philip Reiff's analytic attitude where it presumes that the Freudian analytical attitude, once it has demystified, that it has reached closer to the truth...I don't think you have reached closer to the truth, because after a point you get used to that form of demystification and that becomes justification for new kinds of violence and expropriation. (Nandy and Deftereos, 2006: 13)

There is a distinctive dissenting feature to this analytic attitude that does not end with accepted theories of demystification, but which carries forward a continuing internal critical dynamic. To ensure the critical edge and continuation of this dynamic Nandy advances that, 'any significant psychological or political theory, to be so recognized, must have either an element of self-destructiveness or a subsystem of self-criticism built in' (Nandy, 2004d: 4). It is this 'internal dynamic' that is essential to the analytic attitude that Nandy theorises in this essay and which operates within the psychoanalytic mode underpinning his work more broadly. While the essay does not elaborate further on this inner dynamic, it is the operation of the psychoanalytic mode in his work that provides Nandy with the capacity to raise these very issues. This analytic mode requires an inbuilt self-criticism, which as I have already suggested, includes a confrontation with the boundaries of selfhood. So while Nandy recognises the critical power of the Freudian psychoanalytic experience, it is the ways in which this critical psychoanalytic impulse or dynamic can be domesticated, that he objects. This is more than an intellectual point of difference or objection, but a confrontation and displacement, what can be called *a revolt* against these processes of standardisation and homogenisation. There is a revolt against these efforts to contain or domesticate this analytical attitude or as it operates in Nandy's work and identity as critic, within a psychoanalytic mode.

Julia Kristeva's account of revolt, as a 'constant calling into question the psyche as well as the world' is useful here to describe the psychoanalytic mode underpinning Nandy's work (Kristeva, 2000: 19). Nandy's methods of critique are not predicated on a logic of analytic

mastery, but on a *psychoanalytic mode as revolt*. This process of psychoanalytic questioning 'does not stop with the formal standardised
modes of demystification or unmasking' (Nandy and Deftereos, 2006:
13). In Kristeva's account of revolt these processes of questioning are
dynamic and continuous. By definition, at least in the psychoanalytic
context that Kristeva revives the concept, revolt is only possible as
long as it 'remains a live force and resists accommodation' (Kristeva,
2002b: 38). The concept is also useful because as Kristeva emphasises
it is not the permanence of revolt but the continuing regenerative
possibilities that revolt enables that are important. To this extent the
concept of revolt and the 'culture of revolt' that Kristeva advances is a
call 'to redirect the aggressivity of the drive from the abjection of the
self to the transformation of the social relations' (Chanter and Ziarek,
2005: 2). In Kristeva's account of revolt this regeneration expresses,
'the process, dynamic, and movement of meaning, not reduced to
language but encompassing it' (Kristeva, 2000: 37). Therefore, revolt
is not only a rupturing or de-centering but as Chanter and Ziarek
explain also a renewal and regeneration of, '...psychic life and social
bonds through symbolic re-articulation, which leads to the institution of new forms of social relations, collective identification, and
representations' (Chanter and Ziarek, 2005: 3).

It is worth establishing some qualifications to the application of
Kristeva's concept to characterising the psychoanalytic mode as revolt operating in Nandy's work. The reason for drawing on Kristeva's
concept of revolt is not to enter into the many complex debates surrounding her work.[3] Nor is it my intention to assess the concept of
revolt within her earlier work, particularly *Revolution in Poetic Language* (1984) which commentators like Lechte and Zournazi propose.
This scholarship is well documented. In Chanter and Ziarek's edited
text comprised of a series of essays dedicated to exploring the political
logic of revolt, they suggest that the concept needs to be read alongside
Kristeva's work produced in the 1980s. Chanter and Ziarek argue that
Kristeva's later work on revolt is a departure from an early dialectical conception of revolt based on the law/transgression model and
founded in Freud's Oedipal account of patricide as the obverse of the
paternal law (Chanter and Ziarek, 2005: 4). Instead, I apply certain
aspects of Kristeva's account of revolt to characterise Nandy's mode
of critical intervention. This psychoanalytic mode of revolt enables
Nandy to rupture and regenerate meaning and signification as a consistent feature of his cultural and political criticism, including the
meaning and signification of subjectivity. How though is this process

of revolt, including the self-critique and self-reflexivity that Nandy demonstrates in his work generated?

Psychoanalysis and the Intimacy of Revolt

If Nandy pleads for an analytic attitude to counter the 'rhetoric of wider choice,' then Kristeva's account of revolt demonstrates how this can be achieved (Nandy, 2004d: 3). Consistent with Kristeva's intellectual focus her account of revolt is developed within a psychoanalytic framework. More specifically this account is drawn from transferential features of the Freudian analytic experience. Kristeva shares Nandy's concern for the need to reclaim what he terms is the dissenting features of the Freudian analytic attitude. This account is developed in Kristeva's two texts *The Sense and Non-Sense of Revolt: The Powers and Limits of Psychoanalysis Volume 1* (2000) and her later work *Intimate Revolt: The Powers and Limits of Psychoanalysis Volume 2* (2002). The concept of revolt that she explores is located within the powers and limits of psychoanalysis.

The Sense and Non-Sense of Revolt emphasises two features of the Freudian experience of analytic revolt. In the psychotherapeutic analytic encounter revolt reveals itself as both an Oedipal revolt and as a return to the archaic, to the 'timeless temporality' of psychic life. Kristeva credits Heidegger for the concept of temporalising and Proust whose understanding of timelessness, to 'pure embodied time' also prepares us for benevolence (Kristeva, 2000: 16). In understanding revolt in this way Kristeva displaces and reclaims the concept from its exclusive political foundations and interpretations. In reclaiming revolt this way she explores what she terms is the 'richness of its polyvalence' (Kristeva, 2000: 3). This richness is demonstrated through the return to the archaic described as 'a return to sensations in words under the pressure of unconscious drives.' Kristeva continues that this is 'a return provoking the splitting of the subject between an observant consciousness, on the one hand, and a constellation of words/sensations with the value of reified images, relics of the incorporated object on the other' (Kristeva, 2002a: 175). Psychoanalysis in the clinical setting developed by Freud is where revolt is to be found. For Kristeva one of Freud's key contributions is this notion of 'analytic space as a time of revolt,' in which the transferential experience between analyst and analysand is privileged (Kristeva, 2000: 28). This experience subject to the law of free association involves retrieving memory and entering into the timelessness of unconscious life through processes of anamnesis with the analyst. This dynamic relationship between analyst and analysand is the site of revolt as meanings; signification and representations are regenerated through a psychic re-birth. Revolt as Kristeva describes it, is as Oliver and Edmin note, 'the experience of inclusion through representation, through making language and meaning one's own in order to speak to others' (Oliver and Edmin, 2002: 5).

In *The Sense and Non-Sense of Revolt* (2000), Kristeva details the ways the processes of analytic revolt can be experienced. Revolt can be experienced in three ways: first, as the transgression of a prohibition; second, as repetition, a working-through, or working-out; and third, as displacement or combinative, games. Kristeva illustrates how these experiences take form and are represented in her analysis of three rebellious literary figures *in revolt*: Aragon, Sartre and Barthes. Through this reading Kristeva builds a case for the necessity of revolt, including what she calls a culture of revolt. The necessity of revolt is explained in terms of the function it performs for our individual and collective psychic well-being. Revolt is however, imbued with a specific intensity, for it literally concerns the life and death of the subject. Revolt, including a culture of revolt, keeps us psychically alive by safeguarding our inner capacities for thought. Revolt safeguards psychic life from the dangerous and destructive processes of stagnation and homogenisation that are in Kristeva's terms quite literally the death of the subject. Kristeva explains, 'I see no other role for literary criticism and theory than to illuminate the experiences of formal and philosophical revolt that might keep our inner lives alive' (Kristeva, 2000: 7). The alternative is for Kristeva a psychic regression into barbarity, a life of physical and moral violence in which self other relations and boundaries are violated. Revolt thus at the individual level preserves our psychic well-being, and a perpetual questioning operating within psychic life, while a culture of revolt equally safeguards the collective well-being of the psychic life of a society, in similar ways by fostering this dynamic. For Kristeva what can be discerned from the psychoanalytic setting of listening to human experience is that 'happiness exists only at the price of revolt.' The happiness that she speaks of in terms of safeguarding well-being in psychic life defines the therapeutic features of revolt. Further this happiness or well-being is conditional on having displaced, transgressed or worked through a prohibition (such as a law, authority, ideal, and superego.) To enter into these processes of psychoanalysis as a psychotherapeutic practice is to enter into the processes of revolt.

In *Intimate Revolt* (2002) Kristeva extends on the necessity of revolt in psychic life and its broader social implications. Kristeva explores the political logic of revolt, by contrasting the intimacy of revolt with politics and the social. In safeguarding psychic life, which she calls our most intimate interior space, revolt denotes internal and external processes. However, for Kristeva 'the intimate' she explains, 'is where we end up when we question apparent meanings and values' (Kristeva, 2002a: 43). The intimate interiority of psychic life is where revolt takes place. Celia Sjoholm argues that the intimate becomes the privileged site of revolt for Kristeva. Sjoholm reads this alongside Kristeva's efforts to reclaim the concept of revolt from a political framework, in which ironically the concept denotes a less permanent disruption and increasingly sanitised forms of political unrest. The intimate emerges as a response to the sanitised political domain. Kristeva states,

> The intimate revolt is in fact the only possible revolt, intimacy being that which is the most profound and the most singular in us; the political having become too technocratic, too totalitarian and conflated with the social: the intimate domain evolves as a response. (Kristeva in Sjoholm, 2005: 114)

The intimate evolves as a response to what Kristeva claims are doctrines that have fixed and closed off meaning and representation in the political realm. She also rejects accounts that seek to fix and close off the meaning and representation of the intimate. Such accounts must be rejected because they foreclose the dynamics inherent in the timelessness of psychic life. Kristeva elaborates on this dynamism when she tells us that, 'the liveliest aspect of the intimate—resides precisely in the heterogeneity of the two sensorial/symbolic [and] affect/thought registers' (Kristeva, 2000: 49). Intimate revolt denotes processes that rely on the dynamic interplay of these two registers. Although a more detailed discussion of this is beyond the task here there are four aspects of Kristeva's account of intimate revolt that illustrate the importance of this dynamism and in characterizing the 'intimacy' of the revolt that Nandy enters into as critic. These are first, anamnesis as psychic restructuring; second, the conflicts of resistance: *not wanting to know*; third the necessity for a culture of revolt and finally, the radical evil of standardisation, and homogenisation. Furthermore, these aspects of Kristeva's account of revolt characterise the mode of critical engagement and dissent operating in Nandy's work and identity. The working through that psychoanalysis as psychotherapeutic practice requires of us in order to actuate these processes of revolt, have much to reveal about the tools of the critic and the similarities between Nandy's own working through.

'WORKING THROUGH' THE TOOLS OF THE CRITIC

Anamnesis as Psychic Restructuring

Revolt safeguards the intimate, as a field of possible imaginings and symbolic re-articulations from stagnation and conformity. For Kristeva these features of stagnation, conformity, domestication and homogenisation represent a deeply threatening malaise within contemporary social and political life. This conformity and stagnation of thought within society is captured in Guy Debord's depiction of the 'society of the spectacle' (Debord, 1967). Debord's prophetic reasoning of society was one besieged by the growing standardisation within a society that has lost its capacity to interpret objects and signs. Heidegger makes a similar argument in noting that the conquest of the world as picture is a fundamental feature of the modern age. Kristeva warns that when a society has lost its capacity to regenerate its own symbols and signs, to interpret representation then both individual and collective psychic well-being is compromised. As Kristeva states, 'when all information is virtually image, the spread of information and its crystallisation in the visible prescribe belief in a total consciousness' (Kristeva, 2002a: 140). The society of the spectacle that Debord describes is for Kristeva symptomatic of 'this breakdown of the imaginary… which can be attributed to the surfeit of non-verbal, non-verbalised images which characterise today's spectator society.' To safeguarding against this breakdown of the imaginary and to preserve the life of the subject Kristeva turns to anamnesis. She argues that revolt is 'an invitation to anamnesis in the goal of a rebirth that is psychic restructuring' (Kristeva, 2002a: 7). To enter into these processes of revolt is to accept the invitation for a psychic re-birth. Kristeva emphasises that, 'the possibility of questioning one's own being, searching for oneself (*se quaerere*: 'quaesto mihi factus sum'), is offered by this aptitude for return, which is simultaneously recollection, interrogation, and thought.' (Kristeva, 2002a: 6). The process of retrospection and turning inwards into self in order to confront, rupture, and regenerate psychic life is essential to revolt. Anamnesis, retrospective return, this turning into self, refers to our capacity for questioning and interrogation, or simply stated— thought itself. Anamnesis is a dynamic process of turning back and working through or working out, or displacement through which thought can be regenerated. These processes also regenerate and reconstitute the boundaries of self. In inviting us to confront and work through existing structures, assumptions, beliefs in psychic life, psychic re-birth therefore, also denotes a re-birth of subjectivity. These processes of revolt are dynamic processes inviting us into the possibilities of what Kristeva describes is *infinite re-creation*.

THE CONFLICTS OF RESISTANCE: *NOT WANTING TO KNOW*

The psychoanalytic experience of revolt is for Kristeva accompanied by internal conflicts and resistances. These resistances are a defence mechanism operating within psychic life against the threat of change and the threat of psychic re-birth. These defence mechanisms reveal themselves as denial, disavowal and foreclosure, as a *not wanting to know*. Kristeva explains that revolt is marked by an internal conflict which 'collides with the human being's desire not to know,' especially from knowing truths (about himself/herself or others) that may place him/her *in revolt* (Kristeva, 2002a: 11). This defence mechanism perpetuates denial and a politics of silencing ensuring that the boundaries of self remain unchanged and repeated without question or critical reflection. This state of stagnation extends beyond the psychic life of the individual and is also evident in cultural, social and political configurations. (This denial has also been explored in the precious chapter through Nandy's account of the ways in which this operates within the debates. In responding to his critics Nandy recognises the denial at play in terms of certain critic's inability to engage with his work. He explains this defence using Rollo May's concept of 'pseudo-innocence' or 'inauthentic innocence'. In this chapter, I argue that Nandy is able to recognise this denial in this way because of the analytic mode as revolt operating in his work (May, 1972). Kristeva notes that these defence mechanisms operating in a broader social context can also denote resistance to psychoanalysis. Although explored in any detail here it is interesting to note that the resistance to psychoanalysis can also take place within psychoanalytic societies themselves which she states:

> contribute to discrediting psychoanalysis, with their delicate politics and concern for safeguarding their clinical purity or, on the contrary, an overly aggressive ideological, if not spiritual, orientation, and thereby undermine the Copernican revolution that Freud introduced in the twentieth century and that we increasingly perceive to be the only one that does not turn away from either malady or the revolts of modernity[4]. (Kristeva, 2002a: 11)

She alerts us to the fact that not all societies celebrate the regenerative possibilities of what she terms is a culture of revolt. For Kristeva, revolt brings us face-to-face with this invitation to work through these individual and collective resistances, and in doing so to accept the possibilities of regeneration and a psychic re-birth. Kristeva continues,

> This is where we are: we can either renounce revolt by withdrawing into old values or indeed new ones that do not look back on themselves and do not question themselves or, on the contrary, relentlessly repeat retrospective return so as to lead it to the limits of the representable/thinkable/tenable (to the point of possession), limits made evident by certain advances of the culture of the twentieth century. (Kristeva, 2002a: 7)

THE NECESSITY FOR A CULTURE OF REVOLT

Kristeva argues that to retreat to old values and norms uncritically is to retreat into an established defence mechanism and into the security that certitudes provide. This is to retreat into an existing logic or patterns of thought, associations and identifications that exist individually and collectively. Sjoholm describes this question of certitude as 'an irreconcilable conflict between the subject-in- process and the normative order' (Sjoholm, 2005: 115). Kristeva questions this certitude by posing the following question. 'Just under the surface of this question is another we could legitimately ask: what is the necessity of this culture of revolt?' (Kristeva, 2000: 7). Kristeva provides an answer to this question by stating: 'yet as a transformation of man's relationship to meaning...cultural revolt intrinsically concerns public life and consequently has profoundly political implications. In fact, it poses the question of another politics, that of permanent conflictuality' (Kristeva, 2002a: 11). This regenerated concept of politics as permanent conflictuality does not however eradicate antagonisms, conflicts, contradictions and ambiguity. As Noelle McAfee describes, it is 'the potential for seeing difference as an ontological possibility for subjectivity.' (McAfee in Oliver, 1993: 131). In Kristeva's account it is to our own detriment to repress and deny a culture of revolt, or what McAfee describes as the ontological possibility within this new politics. Kristeva explores this by noting that when the other, the radical stranger or the foreigner is excluded and abjected from politics, and in the absence of a culture of revolt, they are forced to contend with regressive ideologies. These ideologies do not however satisfy their demands for rupture and regeneration of self, and moreover, inclusion. In such situations pathologies or what Kristeva also references as the 'new maladies of the soul' emerge (Kristeva, 1995). For Kristeva their own complicity with their conditions of exclusion

and abjection, leads them to become rioters. To counter these pathologies, politics as a culture of revolt for Kristeva must be understood rather in permanent conflictuality. In this account of politics,
differenced, including the differences of the other are not abjected
or reconciled but are lived with. In *Intimate Revolt* Kristeva affirms
that 'the diversity of cultural models is the only guarantee of respect
for this humanity' for the other (Kristeva, 2002a: 268). As with Nandy
for Kristeva the ability to afford humanity to the other is captured in
the concept of hospitality.[5] Kristeva shares intellectual ground with
Nandy here by noting that 'hospitality should not be a simple juxta-
position of differences, with the domination of one model over all the
others, but, on the contrary, a taking into consideration other logics,
other freedoms, so that each way of being becomes more multiple,
more complex' (Kristeva, 2002a: 268). The culture of revolt captured
in Kristeva's reading of hospitality recognises multiple ways of being
and of subjectivity. This culture fosters a new politics in which the
boundaries of self and other are ruptured and regenerated. To support a culture of revolt is to therefore support the perpetual features
of these processes of revolt. For Kristeva these perpetual processes of
revolt define a culture of revolt that she advocates but more importantly preserves the future of revolt.

THE RADICAL EVIL OF STANDARDISATION AND HOMOGENISATION

In Kristeva's account processes of revolt are what sustain our contin-
ual questioning of ourselves and the world around us. Preserving this
capacity is vital, for it safeguards, against the pathologies of conformity, homogenisation and stagnation. Kristeva notes that foreclosing
revolt and with it the possibility of psychic re-birth ultimately leads
to the death of the subject. Within this account standardisation, homogenisation and stagnation thus takes on a deeper significance. This
significance is expressed for Kristeva in Hannah Arendt's concept of
'radical evil'. In Kristeva's application of the concept radical evil denotes 'the halting of representation and questioning.' Here radical
evil is non-representation and non-questioning and consistent with
Arendt's depiction has its foundations in totalitarianism. For Kristeva,
Arendt rightly acknowledges that totalitarianism is connected to
complete domination. This domination includes psychic domination, and aims to eliminate essential features of our humanity, notably our capacities for questioning and representation. Kristeva states,
'I can never sufficiently emphasize the fact that totalitarianism is the

result of a certain fixation of revolt in what is precisely its betrayal, namely the suspension of retrospective return, which amounts to a suspension of thought' (Kristeva, 2002a: 6). To accept the halting of representation and questioning is to enter into a psychic state of to-talitarianism, an internal stasis within psychic life. Therefore, our capacities to enter into processes of revolt, and cultivate a revolt culture become closed off by this radical evil. Kristeva repeatedly emphasises that this radical evil must be confronted and traversed in order to actuate the therapeutic effects and affects of revolt.

As I have sketched out, revolt references a series of psychoanalytic processes that rupture, regenerate and re-articulate meaning and signification. Like the analytic experience itself within the clinical setting revolt provides the subject in revolt with access to autonomy of thought in questioning and challenging established meanings and norms. This autonomy extends to regenerating the boundaries of self as revolt leads us to a psychic re-birth. Revolt functions as a means of keeping psychic space and the imaginary dynamic and safeguarding well-being within psychic life. Further, revolt functions in keeping the subject alive. The four features of revolt that preserve this well-being within psychic life are: first, retrospection or retrospective return as opening or sensitising us to the possibilities of anamnesis, for psychic re-birth and infinite re-creation; second, in confronting and traversing the internal conflicts and resistance which prevent these processes of rupture and regeneration from taking place in psychic life; third, the necessity for a culture of revolt to preserve our internal capacities for thought and representation; which brings us to fourth, that revolt safeguards against the radical evils of standardisation, homogenisation and conformity within meaning, language, thought and subjectivity. Drawing on key aspects of Kristeva's account, particularly her emphasis on the rupturing and regeneration of meaning and signification (including the meanings and signification ascribed to one's self) as features of revolt. In noting how a psychoanalytic mode of revolt operates within Nandy's work as a means of generating critique, the psychotherapeutic features of this process need to also be taken into account.

Revolt as a psychoanalytic concept denotes a series of processes that safeguard our capacities to rupture, question, confront, and work through established values, norms, and assumptions within psychic life. To this extent revolt regenerates meaning and significance, and, in doing so preserves what Kristeva notes is the well-being of psychic life. These analytic processes lead to the goal of a psychic re-birth, and hence a regeneration of subjectivity, including the boundaries of self. This re-birth is as confronting as it is therapeutic because it places us *in revolt*. The process of being in revolt also draws our attention to our own intimate radical alterity, or the stranger within that marks human subjectivity. This recognition has the effect and affect of sensitising us to our own radical alterity as the decentred subject. Noelle McAfee takes this further in noting that 'an ethics of respect for what cannot be known, for this irreconcilable difference,' takes form as part of subjectivity (McAfee in Oliver, 1993: 118). This informs our ability to extend a hand to the other, having now been exposed to a more complex understanding of subjectivity and the inter-subjective realm. These processes of rupture and regeneration are for Kristeva imbued with the possibility of infinite re-creation. There is a continuing internal dynamism, which resists the dangers and radical evil of homogenisation and stagnation within psychic life. This radical evil of homogenisation carries an additional weight. As Kristeva describes, the suspension of thought leads to the death of the subject. Further to this, Kristeva describes the relationship between abjection and revolt in the following way. Abjection is an affective state that threatens the subject-in-process with the disruption of being lost in the borderlands between subject and object. The suspension of revolt takes us further denoting the end of subjectivity. There is therefore, a therapeutic dimension operating in revolt that preserves the integrity of subjectivity, including the dynamism or as Kristeva prefers, the timelessness of psychic life.

In applying Kristeva's concept of revolt to describe the psychoanalytic mode of revolt operating in Nandy's work, the therapeutic dimension reveals itself in two significant ways. First, it reveals Nandy's ability to actuate perspectives that sensitise us to the therapeutic processes of rupture and regeneration and re-articulation of meaning and signification. Second, the therapeutic reveals itself within Nandy's identity and autonomy of thought that enables him as the *critical analytic intellectual* to actuate these perspectives. The two arguments are symbiotic. The symbiosis between Nandy's identity and mode of critical intervention is not entirely unfamiliar. As previously argued, this relationship informs representations of Nandy in the debates on Indian secularism. Selected critics have demonstrated the ways in which this relationship are conceived in a symptomatic register that polarises debate into a proto and anti-secular logic. Following from this emerges a politics of blame demonstrated in certain critics' responses. Here the threat and disruption of Nandy's intellectual position collapses into a more generalised threat and disruption that Nandy himself as the abject figure carries forward. Cast as the phobic object and with his abject status, his identity and mode of dissent is cast outside. Hence, Nandy is consistently represented as the not yet entitled subject.

What distinguishes Nandy's dissent and attempts to expand the boundaries of debate over secularism, despite not always being audible, simplistically assumed or sufficiently engaged with? Nandy's defiance is also a defiance of the symptomatic register through which many of his criticisms are advanced. Revolt as capturing intimate internal processes therefore; works to redirect the abjection against the self into processes of critical thought and questioning. For Kristeva, these processes provide the conditions for the transformation of social relations. This approach enables Nandy's identity and autonomy of thought to be considered with greater complexity than the symptomatic allows. The critical idiom of his work provides the conditions for Nandy to rupture and regenerate meaning and signification, including the meaning of his own identity. He is able to remake his own subjectivity and in the process resist abjection. In and through these processes he also remakes his intellectual significance. This mode, a mode as revolt, is inherently dynamic and marked by an infinite re-creation; Nandy is able to recreate his subjectivity in very different terms. This also provides him with the capacity for self-reflexivity as an effect of this mode and which in turn informs his work. This has been detailed in terms of the betrayal he enters into in critiquing secularism. Although he claims this betrayal is entered into with 'glee' it is not without its intimately confronting features (Nandy, 2003: 2). For in entering via this mode into processes of retrospection and anamnesis the, '...repetition of inner conflicts and critical analysis [*is*] necessary to overcome the instinctive and unconscious self-protective forces of forgetting, denying, projecting and similar defence mechanisms' (Lifton, 1975: 261).

Nandy's internal confrontation takes place alongside a working through of these defence mechanisms. The expression of glee is therefore, more than just a reactionary and provocative position. It is a position that is arrived at through these intimate processes of retrospection, anamnesis and 'working through,' in confronting these defence mechanisms. Kristeva describes the foreignness and intense confrontation of these processes as 'speaking an*other* language.' Difficult as these processes are, entering into a revolt 'is quite simply the minimum and primary condition for being alive' (Kristeva,

2002a: 254). Kristeva celebrates the foreignness of these 'alternatives' and in 'speaking an*other* language,' which in Nandy's case have been executed with 'glee.' Though the threat and contestation and even incommensurability of Nandy's 'anti-secular' position has been widely commented on by certain critics. If Nandy contends the secular ideal is defended by the intellectually lazy then this seemingly innocuous laziness takes on a deeper meaning. It signifies the reproduction of these defence mechanisms. This is especially the case for critics who may be sympathetic to Nandy's argument, but who are unable to move through these deeply imbedded individual and collective defences. These defences are nonetheless complex for as argued they are intimately connected to selfhood, self-representation, but also to a contested national identity. Revolt in Kristeva's account always makes painful demands on the self, on culture and on society. Kristeva continues that 'to estrange oneself from oneself and to make oneself the smuggler of this continuously recaptured strangeness' are the conditions of revolt (Kristeva, 2002a: 254). These conditions have also been described by Cecilia Sjoholm as a transcendental intuition of the other, which she argues reveals itself as revolt (Sjoholm, 2005: 112). This intuition or recognition of the other and the other within, places Nandy in a psychic space from which to also recognise the subjectivity and humanity of otherness.

A number of scholars have recognised the therapeutic modality of Nandy's social and political criticism. Though as I have suggested this is done so without necessarily accounting for the psychoanalytic impetus within Nandy's voice as critic. For instance Makarand Paranjape notes that Nandy's 'episteme is a modern one, but rather different from the predatory dominant versions' (Paranjape in Lal, 2000: 245). Grounded within the intellectual and ethical commitment to psychoanalysis this mode of critical intervention, despite representations of Nandy as culturalist and traditionalist, is a modern one. What is especially useful about Paranjape's observation is that he understands Nandy to adopt an approach that differs from both a predatory and dominant version of modern critique. This observation is consistent with the account of revolt and its application to describe Nandy's psychoanalytic mode; given that producing predatory and dominant perspectives is equated here with the suspension of thought. In the presence of revolt, and in Nandy's case revolt is present in the operation of the psychoanalytic mode in his work then this suspension of thought is just not possible. Nandy rejects the methods that lead to standardisation, homogenisation, and conformity, along with predatory and dominant discourses. He affirms that 'dissent unless it seeks to subvert the rules of the game and the language, in which the rules are framed, becomes another form of conformity' (Nandy, 2004a: 26). As an intellectual who demonstrates the importance of rupture and regeneration, Nandy in his work encourages a similar response from those who are able to recognise this invitation in his work.

The psychotherapeutic mode of revolt underpinning Nandy's interventions produces a distinct reflexivity. Gustavo Esteva and Madhu Suri Prakash acknowledge this as a feature of Nandy's critique in their introduction to a collected edition of his work (Nandy, 2004a). They argue that, 'these essays continue to challenge us, forcing us to ask ourselves new questions, even as they offer us guidance in the regeneration and re-enchantment of our own selves' (Nandy, 2004a: 1). This reflexivity invites us to replicate these processes of rupture and regeneration as a means of questioning social and cultural life as well as ourselves. Such an approach is an invitation to confront and work through the established, dominant and hegemonic norms, meanings and identities, in order to regenerate and re-articulate meaning and significance. Nandy's work demonstrates a commitment to the therapeutic in the ways in which the recovery of alternatives takes place and is re-claimed as openness in the defiance of the certitudes. These perspectives we can also conclude lead to a recovery of alternatives not only for the self, but always and necessarily in tandem with a recognition of our own radical alterity and otherness. This reflexivity and awareness of otherness (including our own radical otherness) leads to a regeneration of self in relation to the other. More importantly for Nandy, it can lead to a new politics. For in assessing 'the implications of the argument thus far,' Nandy consistent within the operation of the psychoanalytic mode as revolt within his work proposes that, '...openness to voices, familiar or strange, may well have to be the first criterion of the shared self which transcends nation-states, communities, perhaps even cultures themselves' (Nandy, 2004a: 471, 481).

The political logic of revolt operating in the modality of social and political criticism therefore adds a deeper level of significance to what Vinay Lal notes are the 'open futures' advanced in Nandy's writings. This notion of open futures references the outcome of processes of revolt. These futures can only be open when expressed in the therapeutic register. Nandy demonstrates this intellectual and ethical commitment to the therapeutic, as both an effect and affect of his method in his critical reading of dissent through the metaphor of the shaman. This regenerated concept of dissent, consistent with the operation of the psychoanalytic mode as revolt, is for Nandy also necessarily an exercise in the politics of awareness.

METAPHORIC TRANSFERS: THE SHAMAN IN REVOLT

In the essay 'Shamans, Savages and Wilderness: On the Audibility of Dissent and the Future of Civilizations' Nandy develops the argument for the need to rupture and regenerate the concept of dissent (Nandy, 2004a). This is developed through the metaphor of the shaman. In reading this essay I ask to what extent the shaman functions within the essay as a figure *in revolt*. In Nandy's reading the shaman is a figure who is located at the borderlands of society and the borderlands of psychic life. This location is privileged as it imbues the shaman with a sensitivity and capacity to challenge the politics of audibility and inaudibility operating in dissent. Nandy is however, not alone in acknowledging the critical and creative possibilities of the shamanic figure.

The shaman is celebrated as a disruptive figure by a number of contemporary thinkers notably within the work of anthropologists Claude-Lévi Strauss and Michael Taussig and in the work of the Indian psychoanalyst Sudhir Kakar.[6] Although each theorist explores the shaman and shamanism with a different theoretical problematic in mind, all these works explore the shaman as a radical figure that exists at the borderlines of society and culture. The shaman is also celebrated for being at borderline states of subjectivity and at borders of conscious and unconscious life. For instance, in Levi-Strauss' work shamanism shares a number of similarities with psychoanalysis. Lévi-Strauss points out that shamanism, like psychoanalysis, aims to bring 'to a conscious level conflicts and resistances which have remained unconscious' (Lévi-Strauss, 1968: 198). For Kakar in his text exploring healing traditions in India, what shamanism and psychoanalysis have in common is that 'they operate with collective and individual myths' (Kakar, 1982: 116). In both accounts this capacity of the shaman to access these myths, in order to work through unconscious tensions, conflicts and resistances is recognised as a creative and powerful source of critical regeneration. In both accounts it can also be argued that the shaman is a figure in revolt against dominant social and cultural norms and practices. Michael Taussig has explored the shaman's capacity for disruption and regeneration in his account of the shaman's role in the colonial encounter. The shaman becomes central to challenging and confronting the homogenising process of identification and signification within the colonialist gaze. Taussig's ethnographic research details the ways in which the 'wilderness' of the shaman, as a feature of subjectivity and agency, provides a disruption to colonialist modes of representation. This 'wilderness' he argues, 'challenges the unity of the symbol, the transcendent totalisation binding the image to that which it represents' which is ultimately 'the death of signification.' 'Wilderness challenges the unity of the symbol, the transcendent totalisation binding the image to that which it represents. Wilderness pries open this unity and in its place creates slippage…Wilderness is the death of signification' (Taussig, 1986: 219). The strangeness of the shaman, including the wild non-rational and non-modern ways, are for Taussig similarly, a source of creativity and regeneration in the critical encounter.

In Nandy's own analysis it is a combination of these equally disruptive and regenerative features of the shaman that are invoked in his application of this metaphor to theorise dissent. Nandy recognises that these capacities for sensitivity and openness collide with the shaman's strangeness. It is in recognising and acknowledging the radical strangeness that activates the possibility for alternative imaginings of dissent. This is made possible because of the shaman's capacity to speak in languages so foreign and unspeakable, that they are abjected from mainstream society. As an abject figure the shaman, therefore carries the disruptive threat of psychosis. This position of double estrangement demonstrated by the shaman imbues him with the capacity for revolt. Ewa Ziarek reminds us that 'it is here,' in this double estrangement, 'that we seek experiences of revolt' (Ziarek, 2001: 55). The shaman is a fitting metaphor for Nandy's efforts to disrupt existing concepts of dissent and to redirect and regenerate the boundaries of dissent.

The operation of the psychoanalytic mode as revolt within the essay sensitises Nandy to these issues. It also enables him to generate a critical analytic perspective that ruptures and regenerates the concept of dissent. In Nandy's depiction dissent has become foreclosed by the fixed boundaries that constitute what is audible. Nandy issues two warnings against the radical evil that is the suspension of thought. The first warning is levelled against the 'particular narrow and specific form dissent has to take, to be audible or politically non co-optable in our times' (Nandy, 2004a: 470). Nandy laments that for dissent to be audible it must be articulated within a specific form and structure. It must comply with processes of conformity, homogenisation and stagnation in order for it to be heard. The question of the audibility of dissent draws our attention to the inclusions and exclusions operating within the concept. For Nandy these boundaries are fixed and reinforced by what Nandy repeatedly references as the 'global culture of commonsense.' He describes this in the following way:

> And in that commonsense, this shared commonssense if you want to call it so, of the global urban middle class is one way to put it, it cuts across boundaries. It marks out a perimeter within which you operate even as a dissenter, and if you are inside this then you are a sane meaningful worthwhile opponent, then you are a true dissenter. And if you walk out of the perimeters, stay out of it, you are seen as a dissenter who is not only destructive but also not worth looking at because you are flouting the presumed axioms of sanity and rationality in some fundamental sense. And this is what I mean basically when I talk about the structure of global common sense. (Nandy and Deftereos, 2005c: 4)

Another way of expressing this culture of common sense is in relation to modernity. 'Dissent,' Nandy warns, 'To [even] qualify as dissent, must be fully translatable into the idiom of modernity' (Nandy, 2004a: 479). While the audible features of dissent conform to dominant and hegemonic imaginings, Nandy's analysis radically challenges this exclusion.

The second concern outlined in the essay is against the 'strange inaudibility that plagues those who, by design or by default, have become citizens of the dominant global culture' (Nandy, 2004a: 470). There is a link between the global subjects or a global citizen, who in acquiring their global status has willingly and unwittingly, accepted these conditions of inaudibility. This inaudibility is symptomatic for Nandy of a global trans-cultural conformity and stagnation within the culture of modernity, and is not only a cause for concern in India. Is not this inaudibility yet another manifestation of abjecting the wilderness and strangeness of the shaman, thus rendering him outside of accepted dissent? For Nandy, this inaudibility can be understood as part of the defence mechanisms safeguarding the boundaries of dissent. However, what is problematic for Nandy is that the citizen's inner capacity to rupture and regenerate these boundaries disappears from view. There is a loss of a critical capacity within the psychic life of the individual, and collectively within these cultures for imaginary and symbolic re-articulation. This condition confirms the dangers of suspension of thought.

The shaman operates in a similar way to Nandy's account of the non-modern peripheral in Indian political culture, detailed in the discussion of his critique of secularism. Like the non-modern peripheral the shaman is illiterate in the language of modernity and is deemed threatening. Equally threatening is the shaman's willingness to flout 'the presumed axioms of sanity and rationality in some fundamental sense.' This illiteracy and inaudibility go hand in hand coinciding with a lack of political recognition for the non-modern peripheral as entitled subject. The shaman like the non-modern peripheral is afforded a similar status within public life. Nandy takes the metaphor of the shaman seriously in order to redress these concerns and regenerate the concept of dissent in social and political criticism. The shaman is a figure with the capacity to revolt against the homogenisation and standardisation of dissent. The ambiguous position of the shaman as neither an insider nor outsider, and represented with a capacity to access the non-rational is privileged. Nandy explains this in the following way,

> coming out of a transformative experience, and then, claiming to be a testimony to another way of looking at reality and intervening in it, the shaman is a combination of a mystic healer and an exorcist who identifies demons – popular or unpopular, traditional or modern. (Nandy, 2004a: 472)

For Nandy the shaman is a figure who is both exorcist and healer. He is someone who is capable of rupture and someone who has access to regeneration and re-articulation and hence, to the therapeutic. These different ways of seeing, therefore have the capacities to disrupt the particular form dissent takes within this global culture of commonsense. Through the figure of the shaman Nandy undertakes to radically undermine the conformity and stagnation within the concept, to displace this global culture of common sense, and in turn to work through the prescriptive limits of what constitutes audible dissent. Nandy recognises these tasks because of the psychoanalytic mode as revolt operating in his work. It is this mode that provides him with the sensitivity, like the shaman, to acknowledge that,

> The recovery of other selves of cultures and communities, selves not defined by the dominant global consciousness, may turn out to be the first radical task of social criticism and political activism and the first responsibility of intellectual stocktaking in the first decades of the coming century. But that recovery may not be easy. As I have said, radical dissent today constantly faces the danger of getting organised into a standardized form. (Nandy, 2004a: 472)

The recovery that is intellectually and ethically acceptable is to be found in these alternative accounts of individual and collective expressions of selfhood, which remain outside the view of a dominant collective consciousness. Nandy acknowledges the difficulty of activating these processes of revolt. This includes, as discussed, working through internal defences and resistances to change and in traversing internal stasis within psychic life.

Nandy explores the shaman as a 'modest symbol of resistance to the dominant politics of knowledge' (Nandy, 2004a: 472). It is not therefore the heroic symbol of the shaman as the voice of 'all non-co-optable dissent' that he explores (Nandy, 2004a: 472). This qualification is consistent with Nandy's rejection of a single solution to the problematic of dissent. This solution is not possible given the operation of the psychoanalytic mode as revolt within his work. As detailed the analytic mode precludes fixed solutions and the closure of the analytic mode in this way. For Nandy the shaman is a symbol of resistance that perpetually challenges, ruptures and regenerates. Society and culture though is often resistant, and also threatened by the shaman's capacity for change. This can be explained by the fact that the figure of the shaman is already imbued with a number of existing and conflicting symbolic representations within societies. Existing at the borderlands of acceptability and non-acceptability, the shaman evokes a range of responses, as being esteemed and revered, to being a maligned abject figure. Notably, it is the popular image of the shaman as a witchdoctor, a figure with access to the strange and intimate within the self and within culture that is of interest here. In Nandy's work the shaman has the capacity to actuate anamnesis or retrospective return into disavowed parts of individual and collective selfhood. This is possible given his ability to communicate within a number of different metaphysical realms. With 'one foot in the familiar, one foot outside; one foot in the present, one in the future' the shaman represents a disruption to accepted norms of logic and time (Nandy 2004a: 472). The shaman is capable of the kind of 'time travel to a possible self' that Nandy's critique supports (Nandy, 2002b: 157). This time travel includes access to cultural traditions, myths and the unconscious. These qualities lend themselves to processes of rupture and regeneration.

The question remains though, by whom is this mode of dissent recognised and heard? Nandy claims that the shaman's dissent is met with suspicion and resistance. As a figure *in revolt*, who engages with disavowed parts of the self and culture, the shaman's identity and more importantly capacities will not always be represented within mainstream society. This is especially true of modern societies that devalue the mythopoetic, and therefore can only tolerate the shaman as a relic of the past. If he or she does manage to survive in such societies then their subjectivity will be 'rationally' and 'systematically' interpreted as 'belonging to an earlier stage of the evolution of consciousness' (Nandy, 2004a: 473). These representations reveal the threat and anxiety that the shaman provokes. Nandy notes that, 'the shaman may even manage to survive in a historical society as a lunatic, a schizophrenic who should be psychiatrically committed or, if that becomes politically embarrassing, met with deafening silence' (Nandy, 2004a: 473). The embarrassing and inaudible features that the shaman represents are nonetheless valued. It is this value that provides the shaman with the sensitivity and openness fundamental to Nandy's mode of dissent. Further, this embarrassment can be contextualised within the symbolic function that the third world performs within western modernity.

There are however, distinct limits to the metaphor of the shaman. These limitations lay predominantly within the shaman's fear of organised and structured dissent. In this sense 'the shaman often is too anarchic, too individualistic and too suspicious of all formal political processes' (Nandy, 2004a: 474). Yet this inability to conform to formal political processes is what preserves the shaman's ability to maintain access to alternate languages, cosmologies and forms of consciousness. The shaman's inability to conform demonstrates the psychoanalytic mode as revolt in Nandy's essay. Like the shaman whose own mode of dissent is imbedded in a perpetual experience of revolt, Nandy too does not waiver in his commitment to a permanent analytic mode of dissent. The metaphor of the shaman performs an important symbolic function for a thinker and writer like Nandy committed to safeguarding the therapeutic. He reflects on this in the following way: 'what is dissent if it has no place for the unknown, the childlike and the non-rational? And what is the intellectual's job definition if it does not include the ability to be in a minority and at the borderlines of the knowable?' (Nandy, 2004a: 480). Like the shaman, Nandy's ability as a critic to exist at the borderlines of the knowable provides him with this sensitivity and openness to theorise dissent in these ways. For Nandy the boundaries of dissent do not necessarily disappear through this psychoanalytic mode as revolt, but that these boundaries are free from standardisation, homogenisation and conformity. To this we can also add Nandy's sensitivity to positioning of the boundaries between the psychological and the political. As Chanter and Ziarek argue, 'erupting along the fault lines of these supposedly discrete structures, abjection both constitutes and undermines the stable distinctions between the life of the psyche and the life of the polis' (Chanter and Ziarek, 2005: 2). Nandy's capacity to theorise along 'the fault lines' between culture and the psyche, however, extends beyond his critique of secularism, and is also a distinct feature across his work.

Nandy's ability to rupture and regenerate the boundaries between culture and psyche is made possible through this psychoanalytic mode of revolt operating in his work. This analytic mode as revolt imbues Nandy and his work with certain features, namely his ability to resist abjection. Nandy, through this mode, is able to rupture and regenerate meaning and signification, and in the process reclaim and remake his subjectivity and agency as critic. As Kristeva reminds us the concept of revolt, is necessarily an intimate revolt, as a turning inwards into and on oneself. Revolt denotes more that just an analytic attitude of defiance here, by locating itself as a series of processes that activate and safeguard the analytic attitude from homogenisation, standardisation and conformity. These processes of retrospective return and anamnesis, creates a rupturing of norms, values, meanings and identities. Added to these processes are the regenerative possibilities not only in imaginary identifications but also symbolic transformation, in the possibility of transforming social relations. In applying these processes of revolt to describe the psychoanalytic mode Nandy's identity as critic are firmly situated within these concerns. To focus on the operation of the psychoanalytic mode as revolt in Nandy's work and in his identity is to move away from what the *symptomatic* and to enter into this *psychotherapeutic* register. The psychotherapeutic reveals itself in both the disruption but more importantly in the regeneration of meaning. Here dissent itself is continually regenerated not only in the alternative modes of being advanced by the shaman, but in the voice of the critic whose own work exemplifies the metaphoric workings of the shaman. It is in the integrity and permanent features of this psychoanalytic mode of revolt that the consistency in Nandy's interventions can be fully appreciated.

NOTES

1. The analytic attitude is a term coined by Philip Reiff to describe the Freudian endeavour and ranks as Schafer argues, 'as one of Freud's greatest creations,' developed largely in his papers on the techniques of psychoanalysis. A number of theorists, including Reiff have contributed to exploring and characterising this Freudian analytic attitude both in the clinical setting and

in its application to literary theory and cultural studies. For instance see R. Schafer (1983): 3; P. Rieff (1966). E. Erikson (1964); Freud, S. (1974); Elliott, A. and S. Frosh (1995).

2. The relationship between psychoanalysis and hermeneutics is theorised at length in the work of the philosopher Paul Ricoeur. Ricoeur argues that psychoanalysis is a type of hermeneutics and has defined psychoanalysis as a hermeneutics of suspicion. P. Ricoeur (1970).; P. Ricoeur (1981). See also J. Habermas (1971).

3. There are a number of texts contributing to the debates surrounding Kristeva's scholarship. For instance, this includes questioning the political consequences of her work and the social and political implications of the psychoanalytic revolt detailed in her work. For a discussion of these issues refer to S. Beardsworth (2004); T. Chanter, and Ziarek, E. (2005); S. Gambaudo (2007); C. Sjoholm (2005).

4. On this point of resistance to psychoanalysis and psychoanalytic methods see J. Derrida (1998).

5. See J. Kristeva (1991).

6. C. Lévi-Strauss (1968); M. Taussig (1986); S. Kakar (1982).

PART C

Critical Interventions:
Towards the Psychotherapeutic

6

The Psychotherapeutic as
a Mode of Social Criticism

Nandy's interventions extend an invitation to us to enter into processes of retrospective questioning, retrospective return and
anamnesis. These processes of turning inwards— confront, displace,
and work through established norms, meanings, values, projections
and introjections within psychic life. This invitation though is not always readily accepted. For such an invitation brings us face to face
with complex and deeply imbedded defences and resistances within
psychic life. These resistances must be worked through and worked
out, in order to activate the therapeutic possibility of revolt. Revolt
in this respect safeguards our well-being by challenging the radical
evils of stagnation, homogenisation and conformity within psychic
life. The therapeutic emerges then as an effect of this rupturing, to
the incessant movement of revolt. The therapeutic finds expression
through the processes of regeneration, in the infinite re-creation
and psychic re-birth that is made possible through revolt. According
to Kristeva this psychic re-birth takes effect as a rupturing and regeneration of the boundaries of selfhood. From this regeneration of
subjectivity a number of further possibilities then emerge; namely a
changed relationship to the other, along with recognition of our own
radical alterity. The therapeutic appears in these possibilities and alternatives, instituted at the level of the imaginary and re-articulated
in the symbolic.

Nandy's identity, his intellectual significance and autonomy of
thought are firmly located inside these processes of revolt. Therefore,
in suggesting that Nandy enters into these processes of revolt, as the
method to generate social and political criticism, he ruptures and

regenerates meanings, including the meanings attached to his own identity as critic. To this extent, the operation of the psychoanalytic mode as revolt in his work provides him with the capacity to resist abjection. The therapeutic also appears in Nandy's ability to re-direct the abjection towards the self into the transformation of social relations. This transformation takes place for Nandy in his re-positioning of the boundaries between self and other, psychological and political, public and private. This transformation includes the return of possibilities and alternatives in his work, as alternative meanings and aspects of selfhood, even latent aspects of self, are addressed in his work. On another level the therapeutic is equally evident in the effects and affects this psychoanalytic mode of revolt has on others in promoting self-reflexivity and questioning intimately held individual and collective assumptions. These effects include cultivating a reflexivity and self-reflexivity, in order to develop a politics of awareness advanced in Nandy's work. These effects also have the intended consequence of cultivating an analytic attitude previously described.

This chapter draws on two examples to demonstrate Nandy's commitment to radical dissent actuated through a permanent and consistent psychoanalytic mode of revolt. These examples therefore also demonstrate Nandy's ability to resist abjection through this analytic mode as revolt operating in his work. The two examples are taken from different periods in Nandy's intellectual life and also demonstrate the enduring features of his mode over time. On the surface both these examples appear to speak to very different issues, themes and readerships. A case can be made that these differences denote a range within Nandy's oeuvre that should be celebrated according to the criteria of intellectual breadth and depth—criteria which not unusually supports scholarly profiles. Nandy states,

> Frankly, many people tell me about the range of my work, so many things. But actually it is...I would think the range is somewhat narrow in the sense that my primary concern has always been human subjectivity. What makes a human being click? What makes him a master? What makes him a creative artist? What are the inner dynamics of a person? What or how is the person configured? How is the self configured? That has always been my primary interest and in that sense my concerns are not really changed because it is only in a different condition or context that I am looking at it. And even within that you might have noticed that I have always been fascinated by two broad areas of human endeavour - human destructiveness and human potentialities. These two extreme areas; and human potentialities including human creativity, and much of my work flows from this as an oscillation between these two. (Nandy and Defteros, 2005a: 4)

Nandy affirms his psychoanalytic focus, but consistent with this psychoanalytic mode of revolt, he does so through his commitment to working with and working through the complexities of human subjectivity. In focusing on both human destructiveness and human creativity Nandy self-represents his work as being produced from these two analytic positions. Equally significant are the ways in which Nandy engages with a concept of self. The concept of self, subject to the operation of the psychoanalytic mode of revolt in his work, is understood as an infinite recreation. Therefore, the therapeutic effects of Nandy's work are in the regeneration and re-articulation of selfhood.

The two examples discussed in this chapter illustrate how the psychoanalytic mode of revolt operates as a permanent feature of Nandy's work. These examples written over twenty years apart demonstrate the consistency and integrity of his mode of critical intervention. The first example is Nandy's analysis of the loss and recovery of self within the context of colonialism. This is developed in one of Nandy's most well known texts *The Intimate Enemy: Loss and Recovery of Self under Colonialism* (1983a). The text is well-received in a number of intellectual circles but has particular resonance within studies of postcoloniality and postcolonial studies. What is notable about the example is that the same psychoanalytic mode of revolt continues to produce distinct alternatives in the same ways as it has in this earlier point of Nandy's intellectual life. The text radically confronts colonial fantasies of a Western modern and progressive ego ideal operating in colonialist ideology. Nandy radically ruptures and regenerates the positioning of the boundaries between colonial subject and object, coloniser and colonised, perpetrator and victim. As has been emphasised of his work:

> that Nandy consistently advocates a third way (that of the non-player) the way of reconciliation and compassion, of bearing witness and assuming responsibility, even of courage and self-sacrifice, to the point when both the victors and the vanquished may be transformed, seeing themselves in a new light. (Paranjape in Lal, 2000)

Nandy reconfigures colonialism in terms of the subject's conflicting relation to the other within, an enemy who is intimate. In this reading, colonial power as having psychic dimensions enables Nandy to further explore the possibility of rupture and regeneration, as both internal and external processes. These are addressed in *The Intimate Enemy* by re-imagining individual and collective resistance, liberation and self-affirmation alongside questions of cultural survival. The operation of this psychoanalytic mode of revolt therefore actuates this possibility of another structuring of subjectivity, for the individual and for these societies. This regeneration of subjectivity is vital to the recovery that Nandy is interested in re-claiming. This recovery is demonstrated by the possibilities and alternatives throughout the text that safeguard individual and collective psychic life from the dangers of stagnation, homogenisation and conformity.

The second example considered demonstrates the integrity and consistency of Nandy's psychoanalytic mode of revolt over time within the very different context of public debates. These debates are entered into in a selection of five newspaper articles written in 2005–07 and published in *The Times of India*, a national daily broadsheet printed in English. In these articles Nandy continues via the operation of this mode to rupture and regenerate official imaginings of an Indian nation and Indian self. In these articles Nandy radically confronts power relations in order to re-articulate the inclusions and exclusions in Indian culture. The rupture and regeneration of national fantasies draws our attention to the complexity of challenging dominant and fiercely defended concepts of national identity and national integration. These articles demonstrate Nandy's commitment to the recreation of Indian accounts of selfhood not mediated by the Indian nation state. This regeneration also includes the possibility of recognising modes of suffering and trauma, subjective and inter-subjective experiences rendered invisible by a dominant national imaginary. Even within the brief scope of these newspaper articles and at these moments of forced engagement, Nandy's psychoanalytic mode of critical intervention maintains its integrity and moreover, an autonomy of thought. The purpose of reading these five articles then is not to evaluate the alternative imaginaries offered but rather to note the consistency in which each article demonstrates Nandy's psychoanalytic mode of revolt, and in turn his capacity via this mode to produce these alternatives.

LOSS AND RECOVERY OF POSSIBLE SELVES: THE REVOLT AGAINST THE INTIMATE ENEMIES

The Intimate Enemy: Loss and Recovery of Self under Colonialism (1983a) explores the cultural and psychic processes that take form through the psychic life of colonialism. This is a colonialism that colonises minds. As the text affirms it is a colonialism that survives according to the complex rhythms of psychic life, as an intimate enemy well after the demise of empires. This is a colonialism that in Nandy's account won its 'great victories not so much through its military and technological prowess as through its ability to create secular hierarchies incompatible with the traditional order' (Nandy, 1983a: ix). It is a colonialism that succeeded in restructuring imaginary and symbolic forms of identification, processes of subjection, in instituting new forms of social relations and in shifting cultural priorities. For the individuals, cultures and societies involved, this resulted in the internalisation of the West as a dominant psychological category, or political imaginary. The text is an invitation to explore the ways in which human subjectivity and the subjectivity of these societies was shaped by these cultural and political conditions. Consistent though with the operation of the psychoanalytic mode of revolt the invitation by Nandy necessarily denotes both a rupture and rearticulation of these very conditions, and how they may be understood.

The mode of revolt does not however, entail demystifying the colonial condition in order to reveal the truth of this condition. In contrast to the theorist Frantz Fanon who has already exposed 'the truth' as a Manichean reality, Nandy radically destabilises accepted meanings of the colonial experience, including the conditions of psychological subjugation. There is an important point of differentiation that can be made between the work of Fanon and Nandy distinguishable by the operation of different analytic modes within their work. Nandy's own objection to Fanon's work is detailed in the text in terms of the articulation of this mode, and the re-production of an existing logic. For instance he writes that, 'Let us not forget that the most violent denunciation of the West produced by Frantz Fanon is written in the elegant style of a Jean-Paul Sartre' (Nandy, 1983a: xii).[1] Rather there is a distinctive rejection of modes of critical intervention that seek to counter or redress such imbalances. To enter into an oppositional logic to counter that, which is revealed, can easily be co-opted into replicating existing forms of dominance and standardisation. Nandy suggests that this internal logic has dominated anti-colonial thought, and anti-colonial movements, that have sought to redress this power dynamic through a counter response, that replicates a colonial logic. In replicating the internal logic existing within the cultural and psychological pathologies of colonialism can only return us to what Nandy describes are tragic-comic distortions. In claiming that the damaging and destructive effects of colonialism were more harshly experienced by the colonisers than the colonised, he radically

disrupts accepted boundaries between coloniser, colonised; perpetrator, victim; self and other. In Nandy's reading it is the coloniser as a
self-destructive co-victim that subverts the psychological, social and
political conditions of colonialism. To not recognise the degradation
of the coloniser, his own loss of self, loss of psychic wellbeing and
loss of humanity, is to replicate the colonialist fantasy of the superiority of the oppressor. The fantasy of the coloniser's moral, political, economic and psychological superiority is traversed throughout
the text. In recognising that both the coloniser and colonised were
victims of this punitive and overwhelming psychology, Nandy re-
casts colonialism as 'a battle between the de-humanized self and the
objectified enemy' (Nandy, 1983a: xvi). The analysis confronts and
works through images of an Indian colonialism defined by its British
victors and their oppressed Indian counter-parts, by turning to the
internal psychic experiences within the self and within these societies. Therefore accounts of selfhood, self-esteem and self-affirmation,
identifications, projections and representations are the entry points
into the psychic life of colonialism. In Nandy's analysis this survives
within the complexities and contradictions of human subjectivity of
both the coloniser and colonised.

In the text Nandy traverses the narcissistic fantasies of a centrally
located colonial power, primarily in two ways. First, by confronting
and radically questioning the positioning of the boundaries between
colonisers and colonised. He does this by emphasising the loss of self,
and loss of humanity experienced by both perpetrators and victims.
The loss of the self transcends the distinction between colonisers and
colonised, given the psychic costs involved and internalised by the
colonisers. This loss of self was internalised within British culture and
had its own complex set of cultural pathologies to work through. In
doing so, Nandy displaces the authoritarianism of colonialist ideology along with its hyper-masculine forms of identification. Second,
this enables him to work through and regenerate the self's destructive and violent relationship to the other, including identifying with
the aggressor. Implicit within this task is the exploration of psychological resistance to this colonisation of the self, along with questions
of cultural survival. The text focuses on these internal modes of resistance and resilience (internal to the self and to culture) that not only
survive but which challenge the meanings of colonisation in profound ways. Taking the ideas of psychological resistance to colonialism seriously, as Nandy does, is an ethical commitment to preserving
our own intimate critical faculties, the health of our psychic life. This

commitment is all the more imperative in light of the dangers of the nineteenth century dream of the one world that for Nandy continues to, 'haunt(s) us with the prospect of a fully homogenized, technologically controlled, absolutely hierarchised world, defined by polarities like the modern and the primitive, the secular and non-secular...' (Nandy, 1983a: x).

The challenge is to rupture and regenerate this homogenising, standardising and stagnant political imagining. Nandy's analysis ruptures and regenerates the polarities between colonisers and colonised by reconstituting accounts of selfhood and opening us to alternative accounts of subjectivity. The displacement and reconstruction of subjectivity that Nandy enters into via this mode is not simply a counter-response to dominant colonialist ideals. The response that the text validates as ethically acceptable is a far more complex undertaking. The disruption to these ideals is actuated through a revolt resulting in the traversal of colonial fantasies, the negativisation of a hyper-masculine and aggressive colonialist ego, and the affirmation of non-violence. This process is what Kristeva might note is a form of ethical respect for the other and their humanity, emanating from internal transformations within the self. This latter point is significant to the operation of the psychoanalytic mode of revolt. For as Nandy warns, to reproduce structures of violence or to make a case for the creative and psychotherapeutic possibilities within violence reproduces modes of dissent dependent on identification with the aggressor. Such identifications work to reinforce an existing structure of defences, thus creating what Nandy elsewhere has termed is a second-order reality of domination, subjugation and subjection. Even 'when in opposition, that dissent remains predictable and controlled' and ultimately does little to regenerate existing patterns of identification and signification (Nandy, 1983a: xii).

THE RHYTHMS OF RUPTURE

Nandy carries forward his commitment to rupturing established certitudes, meanings and associations. He does this by instructing the reader that the text can be read as a cautionary tale. While 'conventional anti-colonialism can be an apologia for the colonization of minds,' an alternative account can challenge modes of conformity and standardisation. Nandy can distinguish himself from these perspectives with a psychoanalytic mode of revolt that displaces existing meanings, and the meanings attached to subjectivity. In doing so, he unequivocally aligns his work within a more fluid and open critical tradition, as a rupturing and regeneration of ideas, meaning and modes of critical intervention. What is made possible through the operation of the psychoanalytic mode is 'to speak of the plurality of critical traditions and of human rationality,' that his analysis affords (Nandy, 1983a: x). He notes that, 'even if this sounds hopelessly like another case of unresolved counter-transference, I hope this book contributes to that stream of critical consciousness: the tradition of reinterpretation of traditions to create new traditions' (Nandy, 1983a: xii).

Traversing the fantasy of a homogenised world where polarities between [coloniser/colonised, self/other, victimiser/victimised, masculine/emasculated, adult/childlike] must be confronted is pivotal to his contribution to 'critical consciousness'. This critical consciousness is also central to the re-positioning of the boundaries between self and other that Nandy makes within the text. In recognising the alterity that exists within subjectivities and the fluidity in self-definitions of Indianness provides the entry point for this reconfiguration of the self and other. It is in working through the loss and recovery of self that these relationships can be re-imagined and re-constituted. Rupturing these relationships though is a disruptive process. Consequently Nandy intentionally represents a 'distorted view' of Indian historical narrative, including the date of colonialism. If Nandy's psychoanalytic interest is in processes of retrospective questioning made possible through anamnesis, then the concept of time is also subject to the temporalising timelessness of psychic life. Time is radically displaced from a historical linear frame and now subject to the rhythms of psychic life. If, as Nandy declares, the intention is to explore 'the cultural and psychological strategies which have helped [Indian] society to survive the experience [of colonialism]' then the past, present and future collapse into one frame. (Nandy, 1983a: xvi). There is also confrontation with historicism, as Nandy does not hesitate to declare the essays in the text 'to be an alternative mythography of history which denies and defies the [very] values of history [itself]' (Nandy, 1993: xvi).

The *Intimate Enemy* demonstrates the proximity or intimacy between the past, present and future by resisting a linear narrativisation of these experiences with colonialism. Nandy in actuating these processes of anamnesis, of retrospective return and questioning does so as a means of reconstituting these relationships. This aptitude for internal questioning is supplemented by cultural traditions and

Indian accounts of human subjectivity that for Nandy, already carry forward the possibility of re-interpretation and re-construction. For example, he cites that in the case of the Indian folk historian with an understanding of the Indian concept of fatalism, there can be no real disjunction between the past and present. According to the Indian concept of fatalism in the past there are open choices. The past is understood in more fluid terms, open to the reconstruction of that past in terms of a new past or alternative determined future (a new fatalism) (Nandy, 1983a: 58). He confirms that 'the Indian's past is always open; whereas his future is so only to the extent that is a rediscovery or renewal' (Nandy, 1983a: 59). Is the Indian subject then, as depicted here with a tacit understanding of fatalism a figure in revolt? We may very well ask whether the text is a commentary on the ways in which the Indic civilisation is a culture of revolt? Nandy's approach beckons us to ask such questions and therefore, creates a rupturing.

The instability in meaning that Nandy plays with via this mode of analysis is also reflected in the structure of the text. The *Intimate Enemy* comprises two long essays; the first titled 'The Psychology of Colonialism: Sex, Age and Ideology in British India,' and the second, 'The Unconscious Mind: A Post-Colonial View of India and the West.' The feeling of interruption and movement in the text is enhanced by the subdivision of these essays into shorter and seemingly disparate parts. There is a disruptive quality in the structure of the text which does not adhere to a linear logic of re-telling, but rather, is woven and interwoven with a multitude of narratives. The text reads more like a series of vignettes, as Nandy references a variety of protagonists, materials and examples ranging from historical figures, psycho-biographical accounts, life-histories, novels, myths and traditional texts. He therefore oscillates between working with Western and Indian figures, texts, traditions, folkways, myths and personal narratives in order to displace the psychology of colonialism, along with a given idiom of dissent. What is consistent throughout the text is Nandy's focus on human subjectivity as the site of revolt.

While a number of theorists have commented on these processes as a form of hybridisation, the operation of the psychoanalytic mode of revolt is indicative of a different level of complexity. For example, Arif Dirlik argues, 'Nandy utilizes hybridities produced by the colonial encounter as a means to the rediscovery and recovery of authentic pasts' (Dirlik, 2000: 126). In contrast to this reading, hybridisation can be understood as an effect of this mode, in rupturing and re-instituting possibilities and alternatives. Further, these processes of rediscovery cannot be a return to an authentic past or the re-claiming of an authentic Indianness because revolt forecloses the fixity of meaning. Rather, it is in returning to the conditions of this authentic past, and activating retrospective questioning that leads to a possible psychic rebirth of that past. To accept the invitation into this mode of thinking then is to accept that the voice of the author and the analysis offered cannot be understood or articulated within a language of certitudes. It is to accept that this mode of analysis is also a rupturing and regeneration of methods of interpretation through which the possibility of transformation can continue.

Nandy invites the reader into the mode of 'the savage outsider who is neither willing to be a player or counter-player' (Nandy, 1983a: xiv). But we may well ask who this non-player is, who is privileged within the text? And again is this not a figure capable of accessing and actuating processes of revolt? This is the non-player who not only resists and survives within this culture but also does so by preserving his internal capacities for re-imagining his own selfhood and his society's selfhood differently. For Nandy, while 'translating and commenting on the West, these outsiders have smuggled in their own imageries, myths and fantasies' (Nandy, 1983a: xiii). The text therefore celebrates this possibility of instituting an alternative imaginary that not only survives within these accounts of selfhood, but which resists, confronts and reconfigures the dominant parts of self. This capacity for the fluid interplay between what Nandy terms are dominant and the latent parts of the self are fundamental to the wellbeing within psychic life and within culture. What is valued here is the displacement that takes place in meaning when this 'fidelity to one's inner self, as one translates, and to one's inner voice, when one comments' can and does survive (Nandy, 1983: xiii). The examples below affirm the ways this psychoanalytic mode of revolt actuates and institutes alternative meanings, imaginings and representations of the colonial experience.

Loss of Self: *Whose Loss and How?*

Nandy details at length the cultural pathologies that resulted from the experience of colonialism. In the first essay 'The Psychology of Colonialism' the reordering of Indian culture is explored through the importation of British concepts of sex and age. The importation of these concepts and the processes of subjection operating in colonial ideology reconstituted an existing traditional order and social code. This homology between childhood and the state of being colonized that a modern colonial system uses was effective because it resulted in a distinctive change over time in consciousness. Nandy claims that there were far more fluid understandings of masculinity and femininity, in Hindu texts, myths and epics. These accounts have a long critical tradition of the inter-play between masculine and feminine and were replaced by new forms of identification. The concepts of *purusatva* (the essence of masculinity) *naritva* (the essence of femininity) and *kibatva* (the essence of hermaphroditism or emasculation) were radically undermined by colonial ideology and reconstituted by a masculine ego ideal, which the coloniser and colonial order exemplified. The new forms of identification that became central to colonial India resulted in the polarities between masculinity and femininity being supplanted by the antonyms of masculinity and kibatva. This 'femininity-in-masculinity was now perceived as the final negation of a man's political identity, a pathology more dangerous than femininity itself' within colonial culture (Nandy, 1983a: 8). Loss of self reveals itself through this now greatly compromised account of masculinity. What the text laments is the loss of possibility available in process of identification within accounts of human subjectivity. In reconstituting masculinity within an aggressive ego ideal, the effeminate Hindu ego, with his undifferentiated masculinity supplemented by his child like features, provided the psychological conditions through which to reorganise Indian subjectivity. This process also re-affirmed the colonial fantasy of the superiority of the coloniser. The inner conflict caused by this now truncated imago, is for Nandy well-documented, including within literature. This is evident for example in novels such as Rabindranath Tagore's *Car Adhay*, where the heroic protagonist details his own personal movement away from his own categories of identification for political assertion. In Tagore's novel, the protagonist takes on these characteristics of hyper-masculinity instrumentally, but ultimately to his own detriment and loss of self, whereby the re-assertion of hyper masculinity not only confirms political identity and valorises the subject but provides the condition for what Nandy calls, 'a second-order legitimacy to what in the dominant culture of the colony had already become the final differentiate of manliness: aggression, achievement, control, competition and power' (Nandy, 1983a: 9).

The *Intimate Enemy* explores the ways that subjectivity organised around this ego ideal, along with the theory of progress was able to legitimise colonialism by reconstituting the human life cycle. Within

this account the possibilities for self-constitution are greatly truncated. Nandy demonstrates the two responses available to the Indian
subject within this psychology of colonialism. The first is from the
child-like Indian and the second from the childish Indian, though
both responses were subject to the colonialist fantasy of reform, development and progress. In the first instance it is claimed that the
innocent child like Indian whose characteristics included an ignorant, masculine, loyal and corrigible disposition could be reformed
through processes of Westernisation, modernisation and Christiani-
sation. The second response from the childish Indian, who represented an ungrateful, sinful, savage, disloyal and thus incorrigible being,
required a repression of this childish disposition 'by controlling re-
bellion, ensuring internal peace and providing tough administration
and rule of law' (Nandy, 1983a: 16). This psychology was supported
by a number of figures that complied with this colonial culture such
as Michael Madhusudan Dutt who sought to redefine popular Hindu
mythology to fit the changing values under colonialism.[2] Such figures may have contributed to the cultural and political definitions
of selfhood, but these accounts of selfhood did little to preserve self-
esteem and cultural autonomy, or in other words, individual and
collective well-being. The text therefore applauds those who tried
to 'break out of this stagnation' by noting the rupturing of this political imaginary, by individuals who sought to create a new political
awareness (Nandy, 1983a: 27). The restoration of awareness can be
read here as an effort to rupture and regenerate a stagnant imaginary. Nandy cites Iswarchandra Vidyasagar as a figure who sought
to create a new political awareness 'which would combine a critical
awareness of Hinduism and colonialism with cultural and individual
authenticity.' Nandy continues that 'his was an effort to protect not
the formal structure of Hinduism but its spirit, as an open, anarchic
federation of sub-cultures and textual authorities which allowed new
readings and internal criticisms' (Nandy, 1983a: 27). Such interventions or ruptures into this psychology and culture of colonialism are
important for regenerating our understandings of loss of self. These
ruptures are also important for understanding the psychological resistance that Nandy reads into Indian culture.

Another aspect to this loss of self is in the radical claim made within
the text that the coloniser was a co-victim within these processes. Notably what demonstrates the operation of the psychoanalytic mode
of revolt is this invitation to the reader to enter into the mindset and

culture of those equally, if not more so overwhelmed by the experience of being colonial rulers. It is in 'the less well known cultural and psychological pathologies produced by colonization in the colonizing societies' that Nandy explores that the rupture and displacement of the colonial experience is best exemplified (Nandy, 1983a: 32). Nandy radically regenerates our understanding of colonialism by exploring four cultural pathologies that indicate that the 'long term cultural damage colonialism did to the British society was greater.' These pathologies included the colonial order and hierarchy, though in a modified form also applied to British society. Within the society of the coloniser the pathologies created a false sense of cultural homogeneity that is perpetuated by what Nandy terms is an underdevelopment of self. Despite this underdevelopment within individual and collective subjectivity this still encouraged the 'colonizers to impute to themselves magical feelings of omnipotence and permanence' (Nandy, 1983a: 35).

INTERNAL RESISTANCES TO A DOMINANT COLONIAL ORDER

The *Intimate Enemy* takes the displacement of the coloniser further by looking at four different responses to these cultural pathologies. Nandy radically disrupts the fantasy of a unified colonial ego, by focusing on four different British figures and their experiences with colonialism. Nandy also differentiates Indian experiences from the experiences of these Westerners (Nandy, 1983a: 48). The figures of Rudyard Kipling, George Orwell, Oscar Wild and Charles Freer Andrew, each represent a particular response to the internalisation of colonialism within British society. Each in different ways radically displaces the assumption of an integrated colonial ego as each figure deals with the internalisation of colonialism differently. Nandy distinguishes the first two responses by Kipling and Orwell as coming from a direct or indirect exposure to the colonial situation. He suggests that Kipling and Orwell struggled with ideas of authority, responsibility, psychological security, self-esteem, hierarchy, power and evangelism. Kipling capturing the 'pathetic self-hatred and ego constriction which went with colonialism and the latter [Orwell] the relative sense of freedom and critical morality which were the true antithesis of colonialism and which one could acquire only by *working through* the colonial consciousness' (Nandy, 1983a: 36). Wilde and the other members of the Bloomsbury group responded indirectly to colonialism and were not as self-conscious. Andrews represents a 'numerically small but psychologically significant response of many who wholly opted out of their colonizing society and fought for the cause of India' (Nandy, 1983a: 36). Kipling is also the subject of a detailed psychobiography in the second essay of the *Intimate Enemy*, where he is lauded as 'the most creative builder of the political myths which a colonial power needs to sustain its self-esteem' (Nandy, 1983a: 37). According to Nandy, Kipling's image of the colonial subject is however, riddled by resistance, self-hatred, conflict and repression. Kipling is depicted as someone who resisted and consistently fought to disown in self-hatred an aspect of his self that identified with Indianness. For Nandy, the new myths, which Kipling produced about the civilising mission of colonialism is understood as part of the assertion of selfhood. Nandy argues that, 'the pathology of the Westernised Indian's personality, which Kipling so cleverly identified, was rooted in India's encounter with the ego-ideals of Kipling in the first place' (Nandy, 1983a: 84). It is Kipling's investment in the fetishised colonialist stereotypes as effeminate, childlike and savage that also reaffirms an aspect of Kipling's own authenticity, as well as his subjectivity. For Nandy, Kipling's response to colonialism demonstrates a disavowal of his identity. In contrast to this account of self, Orwell's response and resistance is an effort to address this disavowal. If Kipling's efforts where to conceal and repress parts of selfhood then Orwell's resistance was to articulate these openly, becoming an astute critic of the dominant middle-class culture central to the colonialism.

Nandy argues the third response was a protection and defence against the more feminine aspects of British self. This is evidenced in the figure of Wilde and the politicisation and subsequent criminal-ization of his sexual identity. The creativity of this response, which Nandy acknowledges, lies in the ways in which the dominance of hyper-masculinity was resisted against. Wilde's controversy and his marginality were reinforced 'by demonstratively using his homosex-uality as a cultural ideology' which 'threatened to sabotage his com-munity's dominant self-image as a community of well-defined men' (Nandy, 1983a: 44). Andrews' response and resistance to colonialism is expressed in his religiosity and non-conformity to British society. What is interesting about the depiction of Andrews is that he carries the weight of a double identity which Nandy values. Andrews was, as Nandy claims, marked by the ambivalence of being an Indian at heart and at the same time a true Englishman. Andrews developed a critique of British colonialism and mode of resistance informed by Christian ethics as much as it was by the classical universalism of Rabindranath Tagore and the folk-based critical traditionalism of Gandhi. For Nandy, in each of these responses to colonialism, the concept of resistance is displaced and regenerated through these life histories and experiences. It is in turning to the question of human subjectivity and the internalisations within psychic life that resistance is located, and also ruptured and regenerated.

Recovery or 'Liberation for Those Who do not Speak the Language of Liberation'[3]

I have noted that the figure of the non-player, as a subject in revolt is valued within *The Intimate Enemy*. The value of this subject position becomes all the more apparent when questioning the concept of liberation. Consistent with Nandy's mode of critical engagement the value of the non-player is also apparent in his ability to recover self. Within the text, the non-player confronts the cultural pathologies of colonialism by entering into a series of displacements of 'the dyadic relationship' between the rulers and ruled, coloniser and colonised, victimiser and victim (Nandy, 1983a: 7). The non-player confronts the complex defences underpinning these relationships, namely in identifying with the aggressor. In resisting this process of identification the non-player demonstrates a capacity to traverse the colonial fantasy of the superiority of the coloniser. Nandy privileges the non-player in this scenario because of his ability to recognise two crucial tensions at play. These are: first, in acknowledging the loss of self and loss of humanity that the colonial fantasy perpetuates and second, in acknowledging the need to regenerate the concept of recovery and liberation. The loss of self that takes place at a cost as the constitution and articulation of self is truncated by the categories and processes of identification already in place by colonial ideology. The loss of self and loss of humanity, which Nandy explores, represents the processes of standardisation and homogenisation of subjectivity and psychic life. For Nandy the aim, 'of the oppressed should be, not to become a first-class citizen in the world of oppression instead of a second—or third-class one, but to build an alternative world where he can hope to win back his humanity' (Nandy, 1983a: 34). The recovery of self that Nandy's mode of analysis enters into and which is ethically acceptable is intimately tied to winning back this humanity. The concept of humanity is located within psychic life and tied to the capacities to think and imagine something different by reconfiguring subjectivity. The only recovery or liberation that for Nandy is therefore ethically acceptable, consistent with the psychoanalytic mode of revolt, is in rejecting to 'thrive on what psychoanalysis references as secondary gains for the victim from the oppressive system' (Nandy, 1983a: 22). It is only through the rupturing and regeneration of self that recovery and liberation can be claimed.

In keeping with this commitment to psychic rebirth Nandy states that one must side with the slave, not in recognition of enslavement or transcendent suffering but because this subject position represents a higher order cognition. The non-player, the subject in revolt whose intentions are to displace the secondary gains that are reproduced in anti-colonial liberation movements has something to learn from the slave. Nandy's account describes this in the following way: 'one must choose the slave also because he represents a higher order cognition which perforce includes the master as a human, whereas the master's cognition has to exclude the slave as a thing' (Nandy, 1983a: xi). The psychic life of the slave is privileged because of the ways in which the borders of self and other relations are ruptured and regenerated.

RUPTURING AND REGENERATING SELFHOOD: *GANDHI AS A FIGURE IN REVOLT*

This theme of regenerating subjectivity and in recognising the humanity of the other is explored further in the second essay of the text, 'The Uncolonised Mind: A Post-Colonial View of India and the West.' Nandy does this by offering two contrasting psycho-biographical accounts of the psychic lives of Rudyard Kipling and Sri Aurobindo. The primary difference between these figures is for Nandy evidenced in the ways that their identity and selfhood is represented and affirmed. Consistent with the argument developed in Nandy's analysis of colonialism, Aurobindo's case provides a more interesting response to colonialism. For Nandy, Aurobindo similar to Gandhi provided responses to colonialism that demonstrated a greater respect for the selfhood of the other. For Nandy, Aurobindo's case provides a more interesting response to colonialism in that it was a 'cultural self-affirmation, which had a greater respect for the selfhood of the other' (Nandy, 1983a: 85). The essay also reintroduces us to the figure of Gandhi, previously explored in Nandy's work as the bad subject, and now as perhaps the ultimate figure in revolt. What takes place in the text and through these readings then is a hybridisation of experience, as definitions of loss of self are articulated as highly subjective instances within the complexities of psychic life. In Gandhi's case this response is all the more arresting given that his identity is a product of Colonial India. Consistent with Nandy's mode of revolt, 'it was colonial India, still preserving something of its androgynous cosmology and style, which ultimately produced a transcultural protest against the hyper-masculine world view of colonialism, in the form of Gandhi' (Nandy, 1983a: 48).

Gandhi actuates the ethical recovery of the non-player Nandy has in mind. Gandhi is also in revolt, and as Nandy suggests, is a product of a culture in revolt. 'If for the West the present was a special case of an unfolding history, for Gandhi as a representative of traditional India, history was a special case of an all-embracing permanent present, waiting to be interpreted and reinterpreted' (Nandy, 1983a: 57). What Gandhi recognised is that the re-claiming of self and Indianness was central to the recovery or liberation from colonialism. Moreover, he did so without being co-opted as many pre-Gandhian protest movements had already demonstrated by reclaiming a sense of self definition by masculinity, aggression and violence. Gandhi demonstrates that liberation or recovery of self, consistent with the operation of a psychoanalytic mode of revolt, is made possible through our individual and collective capacity to question, think and represent. The liberation or recovery that is advocated is therefore connected to restoring our humanity and the well-being in psychic life. This humanity is also inclusive of the humanity of the other. For Gandhi, as a figure in revolt, there is a distinct rejection of the use of violence in regenerating the relationships between self and other. As Nandy affirms violence 'ties the victim more deeply to the culture of oppression than any collaboration can' (Nandy, 1987a: 34). To condone 'the major technique of oppression in our times, organized violence,' Nandy maintains, 'cannot but further socialise the victims to the basic values of his oppressor' (Nandy, 1987a: 34). Gandhi's account of liberation as non-player best captures this need to reclaim our humanity. This is demonstrated in the way in which Gandhi displaced and regenerated two premises of colonial ideology in British India. These premises were based on sex (the hyper-masculinity of the coloniser against the effeminate Hindu for instance) and age (for example 'the half-child, half-savage Indian Other'). The second part of this discussion in the text turns to the ways these meanings confronted their traditional Indian counterparts and their new incarnations in Gandhi. Gandhi, as a figure in revolt, thus ruptures and traverses the paternal masculine social code of colonial ideology.

The concept of non-violence advocated by Gandhi is central to understanding the rupturing of the masculine social code and the recovery of self offered. Consistent with the operation of the psychoanalytic mode of revolt, Gandhi's concept of non-violence is intimately connected to subjectivity. The liberation and recovery that non-violence provides is not only an external reference point for political mobilisation. This recovery is also predicated on an internal revolt, a rupturing and regeneration of self. In Nandy's account Gandhi challenges the ideology of biological stratification acting as a homologue of—and legitimacy for—political inequality and injustice. Gandhi as a figure in revolt does this by rupturing and regenerating meaning in two ways. First, that for Gandhi androgyny was equated with saintliness, thus privileging this above the categories of masculinity (especially hyper-masculinity) and femininity. Second, that in rupturing the masculine social code in this way, Gandhi regenerates femininity as superior to masculinity, because of its connection to transcendental life. For Nandy, the effect of Gandhi's rupturing and regeneration of the masculine social code is that it also reconfigures our understanding of porous boundaries of self, and ego strength. 'What may look like yet another case of a "weak ego" in the Indian can be viewed as another kind of ego strength'[4] (Nandy, 1987a: 51). Nandy argues that what is perceived as the weak ego of the Indian and Indian culture cannot be equated with an impoverishment of the ego, or a loss of self. Within this re-articulation of self, hyper-masculinity and aggressiveness are removed from the equation. For Nandy, Gandhi's account of 'non-violence gives men access to protective maternity and by implication, to the godlike state of arghanarisvara, a god half-man, half-woman' (Nandy, 1983a: 54). Gandhi's concept of non-violence is therefore, privileged as part of a broader account of selfhood. According to Nandy, Eric Erikson rightly extends upon this by nothing that Gandhi's recovery of self, 'imputes an irreducible minimum humanity [as new possible thought and meaning] to the oppressors and militantly promotes the belief that this humanity could be actualised.'

For Gandhi the orientation towards myth in order to articulate the re-ordering of consciousness was part of a more general orientation to an alternate public consciousness grounded within a different account of the present. Public consciousness was not seen as a causal product of history but as related to history non-causally through memories and anti-memories.' In Nandy's reading, 'from such a viewpoint, the past can be an authority but the nature of the authority is seen as shifting, amorphous and amenable to intervention' (Nandy, 1983a: 57). Subject to the rhythms of rupture and regeneration liberation and recovery within the text can only be claimed if these processes of retrospective return, and retrospective questioning take place.

As *The Intimate Enemy* affirms, the only recovery that is accepted in the text comes through these processes of psychoanalytic revolt. The following passage affirms his commitment to these processes as a mode of critical engagement. Nandy articulates this recovery when he states that; 'one can either call it an Oriental version of the concept of permanent revolution or a practical extension of the mystical concept of timeless time in some Asiatic traditions' (Nandy, 1983a: 63). This commitment to the timelessness of the analytic re-affirms the intellectual and ethical commitment to the therapeutic register. The therapeutic reveals itself in rupturing and regenerating the masculinity of colonialism and in turn, rupturing and regenerating emasculated forms of dissent and practices of psychological resistance that a figure like Gandhi actuates in Nandy's analysis. Gandhi's mode of dissent is celebrated by Nandy here as an example of critical analytic intervention. These interventions succeed in rupturing and regenerating subjectivity and in doing so, regenerate our understanding of both loss and recovery of self for the coloniser and colonised.

RUPTURING AND REGENERATING THE IDEA OF INDIA: *THE PERMANENT PLAY WITH NATIONAL FANTASIES*

The consistency and integrity of Nandy's psychoanalytic mode of revolt, and through this his capacity to generate critical analytic perspectives is evident in a more recent example. I consider five articles written by Nandy where this psychoanalytic mode is applied to contest dominant meanings about the Indian nation state, national integration and Indianness. Nandy ruptures and regenerates official accounts and in doing so plays with a series of national fantasies that underpin the Indian nation state. The five articles published in *The Times of India*, are taken from a selection of Nandy's articles published during 2005–07.[5] Although these articles are short in length, the permanent features of the psychoanalytic mode operating in Nandy's work are evident. The mode of revolt maintains its integrity even in addressing sensitive national issues. At this point of forced engagement Nandy addresses both the complexity of these issues and the ways in which these complexities have been standardised, homogenised and foreclosed within public debates. What each article emphasises are the ways that complex issues have been foreclosed by a dominant account at the expense of alternative possibilities and imaginings. Vinay Lal comments on this tension between rupturing a dominant national imaginary, and regenerating and re-articulating alternatives. Lal explains that, 'Nandy finds himself an inveterate critic of the Indian nation-state, which has little tolerance for dissent and for competing notions of loyalty, but contrawise he is a great admirer of Indian civilization, which has largely been a pluralistic enterprise' (Lal, 2000: 12). These articles illustrate the psychoanalytic mode of revolt as a permanent feature of Nandy's work and identity. It is in this constant rupturing and regeneration that a dominant Indian political imaginary and its accompanying national fantasies can be worked through and recreated.

EMPTY CARNIVAL[6]

Nandy's article 'Empty Carnival' published in March 2007 explores the way in which cricket in India is a sporting game, but equally symbolises passionate national attachments. The game of cricket in India becomes a site or playing field for identification with the nation. Consequently a number of fantasies regarding nation, national identity and national integration are projected onto the game and perpetuated through it. In Nandy's reading cricket becomes interwoven with issues concerning unification and solidarity. Reading cricket in this way enables Nandy to establish that the game is an open-ended projective game for these fantasies, anxieties, fears and threats regarding the Indian nation. The game, however, re-establishes the boundaries of inclusion and exclusion in terms of those who support the Indian cricket team, and in effect India, and those who do not. The cricket playing field then becomes a field of signification where the hyper-competitiveness of the game is intimately tied to over-determined expressions of nationalism. The title 'Empty Carnival' gestures towards Nandy's concern that the dynamism of the game is being increasingly foreclosed by these over-determined nationalistic responses. As he explains 'the stage has been set for heartburn and narcissistic wounds'. What is problematic is that these 'nationalist aspirations… have begun to find pathological expression in cricket in recent years'. The nationalism embodied in Indian cricket as a national symbol justifies an aggression, which is already present in the game but now bears the scars of these 'narcissistic wounds'.[7] In understanding cricket as a projective test, then these aspirations of national unity in victory become dangerous and destructive defences.

Consistent with the rules of the game, a national dominance and unity can only ever be claimed by the winning cricket team. Losing a cricket game therefore, carries the intensity of these narcissistic wounds. The experience of losing a game is experienced as a loss in national unity. It is also experienced as a loss of identity in terms of the integrative function that national identification provides. The over-determined feature of this affective response is evident for Nandy when in losing a game 'cricketers and cricket administrators are [*cast as*] under-patriotic, corrupt, greedy or self-centred'. Losing a game is aligned with not fiercely defending nation and the national interest.

In the article Nandy ruptures and displaces the chain of association operating in these established meanings and representations of cricket. He re-claims the game and notions of gamesmanship as a more open-ended enterprise that resists homogenisation and closure of meaning. In Nandy's analysis cricket as the national game is displaced from the nation's gains and losses and re-generated and re-articulated as a 'subversive game that rebels against the productivity principle.' In contrast to nationalism the game of cricket thrives on its 'built-in-uncertainties'. It is in questioning and working through associations, projections, introjections, meanings and representations that the element of 'chance' central to the game can be reclaimed. The defences that truncate this concept of chance must be worked through for Nandy, including the uncertainties and insecurities that underpin these nationalistic sentiments. The retrospective questioning and working through of these complex individual and collective defences therefore opens up our understanding of cricket in terms of chance. The game of cricket is typically 'Indian' for Nandy because it recognises 'fate' as luck or chance. Like the porous boundaries of Indianness where the interplay between the rational and non-rational in human affairs is more diffuse, open to chance, so too is the meaning of the game regenerated in these terms. Regenerating cricket in this way therefore allows for a more complex psychic association to be established in which the boundaries between security and insecurity, unity and loss become more diffuse. According to Nandy the game then becomes an open-ended projective test that resists the pathologies of nationalism.

Nandy laments the increasing secularisation and professionalisation of the game of cricket. Implicit in these processes are the ways that its players are expected to conform to an existing dominant and standardised image of the cricket player as national hero. This standardised image forecloses the possibilities that the article wants to reclaim on a number of levels. Moreover, it denotes the ways that a player's own subjectivity is foreclosed by these processes. For Nandy, rupturing and regenerating this closure of subjectivity and meanings is vital to the well-being of individual and collective psychic life.

He notes, 'that some cricketers still remain under-professionalised, risk taking, adventurous and happy-go-lucky as a mark of defiance and a tribute to the resilience of human nature'. It is this possibility for defiance or revolt as an expression of the resilience within accounts of selfhood that the article celebrates. It is in the continuing re-creation of self that the relationship between cricket and nation also remains dynamic. For Nandy, the psychological health of the nation, including the health of concepts of national victory, in cricket or otherwise, must retain this dynamic and open-ended feature. When this capacity for rupturing and regenerating meaning and subjectivity is foreclosed, the element of 'chance' in the game becomes over-determined by the pathologies of nationalism. Consequently, what is a dynamic game of chance becomes an empty carnival.

IMAGINARY CITIES[8]

In the article titled 'Imaginary Cities' published in 2006 Nandy explores the ways in which the naming of national cities is fundamental to the boundaries of the Indian nation state. Nandy contrasts the official naming of cities by the nation state with more local definitions and points of reference. The claim advanced in the article is not over which name is true, but that this official naming process forecloses the field of possible names. Expressed in psychoanalytic terms this official process of signification forecloses the field of the imaginary. It is for Nandy these official names instituted by the nation states that dominate the Indian political imaginary. Thus, what is foreclosed by these processes, are other possible imaginary cities. More importantly, the official naming process forecloses our capacity to identify with these cities in alternative and often, conflicting ways. In Nandy's analysis, the naming of cities is connected to questions of subjectivity and identity. The recognition of multiple, co-existing and often conflicting names of cities are thus important for understanding processes of identification and expressions of individual and collective selfhood.

The operation of the psychoanalytic mode of revolt enables Nandy to acknowledge the homogenising and standardising effects of this official naming process. Nandy ruptures the closure of the field of identifications in order to regenerate disavowed names of cities. Moreover, this regeneration of imaginary cities takes place alongside a recovery of the pluralism within Indian cultures, languages and traditions. The article displaces the official and dominant names of cities by arguing, 'local or vernacular names of cities must have official status'. For example, to acknowledge that the Kannadigas call Bangalore 'Bengaluru' is to acknowledge the different vernaculars that exist within Indian culture. National culture, with its emphasis on an official national language and the naming process instituted by the State abjects these alternative accounts from view. For Nandy, to recognise the subjectivity of the Kannadigas, along with their points of reference in the signifier Bengaluru is to extend to the cultural self, democratic rights. The pluralism in these points of reference is therefore connected to democratic pluralism. Within Indian democracy even this cultural self, must be afforded recognition of their rights for self-articulation and signification.

It is not, however, the Indian State's official name that Nandy seeks to rupture but its 'claim to exclusivity', as the dominant name through which identification and signification is expressed. Nandy's invitation to the reader is to challenge and question these claims to exclusivity. The invitation, consistent with his mode of critical intervention is to rupture and regenerate the meanings attached to this exclusive dominant national self. To what extent does this official national self truncate our individual and collective capacity to critically think, question and represent alternatives in these processes of naming? The issue of naming, and in drawing on alternatives within these processes of naming is for Nandy connected to the well-being of psychic life in individuals and in societies. As he claims, 'a great metropolis almost always has more than one name and its wears this plurality as a badge of its greatness'. The concept of pluralism, including democratic pluralism, becomes a corrective against the dangers of homogenisation and standardisation. He affirms that it 'corrects and compensates for the sanitized, de-vernacularised images which can dominate a national imaginary'. Nandy therefore, directly addresses the need for regeneration and infinite recreation for the collective well-being of a society. He states, 'for a great city always hides a number of cities of the mind, associated with different communities, cultures and languages. These imaginary cities are backed by distinctive experiences and different configurations of public memory'.

According to Nandy, we need to recognise the internal and external function the imaginary cities perform in public memory and in keeping the psychic life of the nation dynamic. To ignore these imaginary cities is a disavowal of a vernacular culture that continues to exist alongside official imaginings. Moreover, to ignore these imaginary cities and the possibility of their existence is to ignore our own individual and collective capacities for rupture, regeneration and recreation of meaning.

Birth Pangs[9]

In 'Birth Pangs' published in 2006, Nandy applies his critical psycho-analytic methods to work through the complexities of the Partition of India and the establishment of the Independent Indian Nation State. For Nandy the entry point into these processes of anamnesis and retrospective questioning is through the memories of partition. He turns to the memories of trauma and the experiences of geno-cide that characterised this period. Nandy revisits these memories not to affirm and celebrate the birth of nation, but rather, to rup-ture the dominant meanings attached to this birth which circulated within official accounts of the establishment of the Indian nation state. In doing so, he also radically questions the ways that partition is remembered. For Nandy the regenerated meanings attached to the birth of nation must include a sense of loss that accompanied parti-tion. This loss is definable in two ways. First, by the loss of human life, the genocide, violence and displacement of peoples that took place, and second, that there is a loss of more plural and diverse understand-ing of Indianness. Further, this sense of loss in both its manifestations needs to be publicly acknowledged within narratives of individual and collective trauma. Loss needs to be publicly acknowledged in order to work through the ways in which this birth is remembered, spoken about and represented. Whilst 14 August 1946 marks the birth of the independent countries of India, Pakistan and Bangladesh, Nandy's analysis calls for recognition of the divisiveness, violence and trauma underpinning these experiences.

The article invites us to remember and revisit the memories and trauma of Partition outside of the official narratives of the birth of na-tion. This however, is not an easy invitation to accept. For Nandy this is all the more reason why this process of rupturing and regenerating memories is imperative. As he asserts, 'to disown its significance is to disclaim a part of our collective self'. To disown the significance of partition is to perpetuate a dangerous process of collective for-getting. What is problematic about this collective forgetting is that it maintains existing structures of remembering, including established defences, projections and introjections. This preserves existing struc-tures and patterns of thought within psychic life that can then feed into a number of hostilities. Simply stated, in not working through these associations and defences the scars of trauma, forgetting and the silencing of memories becomes the breeding ground 'to refresh paranoia and self-destructive fantasies of revenge'. This aggressive drive towards the other (the non-Indian, namely Pakistani) is perpetuated through a politics of forgetting. Moreover, in Nandy's analysis this aggressive drive that marks relations to the other, occurs alongside the partitioning of self. The possibility of revisiting and working through this trauma is overshadowed by defensive structures of revenge. This modality of revenge notably characterises India-Pakistan relations. Nandy laments the ways in which the regression into this mode of projection and introjection takes over within a paranoid national imaginary. Once this takes effect then this culture of forgetting acquires a political value that is intimately connected to the national interest and national security. This culture of forgetting thus forecloses these processes of anamnesis and more broadly, revolt from taking place.

In redressing this, Nandy's analysis therefore seeks to rupture and regenerate narratives of trauma in more complex terms. Re-visiting these memories of trauma and entering into processes of remembering through anamnesis is a difficult process. These processes are nonetheless essential in order to rupture the defensive structures outlined. The article displaces these national fantasies of forgetting its birth pangs, which work to safeguard national interests by turning to the memories of individual victims. For Nandy, the day of remembrance of partition becomes a day to rupture and regenerate its significance and the meanings attached to it. It becomes as he states, an opportunity, 'to mourn the victims in a different way'. These alternative expressions of mourning also displace established meanings attached to these individual experiences. For Nandy, this rupturing and regeneration of meaning enables us to publicly acknowledge that the victims 'were not the foot soldiers of a freer-postcolonial world but the cannon fodders for an ideology of state that saw conventional nation-states as the last word in human emancipation'.

Nandy's remembering of victims in this way is therefore radically confronting for it displaces established meanings and official accounts of remembrance. He thus confronts and questions who these victims are and what it is that they should be remembered for. Nandy's critical analytic perspective encourages its readers to reflect, confront and work through the politics of silencing and the politics of remembrance. Once these processes have been entered into then the meanings associated with the remembrance day of partition can be ruptured and regenerated. In Nandy's analysis remembering and commemorating the birth of nation must be accompanied with recognition of the complexities of loss that equally define the birth of the independent Indian nation state.

IMAGINED HOMELAND: SOUTH ASIA AS CIVILISATION AS AGAINST NATION STATE[10]

In 'Imagined Homeland' published in 2005, Nandy questions the role of the nation state within South Asia. He argues that the presence of the nation-state in a region like South Asia has imposed a series of facile differences or inclusions and exclusions that are instituted through the imagined boundaries of the nation-state. Consequently, this logic of difference and differentiation underpins definitions of the nation state. Nandy argues 'most states define themselves not by what they are, but what they are not'. It is through a series of negations and abjections, of what one is not, that the boundaries of national identity can be secured. In the article Nandy radically questions the processes of identification operating through the nation state and which now define the region. This logic acquires a political significance for Nandy through the voices of politicians heralding that, 'India is not Pakistan'. Such claims work to consolidate and further strengthen these processes of national identification, while simultaneously exploiting complex and longstanding national insecurities and defences. These processes of identification are complicated further by the fact that South Asia, particularly prior to the Partition of India was marked by a very different cultural, political, and psychological structure. For Nandy, the pluralism and diversity of the South Asian civilisations were foreclosed by the advent of the nation states and its set of exclusive identity claims. As Nandy explains the 'region looks like a clutch of rather reluctant states, most of which fear that positive self-definition will not take them very far'. The boundaries of the nation state however, in Nandy's analysis remain 'partly artificial'. The role of historians and legal scholars has been to counter this reluctance and artificiality by emphasising the loss of ontological security that the absence of the nation state would lead us towards.

Nandy challenges the dominant view that South Asia emerged as a confederation of nation states in the 1970s. Furthermore he challenges the view that by the 1980s South Asia was deeply ingrained in the political psyche of the region. In contrast to these official and dominant views, South Asian civilisations have a longer and more complex history. Nandy invites us to confront what he terms are the 'hard-boiled' affirmations of nation states. He does this by inviting us to question these affirmations and the dominant role that nation states play in the region's collective imaginary. The nation states of the region he argues are modelled on pre-World War I European states. The emergence of these postcolonial nation states in South Asia coincides with claims for self-determination and recognition on the international stage. This self-determination however, needed to be expressed in a recognizable language, the language of the nation state. The ideal of 'South Asia' emerges from these processes of national consolidation and as a response to other regional groupings on the international stage, such as South East Asia. In Nandy's account these well-established dominant associations and meanings, particularly within the field of international and diplomatic politics are not as secure as they might appear on the surface. Nandy's analysis questions and ruptures the perceived security of the boundaries of the nation state in South Asia, by suggesting there are far more precarious arrangements at play. He suggests that the everyday lives and moral frames of ordinary citizens threaten the official meanings of South Asia. In Nandy's reading, the term South Asia 'remains' 'a compromise'. What is problematic about this compromise is that, 'it has allowed the Indian state to hijack the right to the Indic civilization, forcing other states in the region to seek new bases for their political cultures and disown crucial aspects of their cultural selves'.

It is in articulating and re-claiming these disavowed aspects of this 'other India and its inhabitants' that carries forward the 'subversive potentialities' to regenerate meaning. It is through processes of retrospective return and in turning to question this other India that regeneration of meanings can take place. This is an alternative and regenerated concept of South Asia that is defined by the non-official and dissenting views of ordinary everyday other Indians. This concept of South Asia therefore transcends the boundaries of the nation state and notions of a national self. This takes place because in affirming a collective cultural self, who transcends the nation state, 'the exchange of low-brow cultural artefacts' is made possible. According to Nandy when 'high cultures cannot cross national boundaries, low cultures do'. The article ends with examples of a regenerated image of South Asia defined less by nation states and more by a shared cultural imaginary. This regeneration is attributed to these lowbrow cultural artefacts or mediums that challenge processes of identification. Nandy turns to the examples of Bombay cinema and TV soap opera serials as instituting an alternative imaginary of South Asia. The images and narratives communicated through these mediums challenge an existing dominant imagining of South Asia as a confederation of states, thus transcending facile differences between nation states. These mediums draw upon narratives, images and symbols that a collective cultural self of the region can identify with. These mediums operate on what he terms is 'the basis of cross-national trust, a poor man's version of post-nationalist awareness'. This post-national awareness, along with its regenerated modes of psychic organisation, is reason enough Nandy claims 'for the security community in South Asia to be nervous'. Therefore, these low brow cultural artefacts work to challenge official narratives of the nation-state that dominate the meaning of South Asia. In Nandy's account South Asia as a concept takes on a broader imagining, and in doing so, challenges the dominant status that is afforded the nation state and its fantasies of omnipotence in the region.

THERE'S NO FORGETTING THE TRAUMA[11]

The article 'There's No Forgetting the Trauma' published in 2005, directly addresses the need for individual and collective trauma to be worked through so that a politics of silencing is ruptured. The entry point for this task of anamnesis and retrospective questioning are the collective memories and experiences of the Indian Emergency. Nandy revisits the memories and experiences of the Indian Emergency to emphasise the importance of remembering these political conditions. Moreover, the article can be read as a cautionary reminder of the need for a culture of revolt. The article is written after the thirteenth anniversary of the Emergency and Nandy questions what impact these events have had on a contemporary Indian political imaginary. The Indian Emergency refers to the period from June 1975 until March 1977 when the Indira Gandhi Government suspended civil rights in India. Nandy emphasizes that a whole generation of Indians have survived these events with either no knowledge of them or through a specific national collective memory of them. This generation is either unfamiliar with these political conditions, or simply gesture towards a collective national memory of these events. Nandy asks, what is repressed from this collective national memory? In other words, what are the politics of remembering that underpin contemporary national fantasies of the Emergency? Furthermore, is there a culture of memory of these events, which safeguards us from these events taking place again? For Nandy, the response to these questions

is evident in the authoritarian political culture that continues to linger today. Consistent with the operation of the psychoanalytic mode
of revolt Nandy warns us against the radical evils of this authoritarian
culture. It is a culture that is defined by the suspension of thought
and representation. The suspension of civil rights in India during the
Emergency was also a suspension of democratic questioning, expression and ultimately the suspension of democratic civil rights. The authoritarianism of the then Gandhi government led to the suspension
of quite literally thought itself, and an inability to publicly express
dissenting views.

In remembering the Emergency in these ways Nandy invites the
reader into the processes of rupturing and regenerating the meanings
and significance attached to these authoritarian political conditions.
Nandy's rupturing of the silences and the forgetting provokes us to
question whether these political conditions continue and are present
in India today. He confronts the national fantasy that the Emergency
is an isolated event in India's political history by noting a number
of complicities between the past and the present. Nandy identifies
the continuities between the authoritarian political culture then and
now. He asserts that, 'our law and order machinery remains as compromised as ever and our politicians and bureaucrats have learnt to
negotiate the few institutional changes that were introduced after the
Emergency was lifted'.

He then turns to radically question the ways in which the events
of the Emergency are remembered. There is a correlation established between publicly recognising the seeds of authoritarianism
within political culture today, and the ways in which these experiences are individually and collectively remembered. However, the
question of collective memory is not straightforward. As Nandy highlights there is a fear associated with these processes of remembering.
There is a deep collective resistance of not wanting to know, about
that, which remains located defensively in the past. Such attitudes
must be worked through in order to ensure that the conditions of
authoritarianism can be recognised in their contemporary manifestations. There are nonetheless, deep and complex resistances in collectively remembering the Emergency. This is evident for Nandy in
the fact that 'no Indian historian, sociologist or political scientist has
produced a comprehensive, serious, political or social history of the
Emergency'. While this in part explains the repetition of a culture of
forgetting within public life, Nandy questions whether these traumas
of the Emergency can be repressed from individual memory.

Nandy disrupts the belief that the memories of the Emergency are repressed or forgotten memories. He questions whether trauma and public tragedy can be forgotten when people have been direct victims. These memories continue to survive in psychoanalytic terms as 'recessive or latent layers of our selves and the underside of our public life, outside the reach of formal or official commemorations'. This psychoanalytic questioning into the underside features of self and public life functions as an invitation to enter into these analytic processes of revolt. Nandy's question also raises the concern that 'official commemorations' have foreclosed our individual and collective capacities to remember differently. The article regenerates the occlusion of these memories from the national imaginary by situating these as *alive* and *present* within the underside of political culture. These non-memories, that is memories existing outside of official accounts, must therefore be valued, in order of these processes of inclusion and exclusion at play. According to Nandy, these official accounts allow for a very limited possibility of remembering. To continue to trivialise these memories may be a strategy of collective psychological survival but is also another way of resisting working through these memories and experiences. It is yet another defence against the challenges of retrospective return and processes of anamnesis that needs to take place in order to actuate these alternative possibilities, for remembering differently. For Nandy this alternative remembering affects the ways that we understand the past and the present. Our relationship to the past affects our ability to address present dangers, including the return of this suspension of questioning and thought. This critical analytic approach reminds the reader, that even against these deep and complex internal resistances, memories and anti-memories 'do inform the political choices of our electorate'. The message of the article is that there is a distinctive value in sensitising us to the ever-present dangers of the suspension of thought. This is especially important when the conditions of suspension in the form of authoritarianism or otherwise, cease to be recognised as the suspension of thought in contemporary political life. To this extent the message of the article is that the past has ways of informing the present and revealing itself in the future.

Repetition as a Constant Questioning: The Permanence of the Psychoanalytic Mode of Revolt

I have detailed the ways that the psychoanalytic mode of revolt operates in Nandy's work by analysing two different examples. The first example detailed the ways in which Nandy's mode of critical intervention operates in *The Intimate Enemy*, written in 1983. The text is widely recognised for the originality of Nandy's interventions in rethinking the experiences of colonialism. In my reading, this originality is explained in terms of his critical analytic perspective and what I claim are the enduring qualities of this mode critique over time. It is this psychoanalytic mode that enables Nandy to generate critique that ruptures and regenerates subjectivity, including relations between coloniser and colonised, self and other, victim and perpetrator. The emphasis on the psychology of colonialism enables him to confront, work through and recreate the dominant and official meanings attached to concepts of psychological resistance and cultural survival. In doing so, Nandy radically challenges our understanding of the experiences and representations of internalising an enemy, that is, as he states, intimate. The questioning of the psychology of colonialism and these processes of internalisation extends to both the coloniser and colonised within British and Indian societies. Nandy ruptures the meanings and associations of these internalised experiences in order to regenerate the loss and recovery of self. He does this by challenging the ways in which subjectivity is configured in the ideology of secularism and in exploring the possibility of recovery. Consistent with the features of Nandy's psychoanalytic mode of revolt he offers the reader a number of alternative accounts, meanings, and experiences of colonisation. These are evident in the ways in which figures like Gandhi as a figure in revolt ruptured and regenerated the masculine colonial code. Gandhi actuates the psychoanalytic processes that Nandy advocates in the textin which concepts of recovery are greatly challenged and reconstituted within a framework of non-violence.

The second example discussed was a selection of short newspaper articles that demonstrate Nandy's contributions to public debates during 2005–07. Written more than twenty years after *The Intimate Enemy*, these articles exemplify the repetition and moreover the permanent and enduring features of this psychoanalytic mode of revolt over time. The articles address a range of issues about the Indian nation, national integration and national identity. Nandy, I suggested, plays with national fantasies in order to confront and challenges them. In working through a number of dominant held beliefs and assumptions about the nation state he extends the invitation to the reader to enter into these critical analytic perspectives. The psychoanalytic mode of revolt reveals an uncompromising quality for rupture and regeneration in challenging official accounts, dominant beliefs, meanings, identities, fantasies and projections. Even within the

scope of these brief articles, these processes of revolt redirect signification, as Nandy's perspective ultimately advocates a transformation of not only meaning but also social relations. If we accept the
intention of this mode of critical intervention then the invitation to
the reader is to enter into this logic that promotes receptivity, reflexivity, alternative imaginings and open futures. These futures are ac-
cessible through the creative play with subjectivities, in which new
or rather, alternative psychic and socio-symbolic identifications are
made possible.

The repetition and constant questioning of this psychoanalytic
mode, its incessant movement, are in Kristeva's work described as the
conditions of permanent revolt. This permanent revolt is fundamental to cultivating a culture of revolt. Kristeva warns that this culture is
necessary for 'rather than falling asleep in the new normalizing order,
let us try to rekindle the flame (easily extinguishable) of the culture of
revolt' (Kristeva, 2000: 9). This call to revolt and processes of revolt are
equally present in Nandy's psychoanalytic mode of critical engagement. Through his work, Nandy similarly warns us against the evils of
a normalising order, and the homogenisation and stagnation that accompany dominant official meanings and representations. Through
his work Nandy invites us into the dynamic and permanent features
of this mode of incessant movement. The repetition and the permanence of this repetition, therefore takes place as a constant questioning and encourages reflexivity. This mode of critique is therapeutic
and articulated within a therapeutic register because it facilitates
rupture and re-articulation within psychic life to continue as a dynamic and timeless process. In each of these examples the repetition
of Nandy's psychoanalytic mode of revolt demonstrates these possibilities for psychic re-birth. This psychic re-birth extends beyond
individual experience and in Nandy's work promotes the transformation of social relations. As Kristeva reminds us, regenerating subjectivity also implies a 'rebirth of meaning for the other, which can only
be understood in view of the experience of revolt' (Kristeva, 2000: 8).
This is demonstrated in Nandy's willingness to enter into psychoanalytic processes to generate interventions that resist the effects of the
distortions of a dominant ideology and prevent a normalising logic
or order from taking over. The effect of this in Nandy's work is that
this mode promotes a dynamic permanent questioning. In his work
it also simultaneously advances reflexive and sensitising processes or
approaches to critique.

These reflexive and sensitising approaches are equally present in
Nandy's identity as critic. For in each of these examples this permanent

rupturing and regeneration of the psychoanalytic mode in his work, re-directs 'the aggressivity of the drive from abjection of the self to the transformation of social relations' (Chanter and Ziarek, 2005: 2). The psychoanalytic process of re-making subjectivity and meaning extends to Nandy and his subjectivity and identity as critic. The permanent and incessant movement of this process situates Nandy firmly inside the critical analytic approaches he advocates. These perspectives re-direct the meanings attached to Nandy's identity. For *in* and *through* this mode of critical analytic engagement he resists abjection by being re-made as the critical analytic intellectual. Nandy resists abjection because via this mode of critical analytic engagement he ruptures and re-creates signification, including the signification of his identity as critic.

The permanent and enduring features of this mode institute a dynamic space through which to recreate meaning and signification. Nandy, like Kristeva, endorses the need for a culture of revolt. He warns that conformity and standardisation, as symptoms of modernity, only serve to perpetuate the illusion of one world for all. These processes of homogenisation and standardisation must be resisted and revolted against. Nandy vigorously affirms the importance of these psychoanalytic processes, in his defence of the analysis within a number of places in his work. In his writing in 2002 Nandy re-affirms the need for social and political analysis to confront and resist the fixity and closure of meaning, particularly in light of the dangers of an increasingly dominant global culture of knowledge. This global culture of knowledge is also expressed as a culture of common sense, thus referencing its standardising features. For Nandy, once knowledge is instituted and accepted in normative terms as a culture of commonsense then these processes of psychoanalytic revolt, of rupture and regeneration must be activated. The commitment to these processes of revolt, along with the autonomy of thought which they generate for Nandy is evident in the following comments. He states:

> as the intellectually accessible universe expands, and as we confront disowned cultures and states of consciousness about the presently dominant global middle-class culture of knowledge knows nothing, we need more than ever our capacity to recognise the alternative realities that we are daily coerced to bury. (Nandy, 2002b: 4)

What Nandy identifies as our individual and collective capacity to recognise alternative realities are the effects of this psychoanalytic mode of revolt operating in his work. The intellectual commitment to these psychoanalytic processes of revolt affirms Nandy's commitment to the timelessness and dynamism of psychic life. Nandy thus becomes an intellectual who, through this psychoanalytic mode, consistently demonstrates a sensitivity and capacity to generate interventions that invite us to question our own subjectivity, as much as they do his identity as critic. The invitation to confront and 'work through' these 'intimate enemies' is fundamental to the alternatives that Nandy's writings offer us.

NOTES

1. Chanter and Ziarek (2005).
   There are a number of differences between Fanon's response to colonial oppression and Nandy's. So too are there differences in the political logic of revolt operating in the thinking of these two scholars. My discussion here of a psychoanalytic mode of revolt characterizing the political logic of dissent across Nandy's thinking differs from Ewa Ziarek's efforts to work out the political logic of revolt within Fanon's work. See Ziarek, E. 'Kristeva and Fanon: Revolutionary Violence and Ironic Articulation,' in Chanter, T. and Ewa Ziarek (2005).

2. Nandy (1983a). For a discussion of such figures refer to Nandy (1983). Another example being Ram Mohan Roy whose aggressive criticism of Indian traditions was in the style of the major reform movement of India. As Nandy argues:

   > It was not merely an attempt to explain Indian culture in Indian terms, or even in Western terms, but as an attempt to explain Indian culture in Indian terms, or even in Western terms, but as attempt to explain the West in Indian terms and to incorporate it in the Indian culture as an unavoidable experience.

3. I have already made this point in the previous chapter in discussing Nandy's efforts to re-constitute dissent through the metaphor of the shaman. Nandy argues within that essay that there is a 'language and world-view of those who refuse—or are unable—to speak the language of change, history, revolution and liberation who nonetheless, in their own way and with the help of their own categories, resist domination and theorize about it.'
   See Nandy (2004a).

4. In 'Towards a Third World Utopia' Nandy develops his argument further in establishing that, 'What looks like poor independence training in the non-achieving societies and 'willing subservience' and 'self-castration' in the Hindu may be read also as an affirmation of basic relatedness and a recognition of the need for some degree of reverence in human relations.' Nandy (1987a).

5. Nandy (2007); 'Empty Carnival'; Nandy (2006a); Nandy (2005d). 'There's No Forgetting The Trauma'; Nandy (2006b); Nandy (2006c). 'Imagined Homeland: South Asia as Civilisation as against Nation State'.

6. Nandy (2007). 'Empty Carnival'.
   The quotes that are cited from these articles in the main body of the text are not footnoted individually given the short length of the articles. They do not exceed more than one page in length each.
7. Elsewhere Nandy has developed this argument further by arguing that, 'Nationalism justifies the aggression, which is expressed through the game and the Indians who feel India is being unjustly ranked low in the international pecking order, to whom nationalism itself enjoys some intrinsic legitimacy on that ground, are the first to politicise cricket and to see the game as an area where a nation's fate and status could be determined.' Nandy (1989a). *The Tao of Cricket: On Games of Destiny and the Destiny of Games.*
8. Nandy (2006b). 'Imaginary Cities'.
9. Nandy (2006a). 'Birth Pangs'.
10. Nandy (2006c). 'Imagined Homeland: South Asia as Civilisation as against Nation State'.
11. Nandy (2005d). 'There's No Forgetting The Trauma'.

Conclusion
Re-imaginings in the Cultural Politics of Selfhood

This book has explored key ideas and methods of the Indian political psychologist Ashis Nandy. In addressing the relationship between his ideas and method this book establishes two key arguments, central to understanding Nandy's work and identity as 'intimate enemy' or critic of the state. First, that the ideas advanced in Nandy's critique of secularism, and the alternatives that his work invites us to consider need to be understood alongside the psychoanalytic approach that informs his social and political criticism. This approach is already present in the voice of the political psychologist, although the development of the field of political psychology in India, and Nandy's 'dissident' status within it, has obscured this appreciation. Nandy characteristically turns to the complexities of subjectivity, to external and internal processes, to the borderlands between culture and psyche, in order to address social and political concerns. This capacity and aptitude for critiquing the positioning of internal and external boundaries is though not always recognisable and moreover, remains under theorised as a feature of his social and political criticism. The second argument established in the book is that this appropriation of psychoanalysis manifests through a psychoanalytic mode of revolt operating within Nandy's work, one that enables him to generate distinct interventions and alternatives.

In order to reveal Nandy's approach and its significance, and to further characterise this as a psychoanalytic mode of revolt I engaged with psychoanalytic concepts and methods. Judith Butler's account of the formation of subjectivity in *The Psychic Life of Power* (1997) explores the way the psychic life of power and ideology operate through processes of subjection, in the making of subjectivities. Butler's conceptual framework is useful for understanding the argument Nandy makes about subjectivity, and the making of political identities within Indian political culture. The work of Julia Kristeva was equally relevant for discussing the interplay between external and internal processes in Nandy's work. Kristeva's concepts of the abject and abjection in processes of subject formation speak directly to Nandy's sensitivity to the positioning of boundaries and the inclusions and exclusions that result from these. The abject and abjection, at least as they were applied here, denote fascination and horror as a real and potential threat that can radically disrupt the boundaries of subjectivity. Applying this to Nandy's work allows for a more complex analysis of the positioning of boundaries within subjectivity central to Nandy's work, his intellectual identity and significance. In addition to this are Kristeva's conceptualisation of processes of analytic revolt which characterise Nandy's psychoanalytic mode. Drawing on these concepts in this way added another layer of complexity for considering the way in which the psychoanalytic focus of Nandy's work can be theorised and characterised. Using these psychoanalytic concepts to build a case about Nandy and his work, also affirmed the importance of psychoanalytic methods for social and political criticism.

The inquiry into the psychoanalytic focus of Nandy's work and the methods he adopts to actuate these perspectives was structured by three key questions. First, how the psychoanalytic focus underpinning Nandy's critique of secularism takes form. This was detailed through the confrontations he enters into in critiquing the psychic life of secularism operating in Indian political culture and within political identities. For Nandy the pathologies of secularism are to be found in the way that religious and ethnic identities are made over through processes of subjection. The consequences of these pathologies are many, including secularism's inability to safeguard tolerance and social and political amity. His analysis of secularism details the ways that the effects of the distortions of the ideology perpetuate the political conditions that give rise to xenophobia and fanaticism. Thus his critique of Hindu nationalism also demonstrates the effects of these distortions, through the way concepts of Indianness are made over in monocultural terms as a fixed identity category. This for Nandy forecloses ambivalence and contradiction within human subjectivity and within Indian traditions and culture.

Where a critic like Nandy can be distinguished in the debates of secularism, and where the value of his critique of secularism is to be found, is in his willing confrontation with this dominant secular ideal. Nandy confronts the ways in which the secular ideal operates to define political identities and Indian political culture. In Nandy's account the imposition of the secular ideal into Indian society makes over individual and collective identities according to the aims of this ideal. The dominant ideal defines the boundaries of inclusion and exclusion operating within political identities and in politics. It is these inclusions and exclusions that are confronted in Nandy's account and in doing so; he calls for a re-claiming of concepts of ambivalence within subjectivity and within concepts of Indianness. In confronting the boundaries of secular political culture in these ways Nandy's critique enters into a fascinating, though equally horrifying invitation to challenge the inclusions and exclusions operating in secularism. It is also an invitation to challenge the way in which the debates on secularism are carried out. Nandy, as is characteristic of his approach, equally confronts what can and cannot be publicly acknowledged within this intellectual culture, including the possibilities of imagining alternatives to a dominant secular ideal. Nandy's commitment to confrontation therefore reveals itself in a number of ways. This is evident through Nandy's capacity to confront and moreover, work through dominant and established meanings, identities, ideals, fantasies and projections. This takes place in his critique of secularism, for instance, in the way that he confronts and works through the psychological and viability of secularism in India. However, this capacity for confrontation also extends to his ability to confront and work through the defences operating in the debates on secularism, as he challenges the normative boundaries defining debate and audible dissent.

There are though significant consequences that result from Nandy's capacity to confront and work through the effects of the distortions of the dominant secular ideal. The second question explored in the book, is to ask what consequences result from this? This was explored through a selection of responses and representations of Nandy's work and the significance attacked to his identity as critic within the debates on Indian secularism. Secularism in India particularly since the 1990s, was widely accepted as a state of 'crisis' and was marked by a period of national reflection. It was also a period of forced engagement with the rise of Hindu nationalism and the outbreaks of political violence that radically threatened the secularity of the Indian nation state. The events that unfolded in Ayodhya and Gujarat affirmed for Nandy, that secularism is not only in crisis, but complicit in producing the political conditions for the pathologies of fanaticism and xenophobia to flourish. Nandy's anti-secular position, first detailed in the early 1980s, along with his critique of Hindu nationalism, acquired renewed attentions during this time and more recently, have led to his being a public 'test case' for his arguments.

As a vocal critic of the inherited secular ideal in India, Nandy finds himself cast as a disruptive and threatening voice, as 'intimate enemy' within these debates. This disruption and threat was validated by representations of him as the leading anti-secular and anti-modern voice in India. This anti-secularism was further consolidated by Nandy's perceived culturalism, traditionalism and calls for a return to a pre-modern India, which demonstrated as certain critics argue, his complicity with Hindutva ideology and the politics of the Hindu Right. Although not unfamiliar to controversy and what he describes as 'savage attacks', this renewed interest demonstrated the escalation of threat that Nandy's anti-secular position embodies. In characterising the discursive representations of Nandy's alleged 'anti-secularism' and 'antimodernism', how Nandy's threatening anti-secular position overrides an engagement with the methods he enters into to arrive at such a position, was also discussed. The task is not to offer a correct reading of Nandy's position but to demonstrate how these responses and representations are organised around Nandy's confronting, threatening and disruptive ideas, typically at the expense of acknowledging and engaging with his methods. As Nandy himself concedes confronting the cultural and psychological viability of secularism in India is a complex task.

There is more than academic quibbling at stake as these responses and representations of Nandy take form within a pro and anti-secular symptomatic register. Consistent with the persecutory and narcissistic logic, Nandy's identity as critic is represented in hostile and disruptive terms. For example, as the philosopher Akeel Bilgrami argues Nandy's disruption 'derails all meaningful debate' (Bilgrami, 1994: 1749). As a result such responses and representations are expressed within a symptomatic register, functioning as a defence against the real and perceived threat and danger that Nandy represents. In attempting to marginalise and de-authorise Nandy as a critic in these ways, it is his overwhelming threat of disruption that is defended against. Nandy's identity as a critic is made over, taking on characteristics akin to the Freudian phobic object. Consistent with the operation of phobia in psychoanalytic theory, Nandy's threat is deemed radically threatening and disruptive to concepts of selfhood, or rather accepted and preferred self-understandings and self-representations of self. Nandy's overwhelming threat and disruption was supplemented further by applying Kristeva's concept of abjection. Although this concept denotes a specific moment in pre-symbolic subjectivity, this is a useful concept to think about the way that Nandy is denied subjectivity and intellectual significance within these debates. Cast as the abject figure, Nandy's threat and disruption takes on an additional intensity as that which can disrupt boundaries, including the boundaries between subject and object, thus destabilising (or potentially) destabilising the ontological security of the subject.

The disruption and ambivalence that Nandy addresses in his work and that accompanies his identity as a critic are met with both horror and fascination. Horror is expressed in the representations of Nandy's regressive anti-secularism, the repudiation of his intellectual significance as a scholar, his lack of morality and his complicity with not only an intellectual proto-Gandhian culturalism, but also with pan-Hindu revivalist political forces. Fascination too is never far behind, demonstrated through the level of attention his work continues to receive. This fascination continues despite his status, at least within the debates of secularism as the maligned anti-secularist, anti-modernist, provocateur or romantic voice. Fascination and horror may earmark the subject's state of instability in abjection, but this instability also provides the very conditions for the possibility to rupture and regenerate meaning and subjectivity. Nandy's capacity to confront that, which is deemed abject as a feature of his own work and identity as critic, produces a confronting reflexivity and self-reflexivity that can disarms critics in these over-determined ways.

The question as to how Nandy is able to confront and work through these issues, at the border between culture and psyche has been afforded little attention in existing literature. Although the secondary literature addresses the critical features of Nandy's work and identity, a more complex engagement with the psychoanalytic methods already present in the voice of the political psychologist, is needed. The final part of the book addresses this by characterising the importance of Nandy's psychoanalytic approach as a psychoanalytic mode of revolt. The confrontation and working through that Nandy enters into, is a feature of his work and identity as critic. However, this confrontation and working through and autonomy of thought that his work demonstrates also necessitate a confrontation and working through of self, of Nandy's own identity. Kristeva's concept of revolt was introduced in order to characterise the relationship between ideas, method and the identity of the critic. A key feature of the psychoanalytic mode of revolt operating in Nandy's work was in the ways that this rupturing and regeneration of meaning and subjectivity, informed his identity as critic. Nandy *in* and *through* this mode of critical analytic engagement is able to rupture and regenerate meaning, and hence resist the effects of the distortions of a dominant ideology. This extends to a capacity to resist, rupture, and regenerate the meanings associated with subjectivity, including his identity as critic. Nandy, in and through the psychoanalytic mode of revolt, is also able to resist abjection through these processes of rupturing and regenerating subjectivity.

This psychoanalytic mode of revolt, referencing internal and external processes, is a permanent feature of Nandy's work and identity. Furthermore, how the psychoanalytic mode of revolt operates in two different examples of Nandy's work was considered. As someone whose intellectual identity is firmly inside the issues he responds to, this confronting and working through of self, reveals itself as essential to Nandy's method of dissent. This questioning and regeneration of the possibilities of dissent in Nandy's work are indicative of deeper internal processes at work: more akin to *a revolt*. In regenerating the boundaries of revolt from its exclusively political foundations, Kristeva politicises the psychotherapeutic possibilities within revolt. Situated within psychoanalytic process, revolt denotes processes of anamnesis, of a retrospective questioning and retrospective return in order to regenerate our understanding of ourselves, and in doing so, our relation to ourselves and to others. Revolt as a psychoanalytic concept denotes a series of processes which safeguard our individual and collective capacities to rupture, question, challenge, confront, and work through established values, norms, assumptions, associations within psychic life, and to this extent to regenerate meaning and significance. Through these processes of anamnesis and retrospective questioning, revolt references processes, which lead to the goal of a psychic re-birth. This possibility of a re-birth (of a rupturing and regeneration of self) is however, deeply confronting as much as it is therapeutic, because it places us face to face with our own internal resistances. These resistances if not attended to can foreclose these processes of working through from taking place, and from placing us *in revolt*. For instance, in Kristeva's account, and its application to theorise the defences of secularism in Nandy's work, this is marked by a profound willingness *not to know*. Nonetheless, once these resistances are worked through in the psychoanalytic sense, psychic re-birth, and the regeneration of subjectivity is made possible. This confrontation and traversal of resistances within self, place us *in revolt,* and for Kristeva, enables recognition of our own intimate radical alterity. This in turn facilitates an ability to live with and live through the ambivalence, contradictions and ambiguities that mark human subjectivity.

Nandy too celebrates these critical and reflexive capacities of revolt. Notably there are strong affinities between working through these resistances in a psychoanalytic therapy and the way Nandy works through the cultural and psychic resistances, that otherwise block an appreciation of the damage and distortions that the ideology of the Indian secular state has entailed. The psychoanalytic mode of revolt enables Nandy to question, rupture and regenerate meanings, including subjectivity. These processes are for Kristeva therapeutic processes because they are regenerative and also carry forward the possibility of permanent infinite processes of re-creation and regeneration. To this extent these processes of revolt also safeguard against the dangers and radical evil of homogenisation, standardisation and stagnation within psychic life. Where abjection as an affective state of instability threatens the subject (Kristeva's subject-in-process) with the disruption of being lost in the borderlands between subject and object, '*the not yet entitled subject*', the suspension of revolt, therefore denotes the end of subjectivity. In applying revolt to describe the psychoanalytic mode operating in Nandy's work and identity, the *therapeutic* is also present. This was explored in terms of Nandy's ability to generate perspectives that sensitise us to the therapeutic possibilities of these processes of rupture and regeneration or re-articulation. Nandy is therefore able to produce perspectives, which resist the effects of the distortions of a dominant ideology. This can make us, as Kristeva claims, 'receptive, expectant, mobile…there's a specific kind of humanity…attentive to its own and other people's revolts.' She continues that 'there's a specific kind of humanity that gets up off the therapist's couch, though, attentive to its own and other people's revolts' (Kristeva, 2002b: 68).

Gustavo Esteva and Madhu Prakash affirm that Nandy's perspectives encourage them to ask questions, and to challenge accepted norms as much as they 'offer guidance in the regeneration and re-enchantment of our own selves' (Esteva and Prakash in Nandy, 2004). In Makarand Paranjape's words, 'It helps us think categories, change our perception of things and eventually look at the world afresh' (Paranjape in Lal, 2000) Nandy produces confronting interventions in rupturing and working through dominant and hegemonic norms, meanings, ideas and identities. This rupturing takes place in order to regenerate and re-articulate these meanings and the field of possible significance; what is instituted in alternative political imaginaries. The therapeutic aspect of this psychoanalytic mode of revolt is in the way a recovery of alternatives that takes place in the perspectives that Nandy generates. Perspectives which we can also conclude lead to a recovery of alternatives not only for the self, but always and necessarily in tandem with a recognition of our own radical alterity.

It is worth re-stating that revolt denotes processes that cannot be simplified to those of a contrarian's or reduced to a reactionary voice. Nandy as a thinker and writer *in revolt* is through the operation of this mode, intellectually committed to more complex internal and external processes. This includes building upon a mode of analysis predicated on an internal estrangement from the certitudes of knowledge and certitudes of fixed identities. For estrangement from one's self, from dominant parts of one's self, or as Nandy references from over-socialised parts of oneself are the conditions of revolt. Revolt signifies this complex dialectical process that Nandy notes is the necessary counter-intuitive element within critical social and political criticism. As Celia Sjoholm explains, 'in forcing me towards the other in me, it will push me towards an alterity that will force me to question, interrogate and think, activities that in themselves must be reconsidered' (Sjoholm, 2005: 112). This too bears upon the dynamic of revolt as a 'transcendental intuition of the other'. Sjoholm states that, 'such a transcendental intuition of the other, argues Kristeva, will show itself as revolt' (Sjoholm, 2005: 112). It is therefore, a profoundly therapeutic mode of analysis because it rejects the possibility of defence as meaningful social and political criticism. It also differentiates Nandy's intellectual efforts, as in his critique of secularism from those responses predicated on deeply ingrained resistances to confrontation and in defending the dominant secular ideal. In Nandy's analysis of these continuing defences, defence of the secular ideal must be understood as operating on both individual and collective levels, for it is not separable from deeper fears of democracy, and fears of the post-secular operating in Indian political culture. For Nandy the reproduction of these defences must be confronted and worked through because they limit the play with self-definitions, ego boundaries and identity fragments that are needed to unleash the potentialities of a culture of participatory democracy' (Nandy, 2002b: 4). Even the voice of the 'radical democrat' with this commitment to processes of democratic pluralism needs to be understood alongside the commitment to processes of revolt. Further, they need to be understood alongside safeguarding against processes of stagnation, homogenisation and standardisation and the radical evil of the suspension of thought in psychic life. The defence of democracy and what he terms is 'the democratic art of the possible,' can therefore be conceptualised as a feature and effect of this psychoanalytic mode of revolt, as Nandy brings into his analysis aspects of self and society. Nandy explains this connection in the following way:

> For example, in a democracy there are certain obligations whether you like it or not for 'the democratic art of the possible.' I would have been perfectly comfortable living in a hyper-modern world using that language, because I was brought up in that language. But I know that in 'the democratic art of the possible' you cannot expect that language to go very far. I mean clearly it only enriches drawing room debates and class room debates. (Nandy and Defteros, 2005d: 31)

Is it a happy coincidence we might then ask that I have applied a concept to characterise these critical efforts, which although developed in Julia Kristeva's account of revolt, have their origins in the Indic civilisation? Kristeva in her efforts to regenerate the meaning of revolt within her commitment to psychoanalysis reclaims a meaning of the word that is not just political. She also interprets this word in an etymological sense. Kristeva states, 'the word revolt comes from a Sanskrit root that means to discover, open, but also to turn, to return. This meaning also refers to the revolution of the earth around the sun, for example. It has an astronomical meaning, the eternal return' (Kristeva, 2002b: 100). This offers yet another twist and turn, much like revolt itself, to consider Nandy's identity as critic of the State. To what extent might this psychoanalytic mode of revolt be an effort to return or rather to re-claim aspects of oneself, in this case other selves that still exists within the modern postcolonial Indian intellectual?

SOCIAL AND POLITICAL CRITICISM AND THE FUTURE OF REVOLT

The therapeutic features of this psychoanalytic mode of engagement in Nandy's work provide an approach for social and political criticism that extends beyond the work of the individual. Revolt, Kristeva reminds us 'is the questioning and displacement of the past. The future, if it exists,' she continues, 'depends on it' (Kristeva, 2002a: 5). The concept of revolt as explored within Kristeva's account and in its application to describe the psychoanalytic mode operating in Nandy's work, reinforces the continuities between the past, present and future. To this extent Nandy and his work, particularly *The Intimate Enemy*, which explicitly addresses these continuities within cultural and psychological structures of colonialism, resonate strongly with what passes today as postcolonial theory or postcolonial criticism. Whether or not this is an apt scholarly 'location' for Nandy's work, as Vinay Lal has questioned, remains an open question, though as this book has suggested the continuities between past, present and future that Nandy engages with transcend academic boundaries and territorial anxieties. For Kristeva and Nandy, more importantly, the future does not necessarily contain a predictive test or what we might call a projective test. Celia Sjoholm, writing on these issues further supports this view when she notes the internal dialectic at work within these processes of revolt. Sjoholm argues that, 'the future of the revolt is not futural or a projective vision, but the establishment of a displacing return, a permanence of the function of negativity, challenging and reconstructing given presuppositions' (Sjoholm, 2005: 113). Sjoholm continues to connect these processes of revolt to protecting us from what Freud has cautioned, is the future of an illusion. The future of revolt then consistent within its definition is only made possible through a permanent state of questioning, in the continuation of processes that place us *in revolt*. For Kristeva a culture of revolt is needed, where these permanent processes of questioning are instituted within social and political criticism, as a continuing and dynamic antidote to the suspension of thought and representation. In suggesting that a figure like Nandy demonstrates this commitment through his ability to actuate critical perspectives that contribute to a culture of revolt, I have therefore also commented on the enduring features of this psychoanalytic mode of revolt. As a mode of social and political criticism grounded in a culture of revolt, Nandy's work, his intellectual identity and significance can be evaluated within his capacity to resist the effects of the distortions of a dominant ideology and the future of an illusion. This mode in activating these processes of revolt produces interventions that invite us into this awareness, receptivity, sensitivity, and openness where, human choices and the choices to confront the future of an illusion, are expanded. As Nandy argues '...reconceptualising political, social and cultural ends; by identifying emerging or previously ignored social pathologies that have to be understood, contained or transcended; by linking up the fates of different polities and societies through envisioning their common fears and hopes' (Nandy, 1996a: 638).

In a world where estrangement from others, including estrangement from self is complicated by intimate enemies, threats of terror and ontological insecurity, the methods we adopt to characterise and theorise these threats, is a question that needs to be repeatedly asked. It is a question to which this book has attempted to offer a response, by advancing a case for social and political criticism actuated through a psychoanalytic mode of revolt. Within this mode of generating critique characteristic of Nandy's work, there is also an invitation to radically question where and how inclusions and exclusions are positioned, including within our own subjectivity. For consistent with this critical analytic approach the enemy appears increasingly within; that is within self, within the all too familiar 'culture of commonsense', and within what Nandy warns are the 'accepted myths of our times'. These tensions have been explored in relation to an intimate enemy within India who is cast as a confronting and threatening figure, along with the confronting claims advanced in his work. Through this case study of the Indian political psychologist Ashis Nandy, these confronting features are located within the processes of revolt that underpin the mode of critical intervention he enters into to generate social and political criticism.

It is important to note though, that Nandy's commitment to psychoanalytic processes of revolt does not foreclose his commitment to maintaining the dynamism of these internal resources. The internal resources include the dynamism within the psychic life of the individual and collectively within societies or cultures of revolt. In addition, there is for Nandy, a dynamism within the internal resources of Indian traditions and culture that survives as the underside of Indian political culture. It is within these latent features of Indian traditions and culture that a culture of revolt can be found. This commitment to the internal resources of self and within societies, cultures and traditions that rupture and regenerate meaning and significance, is articulated in a therapeutic register. It is then, we might conclude, a moment of agreeable symmetry in noting that Nandy's work and intellectual identity is not innocent of a double legacy of revolt. This legacy is a modern psychoanalytic concept derived etymologically from a Sanskrit root, but whose inner dynamics continue to question, challenge and twist and turn its constitutive meanings. This is a continuation of the Freudian idea that the return to oneself, actuated through these processes of revolt, can never hide behind the certitudes of inclusions and exclusions, nor within a future of illusions.

For re-imagining the cultural politics of selfhood becomes yet, another starting point for social and political criticism to establish the future of revolt. The invitation that Nandy's work offers to continually regenerate our understanding of the complexities of human subjectivity, self and other relations and what it means to be human, carries an ethico-political commitment. To accept such an invitation is to enter into a mode of social criticism where the possibilities of alternative political imaginings, necessarily begin with the recognition of our own radical alterity.

Bibliography

SELECTED WORKS BY ASHIS NANDY

Books

Nandy, Ashis. (1980a). *At the Edge of Psychology: Essays in Politics and Culture.* New Delhi: Oxford University Press.
———. (1983a). *The Intimate Enemy: Loss and Recovery of Self under Colonialism.* New Delhi: Oxford University Press.
———. (1987a). *Traditions, Tyranny and Utopias: Essays in the Politics of Awareness.* New Delhi: Oxford University Press.
———. (1989a). *The Tao of Cricket: On Games of Destiny and the Destiny of Games.* New Delhi: Viking and Penguin.
———. (1994a). *The Illegitimacy of Nationalism: Rabindranath Tagore and the Politics of Self.* New Delhi: Oxford University Press.
———. (1995a). *Alternative Sciences: Creativity and Authenticity in Two Indian Scientists.* New Delhi: Oxford University Press.
———. (1995b). *The Savage Freud and Other Essays on Possible and Retrievable Selves.* Princeton, New Jersey: Princeton University Press.
———. (1998a). *Return from Exile.* New Delhi: Oxford University Press.
———. (2001). *An Ambiguous Journey to the City: The Village and Other Odd Ruins of the Self in the Indian Imagination.* New Delhi: Oxford University Press.
———. (2002a). *The Romance of the State: And the Fate of Dissent in the Tropics.* New Delhi: Oxford University Press.
———. (2002b). *Time Warps: Silent and Evasive Pasts in Indian Politics and Religion.* New Brunswick, New Jersey: Rutgers University Press.
———. (2004a). 'The Twilight of Certitudes: Secularism, Hindu Nationalism, and Other Masks of Deculturation' in *Bonfire of Creeds: The Essential Ashis Nandy.* New Delhi: Oxford University Press.
———. (2005a). *Exiled At Home: Comprising At the Edge of Psychology, The Intimate Enemy and Creating a Nationality.* New Delhi: Oxford University Press.
———. (2008). *Time Treks: The Uncertain Future of the Old and New Despotisms.* London: Seagull Books.

Edited and Co-Authored Books or Articles

Das, Veena and Ashis Nandy. (eds). (1985). 'Violence, Victimhood and the Language of Silence,' *Contributions to Indian Sociology,* (19): 177–94.

Nandy, Ashis. (ed.). (1990). *Science, Hegemony and Violence: A Requiem for Modernity*. New Delhi: Oxford University Press.

Nandy, Ashis, Sardar Ziauddan and Merryl Wyn Davies (1993). *Barbaric Others: A Manifesto on Western Racism*. London: Pluto Press.

Nandy, Ashis, Shikha Trivedy, Shail Mayaram and Achyut Yagnik. (1995). *Creating a Nationality: The Ramjanmabhumi Movement and Fear of the Self*. New Delhi: Oxford University Press.

Nandy, Ashis and D.L. Sheth. (eds). (1996). *The Multiverse of Democracy: Essays in Honour of Rajni Kothari*. New Delhi: SAGE Publications.

Nandy, Ashis. (ed.). (1998b). *The Secret Politics of our Desires: Innocence, Culpability and Indian Popular Cinema*. New Delhi: Oxford University Press.

Pfaff-Czarnecka, Joanna, Darini Rajasingham-Senanayake, Ashis Nandy and Edmund Teerence Gomez. (1999). *Ethnic Futures: The State and Identity Politics in Asia*. New Delhi: SAGE Publications.

Lal, Vinay and Ashis Nandy. (eds). (2005). *The Future of Knowledge & Culture: A Dictionary for the 21st Century*. New Delhi: Penguin.

———. (2006). *Fingerprinting Popular Culture: The Mythic and Iconic in Indian Cinema*. New Delhi: Oxford University Press.

Selected Essays and Articles

Nandy, A. (1974). 'Between Two Gandhis: Psychopolitical Aspects of the Nuclearisation of India', *Asian Survey*, 14(11): 966–970.

———. (1979). 'Herbert Marcuse: Metapsychologist—A Tribute', *Alternatives*, 5(3): 394–396.

———. (1980b). 'Final Encounter: The Politics of the Assassination of Gandhi,' in Nandy, A. (ed.), *At the Edge of Psychology: Essays in Politics and Culture*. New Delhi: Oxford University Press.

———. (1980c). 'The Popular Hindi Film: Ideology and First Principles', *India International Centre Quarterly*, 8(1): 89–96.

———. (1982). 'A Post-colonial View of the East and the West', *Alternatives*, 8(1): 25–48.

———. (1983b). 'Towards an Alternative Politics of Psychology', *International Social Science Journal*, 35(2): 328–38.

———. (1984a). 'Culture, State and the Rediscovery of Indian Politics', *Economic and Political Weekly*, 19(49): 2078–2083.

———. (1984b). 'Reconstructing Childhood: A Critique of the Ideology of Adulthood', *Alternatives*, 10(3): 359–75.

———. (1985a). 'An Anti-Secularist Manifesto', *Seminar*, October, 1–12.

———. (1985b). 'The Bomb', *Illustrated Weekly of India*, 4 August.

———. (1985c). 'The Shadow State', *Illustrated Weekly of India*, 24 February.

———. (1987b). 'Cultural Frames for Social Transformation: A Credo', *Alternatives*, (12): 113–23.

———. (1987c). 'Development and Authoritarianism: An Epitaph on Social Engineering', *Lokayan Bulletin*, 5(1): 39–50.

———. (1988). 'The Human Factor', *The Illustrated Weekly of India*, 17 January, 20–23.

———. (1989b). 'After the Raj', *Seminar*, September, (361): 26–31.

Nandy, A. (1989c). 'Collapse of a World-View', *Indian Express*, 29 July.

———. (1989d). 'Shamans, Savages and the Wilderness: On the Audibility of Dissent and the Future of Civilizations', *Alternatives*, (14): 263–277.

———. (1989e). 'The Political Culture of the Indian State', *Daedalus*, Fall, 1–26.

———. (1991). 'Hinduism versus Hindutva: The Inevitability of a Confrontation', *The Times of India*, 18 February.

———. (1992). 'Secularism', *Seminar*, June (394): 29–30.

———. (1994b). 'Culture as Resistance: Violence, Victimhood and Voice', *The Times of India*, 10 December.

———. (1994c). 'Culture, Voice and Development: A Primer for the Unsuspecting', *Thesis Eleven*, (39): 1–18.

———. (1994d). 'Fear in the Air: The Inner Demons of Society', *The Times of India*, 14 October.

———. (1994e). 'Human Rights Today: A View from the West and East', *The Times of India*, 28 December.

———. (1994f). 'Philosophy of Coca-Cola: The Simple Joy of Living', *The Times of India*, 27 August.

———. (1994g). 'The Fear of Gandhi: Nathuram Godse and His Successors', *The Times of India*, 27 April.

———. (1994h). 'Value of Politics: The Greedy Road to Success', *The Times of India*, 10 September.

———. (1994i). 'Violence in Our Times: In Search of Total Control', *The Times of India*, 29 October.

———. (1995c). 'Culture of Consumerism: Targeting the Lonely Individual', *The Times of India*, 6 March.

———. (1995d). 'History's Forgotten Doubles', *History and Text*, May (34): 44–66.

———. (1995e). 'Popular Cinema: A Slum's View of Indian Politics', *The Times of India*, 2 February.

———. (1995f). 'Responses to Development: Dissent and Cultural Destruction', *The Times of India*, 15 April.

———. (1995g). 'The Future University', *Seminar*, January (425): 95–96.

———. (1996a). 'Bearing Witness to the Future', *Futures*, (28): 6–7 August–September, 636–639.

———. (1996b). 'Future of Poverty: Development and Destitution', *The Times of India*, 16 February.

———. (1997a). 'A Report on the Present State of Health of the Gods and Goddesses in South Asia', *Manushi*, March–April (99): 5–9.

———. (1999). 'The Invisible Holocaust and the Journey as an Exodus: the Poisoned Village and the Stranger City', *Postcolonial Studies*, 2(3): 305–329.

———. (2002c). 'Obituary of a Culture', *Seminar*, 513(15): 1–7.

———. (2002d). 'Enlightened Scholar', *The Hindu*, 31 March.

———. (2002e). 'Telling the Story of Communal Conflicts in South Asia: Interim Report on a Personal Search for Defining Myths,' *Ethnic and Racial Studies*, 25(1): 1–19.

———. (2004b). 'The Beautiful Expanding Future of Poverty: Popular Economics as a Psychological Defence', *Economic and Political Weekly*, 39(1): 94–99.

———. (2005b). 'Allure of the Demonic', *Outlook*, 22 August.

Nandy, A. (2005c). 'The Idea of South Asia: A Personal Note on Post-Bandung Blues', *Inter-Asia Cultural Studies*, 6(4): 541–545.

———. (2005d). 'There's No Forgetting the Trauma', *The Times of India*, 9 July.

———. (2006a). 'Birth Pangs', *The Times of India*, 14 August.

———. (2006b). 'Imaginary Cities', *The Times of India*, 7 November.

———. (2006c). 'Imagined Homeland: South Asia as Civilisation as against Nation State', *The Times of India*, 9 March.

———. (2006d). 'Nationalism, Genuine and Spurious: Mourning Two Early Post-Nationalist Strains in India', *Economic and Political Weekly*, 41(32): 3500–3504.

———. (2007). 'Empty Carnival', *The Times of India*, 24 March.

———. (2008). 'Blame the Middle Classes', *The Times of India*, 8 January.

———. (2010). 'The Judges Have Been Injudicious Enough to Create a Space for Compassion and Humane Sentiments,' *Tehelka Magazine*, 7(44), 6 November.

Conference Papers

Nandy, A. (2002f). 'Humiliation: Politics and Cultural Psychology of the Limits of Human Degradation, Keynote Address at Humiliation Conference', Ranikhet: Centre for the Study of Developing Societies and Nirman Foundation.

———. (2004c). 'Modernity and the Sense of Loss', Berlin: Deutsche Gesellschaft fur Technische Zusammenarbeit.

———. (2005e). 'Nationalism, Genuine and Spurious: A Very Late Obituary of Two Early Post-Nationalist Strains in India', Third Mehta Memorial Lecture, Mumbai: Nehru Centre.

———. (2005f). 'The Return of The Sacred: Post-Secular Reflections on the Language of Religion and the Fear of Democracy', Kyoto: Kyoto International Culture Forum.

Selected Articles Published Online

Nandy, A. (2000a). 'Gandhi after Gandhi after Gandhi', available at http://www.littlemag.com/2000/nandy.html 1(1). 6 April 2012.

———. (2000b). 'India: State, History and Self', available at http://www.littlemag.com/midclass/nandy.html 1(3). 2 April 2012.

———. (2000c). 'Nostalgia Isn't What It Used To Be', available at http://www.littlemag.com/vox/nandy.html 1(5). 3 February 2012.

———. (2002g). 'Obituary of a Culture', available at http://www.india-seminar.com/2002/513. 6 April 2012.

———. (2002h). 'Closing The Debate On Secularism: A Personal Statement', available at http://vlal.bol.ucla.edu/multiversity/Nandy/Nandy.htm. 6 April 2012.

———. (2003). 'Unclaimed Baggage', available at http://www.littlemag.com/faiths/nandy.html 3(2). 3 February 2012.

———. (2004d). 'Freud, Modernity and Postcolonial Violence: Analytic Attitude, Dissent and the Boundaries of the Self', available at http://www.littlemag.com/looking/ashisnandy.html 4(5&6). 5 April 2012.

———. (2004e). 'A Billion Gandhi's', available at http://www.outlookindia.com/article.aspx?224252. 10 May 2012.

Nandy, A. (2006e). 'Narcissism and Despair', available at http://www.littlemag.
com/security/ashisnandy.html 7(3&4). 5 April 2012.

Works Containing Contributions by Ashis Nandy

Assayag, Jackie and Veronique Benei. (eds). (2003). *At Home in Diaspora: South
Asian Scholars and the West.* Bloomington: Indiana University Press.
Bhargava, Rajeev. (ed.). (1998). *Secularism and its Critics.* New Delhi: Oxford
University Press.
Das, Veena. (ed.). (1990). *Mirrors of Violence: Communities, Riots and Survivors in
South Asia.* New Delhi: Oxford University Press.
Majid, Rahnema and Victoria Bawtree. (eds). (1997). *The Post-Development
Reader.* London: Zed Books.
Marglin, Frederique Apfell and Stephen Marglin. (eds). (1990). *Dominating
Knowledges: Development, Culture and Resistance.* New Delhi: Oxford
University Press.
Miller, Don. (ed.). (1999). *Neighbours and Strangers.* New Delhi: Rainbow
Publishers.
Nigam, Aditya. (2009). 'The Oppressed Have no Obligation to Follow the
Rules of the Game', available at http://criticalencounters.wordpress.
com/2009/01/19/%E2%80%9Cthe-oppressed-have-no-obligation-to-follow-
the-rules-of-the-game%E2%80%A6%E2%80%9D-ashis-nandy/ 19 January.
Sengupta, Debjani. (ed.). (2003). *Mapmaking: Partition Stories from 2 Bengals.*
New Delhi: Srishti.

Published Interviews with Ashis Nandy

Darby, Phillip. (ed.) (2006). *Postcolonising the International: Working to Change
the Way We are.* Honolulu: University of Hawaii.
Kothari, Smitu. (2004). 'Revisiting the Violence of Development: An Interview
with Ashis Nandy,' *Development,* 47(1): 8–14.
Lal, Vinay. (ed.). (2000). *Dissenting Knowledges, Open Futures: The Multiple Selves
and Strange Destinations of Ashis Nandy.* New Delhi: Oxford University Press.
Nandy, Ashis and Ramin Jahanbegloo. (2006). *Talking India: Ashis Nandy in Con-
versation with Ramin Jahanbegloo.* New Delhi: Oxford University Press.
Papastergiadis, Nikos. (1998). *Dialogues in The Diasporas: Essays and Conversa-
tion on Cultural Identity.* London: Rivers Oram Press.
Pinney, Christopher. (1995). 'Hindu Cinema and Half-Forgotten Dialects: An In-
terview with Ashis Nandy,' *Visual Anthropology Review,* Fall (2): 7–16.
Ramos, Jose Maria. (2005). 'Memories and Methods: Conversations with Ashis
Nandy, Ziauddin Sardar and Richard Slaughter,' *Futures,* (37): 433–444.

Transcripts of Unpublished Interviews with Ashis Nandy

Nandy, Ashis and Christine Deftereos, 2005a. *Conversations with Ashis Nandy:
Session I,* Unpublished Interviews, New Delhi, India: 1–27.

Nandy, Ashis and Christine Deftereos. (2005b). *Conversations with Ashis Nandy: Session II,* Unpublished Interviews, New Delhi, India: 1–12.

———. (2005c). *Conversations with Ashis Nandy: Session III,* Unpublished Interviews, New Delhi, India: 1–33.

———. (2005d). *Conversations with Ashis Nandy: Session IV,* Unpublished Interviews, New Delhi, India: 1–35.

———. (2006). *Conversations with Ashis Nandy: Session V,* Unpublished Interviews, Melbourne, Australia, 1–16.

Transcripts of Unpublished Interviews about Ashis Nandy

Deftereos, Christine. (2005a). *Conversations on Ashis Nandy: Shail Mayaram with Christine Deftereos.* Unpublished Interviews, New Delhi, India: 1–13.

———. (2005b). *Conversations on Ashis Nandy: Abhay Kumar Dubey with Christine Deftereos.* Unpublished Interviews, New Delhi, India: 1–17.

———. (2005c). *Conversations on Ashis Nandy: Shankar Ramaswami with Christine Deftereos.* Unpublished Interviews, New Delhi, India: 1–6.

———. (2005d). *Conversations on Ashis Nandy: Vinay Lal with Christine Deftereos.* Unpublished Interviews, New Delhi, India: 1–60.

———. (2005e). *Conversations on Ashis Nandy: D.L. Sheth with Christine Deftereos.* Unpublished Interviews, New Delhi, India: 1–19.

———. (2006). *Conversations on Ashis Nandy: Don Miller with Christine Deftereos.* Unpublished Interviews, Melbourne, Australia: 1–22.

———. (2007). *Conversations on Ashis Nandy: Phillip Darby with Christine Deftereos.* Unpublished Interviews, Melbourne, Australia: 1–35.

Works Referencing Ashis Nandy

Alinejad, Mahmoud. (2003). 'Book Review: Time Warps, Silent and Evasive Pasts in Indian Politics and Religion' by Ashis Nandy, *Commonwealth & Comparative Politics,* 41(3): 86–89.

Baber, Zaheer. (1996). 'After Ayodhya: Politics, Religion and the Emerging Culture of Academic Anti-Secularism in India', *Dialectical Anthropology,* (21): 317–343.

———. (1998). 'Communal Conflict and the Nostalgic Imagination in India', *Journal of Contemporary Asia,* 28(1): 27–44.

———. (2004). 'Race, Religion and Riots: The "Racialisation" of Communal Identity and Conflict in India', *Sociology,* 38(4): 701–718.

Beteille, André. (2001). 'Seeding the Topsoil', *Outlook,* 20 August.

Bhargava, Rajeev. (ed). (1998). *Secularism and its Critics.* New Delhi: Oxford University Press.

———. (2002). 'On the Majority-Minority Syndrome, *The Hindu,* 9 July.

Bilgrami, Akeel. (1994). 'Two Concepts of Secularism: Reason, Modernity and Archimedean Ideal', *Economic and Political Weekly,* 9 July: 1749–1761.

———. (1997). 'Secular Liberalism and Moral Psychology of Identity', *Economic and Political Weekly,* 4 October: 2527–2540.

Calhoun, Craig. (2002). 'The Class Consciousness of Frequent Travelers: Toward a Critique of Actually Existing Cosmopolitanism', *The South Atlantic Quarterly*, 101(4): 869–97.

Caroll, J. Jr., (2001). 'Secularism in India', in Sharma, A. (ed.) *Hinduism and Secularism After Ayodhya*. New York: Palgrave.

Chakrabarty, Dipesh. (2002). *Habitations of Modernity: Essays in the Wake of Subaltern Studies*. Chicago: The University of Chicago.

Chakrabarty, Dipesh in Lal, Vinay. (ed.). (2000). *Dissenting Knowledges, Open Futures: The Multiple Selves and Strange Destinations of Ashis Nandy*. Oxford University Press, Delhi: 250.

Chakrabarty, Dipesh, Majumdar, Rochona and Sartori, Andrew. (2007). From the Colonial to the Post-colonial: India and Pakistan in Transition. New Delhi: Oxford University Press.

Chatterjee, Partha. (1994). 'Secularism and Toleration', *Economic and Political Weekly*, 9 July, 1768–1777.

Chaudhuri, Amit. (2003). 'On the Nature of the Indian Gothic', *The Hindu*, 6 April.

———. (2004a). 'Distant Thunder', *Outlook*, 2 August.

———. (2004b). 'Natural Proclivities: So Little Fruitful Dissent, So Much Private Discontent', *The Telegraph*, 14 August.

Darby, Phillip. (2005). 'The Alternative Horizons of Ashis Nandy', *Overland*, (179): 53–57.

———. (2008). *The Institute of Postcolonial Studies Newsletter*, March (25):1–6.

Das, Veena. (1995). *Critical Events: An Anthropological Perspective on Contemporary India*. New Delhi: Oxford University Press.

Dasgupta, Swapan. (2004). 'Cultural Cringe: Reducing Colonialism to a Single Design is Poor History', *The Telegraph*, 13 August.

Desai, Radhika. (1999). 'Culturalism and Contemporary Right: Indian Bourgeoisie and Political Hindutva', *Economic and Political Weekly*, 20 March, 695–712.

———. (2004). *Slouching Towards Ayodhya: From Congress to Hindutva in Indian Politics*. New Delhi: Three Essays Press.

Gatade, Subhash. (2008). 'Why Narendra Modi Loves to Hate Prof. Ashis Nandy?' available at http://www.countercurrents.org/gatade180608.htm.

Jayal, N. G. (2006). 'Revisiting Nationalism', *Economic and Political Weekly*, 41(2): 4513–4515.

Joseph, Sarah. (1997). 'Politics of Contemporary Indian Communitarianism', *Economic and Political Weekly*, 4 October: 2517–2523.

Joshi, Sanjay. (2001). *Fractured Modernity: Making of a Middle Class in Colonial North India*. New Delhi: Oxford University Press.

Keddie, Nicki. (2003). 'Secularism and its Discontents', *Daedalus*, 132(3): 14–31.

Kesavan, Mukul. (2001). *Secular Common Sense*. New York: Penguin Books.

Kumar, D. (1994). 'Left Secularists and Communalism', *Economic and Political Weekly*, 9 July: 1803–1809.

Kumar, Manasi. (2006). 'Rethinking Psychology in India: Debating Pasts and Futures', *Annual Review of Critical Psychology*, (5): 236–356.

Lal, Vinay. (1999). 'Gandhi, The Civilisational Crucible and the Future of Dissent', *Futures*, (31): 205–219.

Lal, Vinay. (2001). 'Subaltern Studies and its Critics: Debates over Indian History', *History and Theory*, 40 February: 135–148.

———. (2002). 'The Disciplines in Ruins: History, the Social Sciences, and Their Categories in the "New Millennium"', *Emergences*, 12(1): 139–155.

———. (2003). *The History of History: Politics and Scholarship in Modern India*. New Delhi: Oxford University Press.

———. (2005). 'The Tragi-Comedy of the New Indian Enlightenment: An Essay on the Jingoism of Science and the Pathology of Rationality', *Social Epistemology*, 19(1): 77–91.

———. (2006). 'Civilisational Dialogues [Book Review]' *Economic and Political Weekly*, 41(45): 4751–4752.

Larson, Gerald James. (1995). *India's Agony over Religion*. Albany: State University of New York Press.

Malik, Y. K. and V. B. Singh. (1994). *Hindu Nationalists in India: The Rise of the Bharatiya Janata Party*. Boulder: Westview Press.

McGuire, J., Peter Reeves and Howard Brasted. (1996). *Politics of Violence: From Ayodhya to Behrampada*. New Delhi: SAGE Publications.

Miller, Don. (1998). 'Nandy: Intimate Enemy Number One', *Postcolonial Studies*, 1(3): 299–303.

Mufti, Aamir. (2000). 'The Aura of Authenticity', *Social Text*, 18(3): 87–103.

Nanda, Meera. (2004a). *Prophets Facing Backward: Postmodern Critiques of Science and Hindu Nationalism*. New Jersey: Rutgers University Press.

———. (2004b). 'Responses to My Critics', *Social Epistemology*, 19(1): 147–191.

———. (2005). *The Wrongs of the Religious Right: Reflections on Science, Secularism and Hindutva*. New Delhi: Three Essays Press.

———.(2006). 'How Modern Are We? Cultural Contradictions of India's Modernity', *Economic and Political Weekly*, 11 February.

Nayar, Kuldip. (2004). 'Abhor Singularity!' *Outlook*, 31 May.

Needham, Anurandha Dingwaney and Rajeswari Sunder Rajan. (eds). (2007). *The Crisis of Secularism in India*. Durham: Duke University Press.

Pandey, Gyanendra. (ed). (1993). *Hindus and Others: The Question of Identity in India Today*. New Delhi: Penguin.

———. (1992). 'In Defense of the Fragment: Writing About Hindu-Muslim Riots in India Today', *Representations*, 37(Winter): 30–47.

———.(2001). *Remembering Partition: Violence, Nationalism and History in India*. New York: Cambridge University Press.

Pantham, Thomas. (1997). 'Indian Secularism and its Critics: Some Reflections', *The Review of Politics*, 59(3): 523–544.

Reddy, Sheela. (2007). 'The Soothsayer: The Nandy Bull Rages on, and Now the Fukuoka award,' *Outlook Magazine*, 13 August.

Sarkar, Sumit. (1994). 'The Anti-Secular Critique of Hindutva: Problem of a Shared Discursive Space', *Germinal*, 1.

Subramaniam, Banu. (2000). 'Archaic Modernities: Science, Secularism and Religion in Modern India', *Social Text*, 18(3): 67–86.

Subrahmanyam, Sanjay. (2004a). 'A Guru And His Followers: A Colonial Thinker', *The Telegraph*, 8 August.

Subrahmanyam, Sanjay. (2004b). 'Our Only Colonial Thinker', *Outlook*, 5 July.

Tharamangalam, Joseph. (1995). 'Indian Social Scientists and Critique of Secularism', *Economic and Political Weekly*, 4 March: 457–461.

Upadhyaya, P. C. (1992). 'The Politics of Indian Secularism', *Modern Asian Studies*, 26(4): 815–853.

Vanaik, Achin. (1997). *Communalism Contested: Religion, Modernity and Secularisation*. New Delhi: Vistaar Publications.

Visvanathan, Shiv and Susan Visvanathan. (1992). 'The Problem', *Seminar*, June (394): 12–15.

SECONDARY SOURCES

Adeney, Katherine and Lawrence Saez. (eds). (2005). *Coalition Politics and Hindu Nationalism*. London: Routledge.

Agnes, F. (2007). 'The Supreme Court, the Media and the Uniform Civil Code Debate in India', in Needham, A. D. and R.S. Rajan (eds), 2007. *The Crisis of Secularism in India*. Durham: Duke University Press.

Anderson, Walter K. and Sridhar D. Damle. (1987). *The Brotherhood in Saffron: The Rashtriya Swayamsevak Sangh and Hindu Revivalism*. New Delhi: Vistaar.

Anderson, Warwick, Deborah Jenson and Richard C. Keller. (eds). (2011). *Unconscious Dominions: Pscyhoanalysis, Colonial Trauma and Global Sovereignties*. Durham: Duke University Press.

Arendt, Hannah. (1951). *The Origins of Totalitarianism*. New York: Harcourt, Brace.

———. (1964). *Eichmann in Jerusalem; A Report on the Banality of Evil*. New York: Viking Press.

Asad, Talal, Wendy Brown, Judith Butler and Saba Mahmood. (2009). *Is Critique Secular? Blasphemy, Injury and Free Speech*. Berkeley: University of California Press.

Basu, Tapan, Padip Datta, Sumit Sarkar, Tanika Sarkar and Sambuddha Sen. (1993). *Khaki Shorts Saffron Flags*. New Delhi: Orient Longman.

Bauman, Zigmund. (1989). *Modernity and the Holocaust*. Cambridge: Polity Press.

———. (2004). *Wasted Lives: Modernity and its Outcasts*. Cambridge: Polity Press.

Baxi, U. (2007) 'Citing Secularism in the Uniform Civil Code: A Riddle Wrapped Inside an Enigma?' in Needham, A.D. and R.S. Rajan (eds), *The Crisis of Secularism in India*. Durham: Duke University Press.

Beardsworth, Sarah. (2004). *Julia Kristeva: Psychoanalysis and Modernity*. Albany: State University of New York Press.

Becker-Leckrone, Megan. (2005). *Julia Kristeva and Literary Theory*. Houndsmills: Palgrave Macmillan.

Benhabib, Seyla. (1992). *Situating the Self: Gender, Community, and Postmodernism in Contemporary Ethics*. New York: Routledge.

———. (ed.). (1996). *Democracy and Difference: Contesting the Boundaries of the Political*. Princeton: Princeton University Press.

———. (2008). *Another Cosmopolitanism*. New York: Oxford University Press.

Breckenridge, Carol A., Sheldon Pollock, Homi K. Bhabha and Dipesh Chakrabarty. (eds). (2002). *Cosmopolitanism*. Durham: Duke University Press.

Bhargava, Rajeev. (1994). 'Giving Secularism Its Due', *Economic and Political Weekly*, 9 July: 1784–1791.

Bharucha, Rustom. (1998). *In the Name of the Secular: Contemporary Cultural Activism in India*. New Delhi: Oxford University Press.

Bhatt, C. and P. Mukta. (2000). 'Hindutva in the West: Mapping the Antinomies of Diaspora Nationalism', *Ethnic and Racial Studies*, 23(3): 407–441.

Bhattacharya, Neeladri. (2009). 'Teaching History in Schools: the Politics of Text-books in India', *History Workshop Journal*, 67(1): 99–110.

Bilgrami, Akeel. (2003). 'The Clash with Civilizations,' *Daedalus*, 132(3): 88–94.

———. (2006). 'Notes Towards the Definition of "Identity"', *Daedalus*, 135(4): 5–14.

Brass, Paul K. and Achin Vanaik. (eds). (2002). *Competing Nationalisms in South Asia: Essays for Asghar Ali Engineer*. New Delhi: Orient Blackswan.

Butler, Judith. (1997). *The Psychic Life of Power: Theories in Subjection*. Stanford: Stanford University Press.

———. (2004). *Precarious Life: The Powers of Mourning and Violence*. London: Verso.

———. (2005). *Giving an Account of Oneself*. New York: Fordham University Press.

Butler, J., E. Laclau and S. Zizek. (2000). *Contingency, Hegemony, Universality: Contemporary Dialogues on the Left*. London: Verso.

Butler, J. and G.C. Spivak. (2007). *Who Sings the Nation State? Language, Politics, Belonging*. London: Seagull Books.

Carver, T. and S.A. Chambers. (eds). (2008). *Judith Butler's Precarious Politics: Critical Encounters*. London: Routledge.

Chakrabarty, Dipesh. (2000). *Provincialising Europe: Postcolonial Thought and Historical Difference*. Princeton: Princeton University Press.

Chakrabarty, D. (2002). *Habitations of Modernity: Essays in the Wake of Subaltern Studies*. Chicago: The University of Chicago.

Chakravarti, Uma. (1998). 'Saffronizing the Past: Of Myths, Histories and Right-Wing Agendas', *Economic and Political Weekly*, 31 January: 225–232.

Chanter, T. and E.P. Ziarek. (eds). (2005). *Revolt, Affect, Collectivity: The Unstable Boundaries of Kristeva's Polis*. Albany: State University of New York Press.

Carse, J. P. (1986). *Finite and Infinite Games: A Vision of Life as Play and Possibility*. New York: Ballantine Books.

Chatterjee, P. (1994). 'Secularism and Toleration', *Economic and Political Weekly*, 29(28), 9 July: 1768–1777.

Chatterjee, Partha and Gyanendra Pandey. (eds). (1992). *Subaltern Studies VII: Writings on South Asian History and Society*. New Delhi: Oxford University Press.

Chaudhuri, Amit. (2003). 'Wage A War To Win Your Peace', *Outlook*, 27 January.

———. (2004). 'In The Waiting-Room of History', *Outlook*, 9 August.

———. (2005). 'The East as a Career: Two Questions That Indian Writers in English are always asked', *The Telegraph*, 1 May.

———. (2005). 'Argufying', *Outlook*, 30 September.

Christensen, Ellen. (2003). 'Chapter 9: Reclaiming Sacred Hindu Space at Ayodhya: The Hindu Right and the Politics of Cultural Symbolism in Contemporary India,' in Toffolo, C.E. (ed.), *Emancipating Cultural Pluralism*. Albany: State University of New York Press.

Crooks, Kalpana Seshadri. (1994). 'The Primitive as Analyst: Postcolonial Feminism's Access to Psychoanalysis', *Cultural Critique*, 28: 175–218.

Crossman, Brenda and Ratna Kapur. (1999). *Secularism's Last Sigh? Hindutva and the (mis)rule*. New Delhi: Oxford University Press.

———. (1996). 'Secularism: Bench-Marched by Hindu Right', *Economic and Political Weekly*, 31(38), 21 September: 2613–2630.

Dacey, A. (2008). *The Secular Conscience: Why Belief Belongs in Public Life*. Amherst: Prometheus Books.

Darby, Phillip. (2003). 'Reconfiguring the International: Knowledge Machines, Boundaries and Exclusions', *Alternatives*, (28): 141–166.

Das, Gurcharan. (2004). 'Privatise Secularism!', *Outlook*, 12 April.

Das, Runa. (2008). 'Nation, Gender and Representations of (In)Securities in Indian Politics: Secular-Modernity and Hindutva Ideology', *European Journal of Women's Studies*, 15(3): 203–221.

Das, Veena. (1996). 'Language and Body: Transactions in the Construction of Pain', *Daedalus*, 125 (Winter), 67(25).

———. (2000). *Violence and Subjectivity*. Berkeley: University of California Press.

———. (2001). *Remaking a World: Violence, Social Suffering and Recovery*. Berkeley: University of California Press.

Debord, Guy. [2002] (1967). *The Society of the Spectacle*. Detroit: Black & Red.

Derrida, Jacques. (1979). *Spurs: Nietzsche's Styles*. Chicago: The University of Chicago Press.

———. (1998). *Resistances to Psychoanalysis*. Stanford: Stanford University Press.

Dhavan, Rajeev. (1992). 'The Sound of Thunder', *Seminar*, June (394): 31–34.

Dirlik, Arif. (1997). *The Postcolonial Aura: Third World Criticism in the Age of Global Capitalism*. Boulder, Colorado: Westview Press.

———. (2000). *Postmodernity's Histories: the Past as Legacy and Project*. New York: Rowman & Littlefield.

Dube, Saurabh. (2002). 'Introduction: Enchantments of Modernity', *The South Atlantic Quarterly*, 101(4): 729–55.

———. (2004). *Stiches on Time: Colonial Textures and Postcolonial Tangles*. New Delhi: Oxford University Press.

Dumant, S. and R. Porter. (eds). (1996). *The Age of Anxiety*, London: Virgo Press.

Elliott, Anthony and Stephen Frosh. (eds). (1995). *Psychoanalysis in Contexts: Paths between Theory and Modern Culture*. London: Routledge.

Elliott, Anthony. (2002). 'The Social Imaginary: A Critical Assessment of Castoriadis's Psychoanalytic Social Theory', *American Imago*, 59(2): 141–170.

———. (2004). *Social Theory since Freud: Traversing Social Imaginaries*. London: Routledge.

Engineer, Asghar Ali. (ed.). (1984). *Communal Riots in Post-Independence India*. Hyderabad: Sangam Books.

Erikson, Eric. (1964). *Insight and Responsibility: Lectures on the Ethical Implications of Psychoanalytic Insight*. New York: W.W. Norton.

Fanon, Frantz. (1967). *Black Skin, White Masks*. New York: Grove Press.

Fletcher, John and Andrew Benjamin. (eds). (1990). *Abjection, Melancholia and Love: The Work of Julia Kristeva*. Warwick Studies in Philosophy and Literature, London: Routledge.

French, Patrick and Roland-Francois Lach. (eds). (1998). *The Tel Quel Reader*. London: Routledge.

Foucault, Michel. (1997). *Society Must Be Defended*. London: Allen Lane.

Freitag, Sandria B. in Ludden, David. (ed.). (2005). *Making India Hindu: Religion, Community, and the Politics of Democracy in India*. New Delhi: Oxford University Press.

Freud, Sigmund. (1936). *The Problem of Anxiety*. New York: The Psychoanalytic Quarterly Press.

———. (1974). *Introductory Lectures on Psychoanalysis*. Harmondsworth, Middlesex: Penguin.

Gambaudo, S. (2007). *Kristeva, Psychoanalysis and Culture: Subjectivity in Crisis*. Hampshire: Ashgate Publishing Limited.

Gandhi, Leela. (2001). 'Other(s) Worlds: Mysticism and Radicalism at the Fin de Siècle', *Critical Horizons*, 2(2): 227–253.

———. (1998). *Postcolonial Theory: A Critical Introduction*. Sydney: Allen and Unwin.

Gandhi, Mohandas K. (1982). *An Autobiography or the Story of My Experiments with Truth*. London: Penguin.

Gandhi, Ramachandra. (1992). *Sita's Kitchen: A Testimony of Faith and Inquiry*. Albany: State University of New York Press.

Gandhi, Sonia. (2002). 'Secularism Is India's Destiny', *Outlook*, 10 December: 1.

Ganguly, Sumit. (2003). 'The Crisis of Indian Secularism', *The Journal of Democracy*, (14.4): 11–25.

Gaonkar, D. P. (ed.). (2001). *Alternative Modernities*. Durham: Duke University Press.

Gay, Peter. (ed.). (1995). *The Freud Reader*. London: Vintage.

German, M. (2007). *The Paper and the Pew: How Religion Shapes Media Choices*, Lanham: University Press of America.

Guberman, Ross Mitchell. (ed.). (1996). *Julia Kristeva Interviews*. New York: Columbia University Press.

Guha, Ranajit. (ed.). (1984). *Subaltern Studies III: Writings on South Asian History and Society*. New Delhi: Oxford University Press.

———. [2005]. (1947). 'Degrees of Blame', *Outlook*, 27 June.

Gupta, Dipankar. (2000). *Mistaken Modernity: India between Worlds*. New Delhi: HarperCollins Publishers India.

Gustavo Esteva and Prakash Madu in Nandy Ashis. (2004). *Bonfire of Creeds: The Essential Ashis Nandy*. New Delhi: Oxford University Press.

Habermas, J. (1971). *Knowledge and Human Interests*. Boston: Beacon Press.

Hansen, Thomas Blom. (1999). *The Saffron Wave: Democracy and Hindu Nationalism in Modern India*. Princeton: Princeton University Press.

Humphrey, Michael. (2002). *The Politics of Atrocity and Reconciliation: From Terror to Trauma*. New York: Routledge.

Iyengar, Shanto and William J. McGuire. (eds). (1993). *Explorations in Political Psychology*. London: Duke University Press.

Jaffrelot, Christophe. (ed). (2007). *Hindu Nationalism: A Reader*. Princeton: Princeton University Press.

———. (2008). 'Hindu Nationalism and the (Not So Easy) Art of Being Outraged: The *Ram Setu* Controversy', *South Asia Multidisciplinary Academic Journal* available at http://www.samaj.revues.org/index1372.html.

Jakobsen, J. R. and A. Pellegrini. (2000). 'World Secularisms at the Millennium', *Social Text*, 18(3): 1–27.

Kakar, Sudhir. (1982). *Shamans, Mystics and Doctors: a Psychological Inquiry into India and its Healing Traditions*. New York: Alfred A. Knopf.

———. (1991). *The Analyst and the Mystic*. New Delhi: Penguin Books.

———. (1996a). *The Colors of Violence: Cultural Identities, Religion and Conflict*. Chicago: The University of Chicago Press.

———. (1996b). *Culture and Psyche: Selected Essays*. New Delhi: Oxford University Press.

———. (1996c). *The Indian Psyche*. New Delhi: Oxford University Press.

———. (2011). *The Essential Sudhir Kakar*. New Delhi: Oxford University Press.

Kaplan, R. D. (2009). 'India's New Face', The Atlantic, April, available at http://www.theatlantic.com/doc/200904/india-modi.

Kapur, R. A. (1986). *Sikh Separatism: The Politics of Faith*. London: Allen and Unwin.

Khilnani, S. (2002). 'A New Cultural Lexicon', *The Hindu*, 1 September.

Kothari, R. (1970). *Politics in India*. New Delhi: Orient Longman.

Kristeva, J. (1982). *Powers of Horror: An Essay on Abjection*. New York: Columbia University Press.

———. (1984). *Revolution in Poetic Language*. New York: Columbia Press.

———. (1991). *Strangers to Ourselves*. New York: Columbia University Press.

———. (1995). *New Maladies of the Soul*. New York: Columbia University Press.

———. (2000). *The Sense and Non-Sense of Revolt: The Powers and Limits of Psychoanalysis Volume 1*. New York: Columbia University Press.

———. (2001). *Hannah Arendt: Life as Narrative*. Toronto: Toronto University Press.

———. (2002a). *Intimate Revolt: The Powers and Limits of Psychoanalysis Volume 2*. New York: Columbia University Press.

———. (2002b). *Revolt, She Said*. Los Angeles: Semiotext(e).

Kuklinski, James. (ed.). (2002). *Thinking About Political Psychology*. Cambridge: Cambridge University Press.

Lal, Vinay. (2002a). *Empire of Knowledge: Culture and Plurality in the Global Economy*. London: Pluto Press.

———. (2002b). 'On the Rails of Modernity: Communalism's Journey in India, *Emergences*, 12(2): 297–311.

Layman G. C. and E. G. Carmines. (1997). 'Cultural Conflict in American Politics: Religious Traditionalism, Postmaterialism and U.S. Political Behavior', *The Journal of Politics*, 59(3): 751–777.

Lechte, John. (1990). *Julia Kristeva*. London: Routledge.

Lechte, John and Mary Zournazi. (1998). *After the Revolution: On Kristeva*. Sydney: Artspace.

———. (eds). (2003). *The Kristeva Critical Reader*. Edinburgh: Edinburgh University Press.

Lévi-Srauss, Claude. (1968). *Structural Anthropology*. London: Allen Lane the Penguin Press.

Lifton, Robert J. (ed.). (1975). *Explorations in Psychohistory: The Wellfleet Papers*. New York: Simon and Schuster.

———. (1987). *The Future of Immortality and other Essays for a Nuclear Age*. New York: Basic Books.

Ludden, David. (ed). (2005). *Making India Hindu: Religion, Community, and the Politics of Democracy in India*. New Delhi: Oxford University Press.

Lutgendorf, Phillip. (1990). 'Ramayan: The Video', *Drama Review*, 34: 127.

Madan, T. N. (1992). 'Fundamentalism', *Seminar*, June (394). 23–25.

———. (1997). *Modern Myths, Locked Minds: Secularism and Fundamentalism in India*. New Delhi: Oxford University Press.

Mahmood, Saba. (2006). 'Secularism, Hermeneutics and Empire: The Politics of Islamic Reformism', *Public Culture*, 18(2): 323–47.

Makari, George. (2008). *Revolution in Mind: The Creation of Psychoanalysis*. Melbourne: Melbourne University Press.

Malik, Y. K. and V. B. Singh. (1994). *Hindu Nationalists in India: The Rise of the Bharatiya Janata Party*. Boulder: Westview Press.

Maslow, Abraham. (1973). *Dominance, Self-Esteem, Self Actualization: Germinal Papers, Monterey*. California: Brooks/Cole Publishing.

May, Rollo. (1972). *Power and Innocence: A Search for the Sources of Violence*. London: Souvenir Press.

Mayaram, Shail. (2003). *Against History, Against State: Counterperspectives from the Margin*. New York: Columbia University Press.

McAfee, Noelle. (1993). In Oliver, Kelly (ed.), *Ethics, Politics and Difference in Julia Kristeva's Writing*, p. 131. New York: Routledge.

———. (2000). *Habermas, Kristeva and Citizenship*. Ithaca: Cornell University Press.

———. (2004). *Julia Kristeva*. New York: Routledge.

Miller, Don. (1992). *The Reason of Metaphor: A Study in Politics*. New Delhi: SAGE Publications.

Moi, Tori. (ed.). (1986). *The Kristeva Reader*. Oxford: Basil Blackwell.

Mouffe, Chantal. (2000). *The Democratic Paradox*. London: Verso.

———. (1998). 'Deliberative Democracy or Agaonistic Pluralism?', *Dialogue International Edition*, (7–8): 9–21.

———. (2005a). *On the Political*. London: Routledge.

———. (2005b). *The Return of the Political*. London: Verso.

Nanda, B. R. (2002). *In Search of Gandhi: Essays and Reflections*. New Delhi: Oxford University Press.

Nanda, Meera. (2002a). *Breaking the Spell of Dharma and Other Essays*. New Delhi: Three Essays Press.

———. (2005b). 'Intellectual Treason', *New Humanist*, 7 January.

Nauriya, A. (2003). 'Gandhi on Secular Law and State', *The Hindu*, 22 October.

Nayar, K. and K. Singh. (1984). *Tragedy of Punjab: Operation Bluestar and After*. New Delhi: Vision Books.

Needham, A. D. and R. S. Rajan. (eds). (2007). *The Crisis of Secularism in India*, Durham: Duke University Press.

Oliver, Kelly. (ed.). (1993). *Ethics, Politics and Difference in Julia Kristeva's Writing*. New York: Routledge.

Oliver, Kelly and Steve Edmin. (2002). *Between the Psyche and the Social: Psycho-analytic Social Theory*. New York: Rowman and Littlefield.

Omvedt, Gail. (2003a). 'Pseudo-Secularism I', *The Hindu*, 20 January.

———. (2003b). 'Pseudo-Secularism II', *The Hindu*, 21 June.

Panikkar, K. N. (1992). 'Conceptualizing Communalism', *Seminar*, June (394): 26–28.

Paranjape, Makarand in Lal, Vinay. (ed.). (2000). *Dissenting Knowledges, Open Futures: The Multiple Selves and Strange Destinations of Ashis Nandy*, pp. 233–248. New Delhi: Oxford University Press.

Pathak, Avijit. (1998). *Indian Modernity: Contradictions, Paradoxes and Possibilities*. New Delhi: Vandams Books.

Perrett, R. W. (1997). 'Religion and Politics in India: Some Philosophical Perspectives', *Religion Studies*, 33(April): 1–14.

Raimundo, P. (2005). 'Presidential Address', *Second International Conference on Religions and Cultures in the Indic Civilization*. New Delhi.

Ramaswamy, Sumathi. (2010). *The Goddess and the Nation: Mapping Mother India*. Durham: Duke University Press.

Rajagopal, Arvind. (1994). 'Ram Janmabhoomi, Consumer Identity and Image-base Politics', *Economic and Political Weekly*, 29: 1659–1668.

Reineke, M. J. (1997). *Sacrificed Lives: Kristeva on Women and Violence*. Bloomington: Indiana University Press.

Ricoeur, Paul. (1970). *Freud and Philosophy: An Essay on Interpretation*. New Haven: Yale University Press.

———. (1981). *Hermeneutics and the Human Sciences: Essays on Language, Action and Interpretation*. Cambridge: Cambridge University Press.

Rieff, Phillip. (1966). *The Triumph of the Therapeutic: Uses of Faith after Freud*. New York: Harper Row.

Rummel, R. J. (1994). *Death by Government: Genocide and Mass Murder since 1900*. West Hanover: Christopher Publishing.

Rustom, Bharucha. (1998). 'Mapping the Secular' in *In the Name of the Secular: Contemporary Cultural Activism in India*. New Delhi: Oxford University Press.

Said, Edward. W. (2003). *Freud and the Non-European*. London: Verso.

———. (2004). *Humanism and Democratic Criticism*. Houndsmills: Palgrave Macmillan

Salih, Sarah with Judith Butler. (eds). (2004). *The Judith Butler Reader*. Oxford: Blackwell Publishing.

Sardar, Ziauddin. (1997). 'Why you Can't Read these Stars of India', *New Statesman*, 126(4320): 47.

Sardar, Ziauddin in Lal, Vinay. (ed.). (2000). *Dissenting Knowledges, Open Futures: The Multiple Selves and Strange Destinations of Ashis Nandy*, New Delhi: pp. 211–232. Oxford University Press. Delhi.

Sarkar, Sumit. (2002). *Beyond Nationalist Frames: Postmodernism, Hindu Fundamentalism, History*. Bloomington, Indianapolis: Indiana University Press.

Savarkar, V. D. [1923] (2003) *Hindutva: Who is a Hindu?* Delhi: Hindi Sahitya Sadan.

Schafer, Roy. (1983). *The Analytic Attitude*. New York: Basic Books.

Shapiro, M. and H. Alker. (eds). (1995). *Challenging Boundaries: Global Flows, Territorial Identities*. Minneapolis: University of Minnesota Press.

Schwab, Gabrielle. (2004). 'Haunting Legacies: Trauma in Children of Perpetrators', *Postcolonial Studies*, 7(2): 177–195.

Sen, Armatya. (2005). *The Argumentative Indian: Writings on Indian History, Culture and Identity*. London: Penguin Books.

Sharma, Arvind. (ed.). (2001). *Hinduism and Secularism After Ayodhya*. New York: Palgrave.

Sjoholm, Celia. (2005). *Kristeva and the Political*. London: Routledge.

Smith, Ann-Marie. (1998). *Julia Kristeva: Speaking the Unspeakable*. London: Pluto Press.

Smith, David. (2003). *Hinduism and Modernity*. New Delhi: Oxford University Press.

Stavrakakis, Yiannis. (2003). 'Re-activating the Democratic Revolution: The Politics of Transformation Beyond Reoccupation and Conformism', *Parallax*. 9(2): 56–71.

Tally, Robert T., Jr. (2007). 'The Agony of the Political: A Review of Chantal Mouffe', *On the Political, Journal of Postmodern Culture*, 17(2), January.

Taussig, Michael. (1986). *Shaminism, Colonialism and the Wild Man: A Study in Terror and Healing*. Chicago: Chicago University Press.

Taylor, C. (2007). *A Secular Age*. Cambridge: Harvard University Press.

Thapar, Romila. (2000). 'Hindutva and History: Why do Hindutva Ideologues Keep Flogging a Dead Horse?', available at http://www.hinduonnet.com/fline/fl1720/17200150.htm.

———. (2009). 'The History Debate and School Textbooks in India: A Personal Memoir', *History Workshop Journal*, 67(1): 87–98.

Tilak, Srinivas. (2001). 'The Indian Secularists' Metaphor for Illness and Perversion', in Sharma, Arvind (ed.), *Hinduism and Secularism: After Ayodhya*. New York: Palgrave.

Toffolo, Chris E. (ed.). (2003). *Emancipating Cultural Pluralism*. Albany: State University of New York Press.

Tyabji, Nasir. (1994). 'Political Economy of Secularism: Rediscovery of India', *Economic and Political Weekly*, 9 July: 1798–1802.

Vaidyanathan, T.G. and Jeffrey J. Kripal. (eds). (1999). *Vishnu on Freud's Desk: A Reader in Psychoanalysis and Hinduism*. New Delhi: Oxford University Press.

Vanaik, Achin. (1994). 'Situating the Threat of Hindu Nationalism: Problems with a Fascist Paradigm', *Economic and Political Weekly*, 9 July: 1729–1748.

Van der Veer, Peter. (1994). *Religious Nationalism: Hindus and Muslims in India*. Berkeley: University of California Press.

Vice, Sue. (ed.). (1996). *Psychoanalytic Criticism: A Reader*. Cambridge: Polity Press.

Zavos, John. (2005). 'The Shapes of Hindu Nationalism', in Adeny, Katherine and Lawrence Saez (eds), *Coalition Politics and Hindu Nationalism*. London: Routledge.

Ziarek, Ewa Plonowska. (2001). *An Ethics of Dissensus: Postmodernity, Feminism and the Politics of Radical Democracy*. California: Stanford University Press.

Zizek, Slavoj. (2008). *Violence: Six Sideways Reflections*. London: Profile Books.

ONLINE SOURCES

Anti-History/In Another Life http://antihistory/blogspot.com
Ashis Nandy-Solidarity http://ashisnandysolidarity.blogspot.com.au
Bajrang Dal http://www.hinduunity.com/bajrangdal.html
Bharatiya Janata Party http://www.bjp.org
Butterflies and Wheels: Fighting Fashionable Nonsense
    http://www.butterfliesandwheels.com
Centre for the Study of Developing Societies http://www.csdsdelhi.org
Economic and Political Weekly http://www.epw.org.in
Frontline Magazine http://www.frontlineonnet.com
Hindutva: The Hindu Way of Life http://www.hindutva.org
India Express http://www.indiaexpress.com
India Forum http://www.india-forum.com
IndiaStar Review of Books http://www.indiastar.com
India Together http://www.indiatogether.org
Julia Kristeva http://www.kristeva.fr
Kamat's Pot pourri on Indian Culture
    http://www.kamat.com/indica/culture/sub-cultures/rss.htm
Manas http://www.sscnet.ucla.edu/southasia/index.html
Manushi: More than a Magazine a Cause http://www.manushi-india.org
Multiversity http://www.multiworld.org/mversity.htm
Open Democracy: Free Thinking for the World http://www.opendemocracy.net
Outlook India Magazine http://www.outlookindia.com
Psychoanalytic Electronic Publishing http://www.p-e-p.org
Rashtriya Swayamsevak Sangh (RSS) http://www.rss.org
Sangh Parivar http://sanghparivar.org
South Asia Citizens Web http://www.sacw.net
The Hindu Newspaper http://www.hinduonnet.com
The Times of India http://timesofindia.indiatimes.com/
Vishwa Hindu Parishad http://www.vhp.org

Index

About the Author

Christine Deftereos is a social theorist whose writings explore the relationship between self and society. Her research interests take place at the intersection between contemporary social and political criticism, psychoanalytic theory and the politics of selfhood. With a specialized interest in postcolonial identities and South Asian politics, her work also explores processes of identification and the limits of identity politics.